RETURN TO VIETNAM

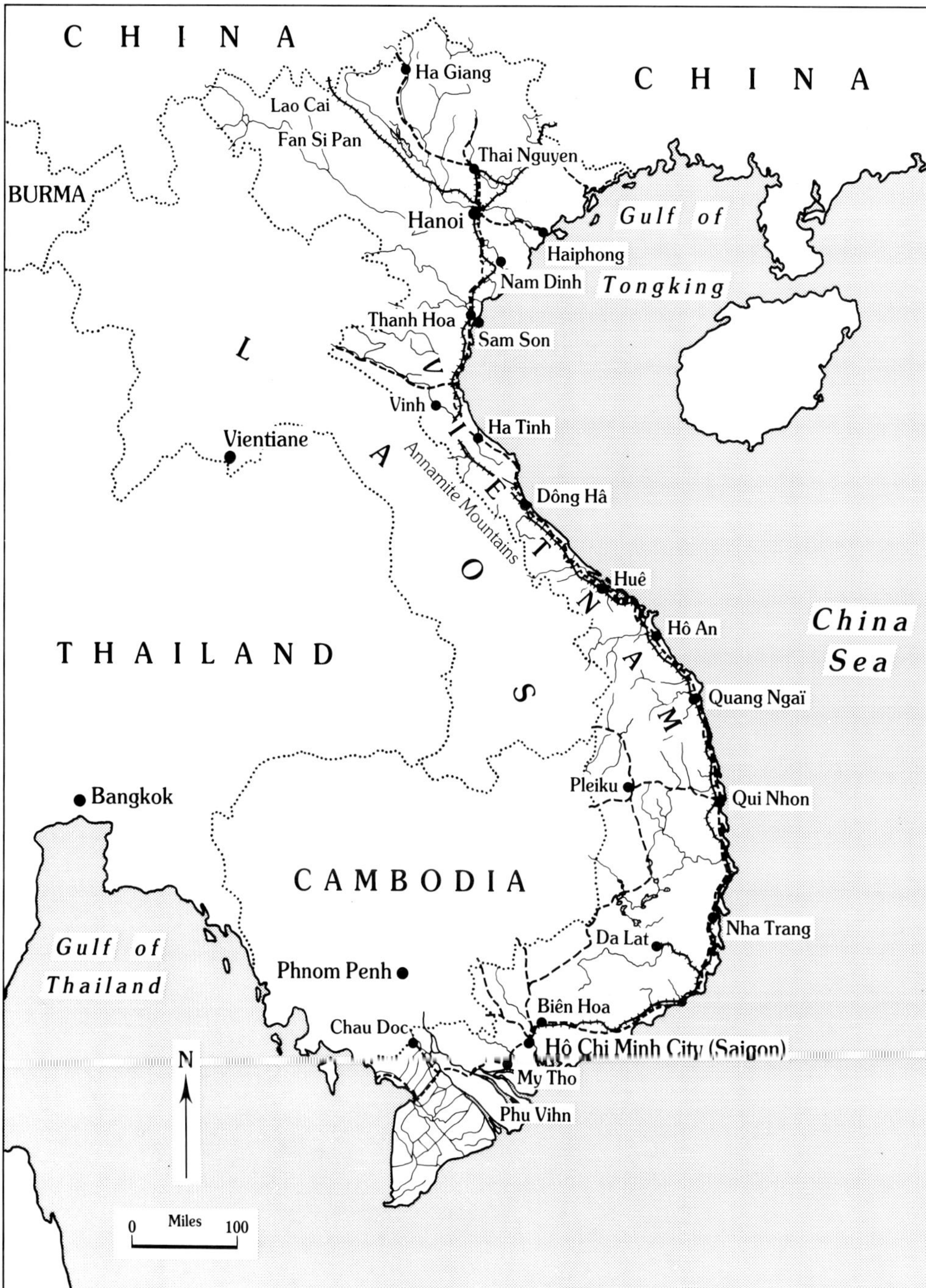

CHINA
CHINA
BURMA
Ha Giang
Lao Cai
Fan Si Pan
Thai Nguyen
Hanoi
Haiphong
Gulf of Tongking
Nam Dinh
Thanh Hoa
Sam Son
LAOS
Vinh
Ha Tinh
Vientiane
Annamite Mountains
VIETNAM
Dông Hâ
Huê
Hô An
China Sea
THAILAND
Quang Ngaï
Pleiku
Qui Nhon
Bangkok
CAMBODIA
Nha Trang
Da Lat
Gulf of Thailand
Phnom Penh
Biên Hoa
Chau Doc
Hô Chi Minh City (Saigon)
My Tho
Phu Vihn
N
0 Miles 100

RETURN TO VIETNAM

JEAN-CLAUDE GUILLEBAUD

Photographs by

RAYMOND DEPARDON

Translated by

JOHN SIMMONS

VERSO

London · New York

First published by Verso 1994

First published as *La colline des Anges: Retour au Vietnam*

Published with the financial assistance of the French Ministry of Culture.

Verso
UK: 6 Meard Street, London W1V 3HR
USA: 29 West 35th Street, New York, NY 10001-2291

Verso is the imprint of New Left Books

ISBN 0-86091-418-6
ISBN 0-86091-643-X (pbk)

British Library Cataloging in Publication Data
A catalogue record for this book is available from the British Library

Library of Congress Cataloging-in-Publication Data
Guillebaud, Jean-Claude.
[Colline des anges. English]
Return to Vietnam / Jean-Claude Guillebaud; photographs by Raymond Depardon; translated by John Simmons.
p. cm.
ISBN 0-86091-418-6. – ISBN 0-86091-643-X (pbk.)
1. Vietnam—Description and travel. I. Depardon, Raymond. II. Title.
DS556.39.G8513 1994 94–22121
915.9704'44—dc20 CIP

Typeset by Solidus (Bristol) Limited
Printed and bound in Great Britain by
B.A.S. Printers, Over Wallop, Hampshire

TRANSLATOR'S ACKNOWLEDGEMENT

I am deeply grateful to Jocelyne Barque for answering countless questions with great patience. My thanks also to Malcolm Imrie, who initiated this project at Verso, as well as to Liz Heron and Donald Nicholson-Smith.

LOOKING BACK

We went back to Vietnam, exactly twenty years after. The round number had symbolic value. We had no intention of wallowing in nostalgia, or playing the role of veteran war correspondents. But it seemed to us that Vietnam was not a story you could just finish watching, switch off and forget. To put it simply, it was essential to return.

Twenty years? I had left Saigon for the last time in May 1972, just after the Giap offensive along the 17th parallel, and the fall and subsequent recapture of An Lôc and Quang Tri. Fierce battles now forgotten, 'the Verduns of Vietnam'. Raymond Depardon made his last trip to South Vietnam that same year. I was subsequently forbidden to visit Mr Thieû's South Vietnam. But for years Raymond and I knew that one day we would again take a plane to Saigon. As though retracing our steps, with a certain trepidation.

We knew this would be no ordinary journey. Which is probably why we spoke little of Vietnam during the seventeen hours of the flight. The word was a bit intimidating and we avoided the subject. We lingered in an illusory 'bubble', loath to uproot ourselves from the problems of an ordinary week – 'urgent' meetings, family, work-in-progress. Long after take-off we were still scouring the daily papers and weekly magazines. As if we instinctively wanted to put off the moment. It took several hours of flying for us to allay this bizarre anxiety and these dilatory concerns. It wasn't until the stopover in Bombay that, caught off guard at last by the sudden, sweltering heat in the transit lounge, we began coming to our senses, to this slightly drunken frivolity: the real departure this time was going to be – necessarily – a look back at ourselves.

Several hours later, day was breaking on the Saigon River.

TWENTY YEARS AFTER

Tan Son Nhut, the Hô Chi Minh City airport, towards the end of May 1992. Slender Vietnamese women, with jet-black, bobbed hair, accost male visitors and slip then an unexpected message: calling cards for a night spot, or 'VIP Club'. Quite openly. On the roof of the terminal, a rather cheerful crowd strains against the barrier, everyone looking for a familiar face, a potential customer. A flurry of reunions all over the building. The customs officials – 'Northerners' – inspect the baggage less carefully than anticipated. Our flight, it is true, is bringing back several groups of Vietnamese from abroad – excited and staggering under the weight of brand-new luggage. My neighbour on the plane, an old man of eighty-five living in Montreal, has not been back to Vietnam since 1974. In arrivals I see him shuffling along, rolling his French Canadian r's beneath the rafters of Tan Son Nhut.

Once outside the airport I take a close look at the swarm of two-wheelers, the Honda motorbikes and pedicabs, which converge on us at every red light, as well as the buildings, the street merchants, all the coral trees in bloom. Are we moved by Vietnam itself or by the passing of the years? Skirting what was formerly Tu Do Street to reach the Continental Palace Hotel – by the rear – our taxi passes an incredible couple. Were they waiting for us too? A big, greying American in a red cap, and on his arm, a tiny Vietnamese woman in high heels. It is an image from the past, with the woman repeating, gesture for gesture, in every sashay and strut, a scene endlessly encountered twenty years ago: a GI on leave, with a bar hostess from Mimi's or Chez Carine trotting along by his side. Huge, sandy-haired beasts being led by the nose to the nearest watering hole by tiny whores. We're not dreaming: former American servicemen have been coming back recently to wander the streets of Saigon. (I say 'Saigon' because nobody uses 'Hô Chi Minh City' any more; the name has been impugned, just as Leningrad has once again become St Petersburg or Gorki, Nizhni-Novgorod.) Their frames are thicker,

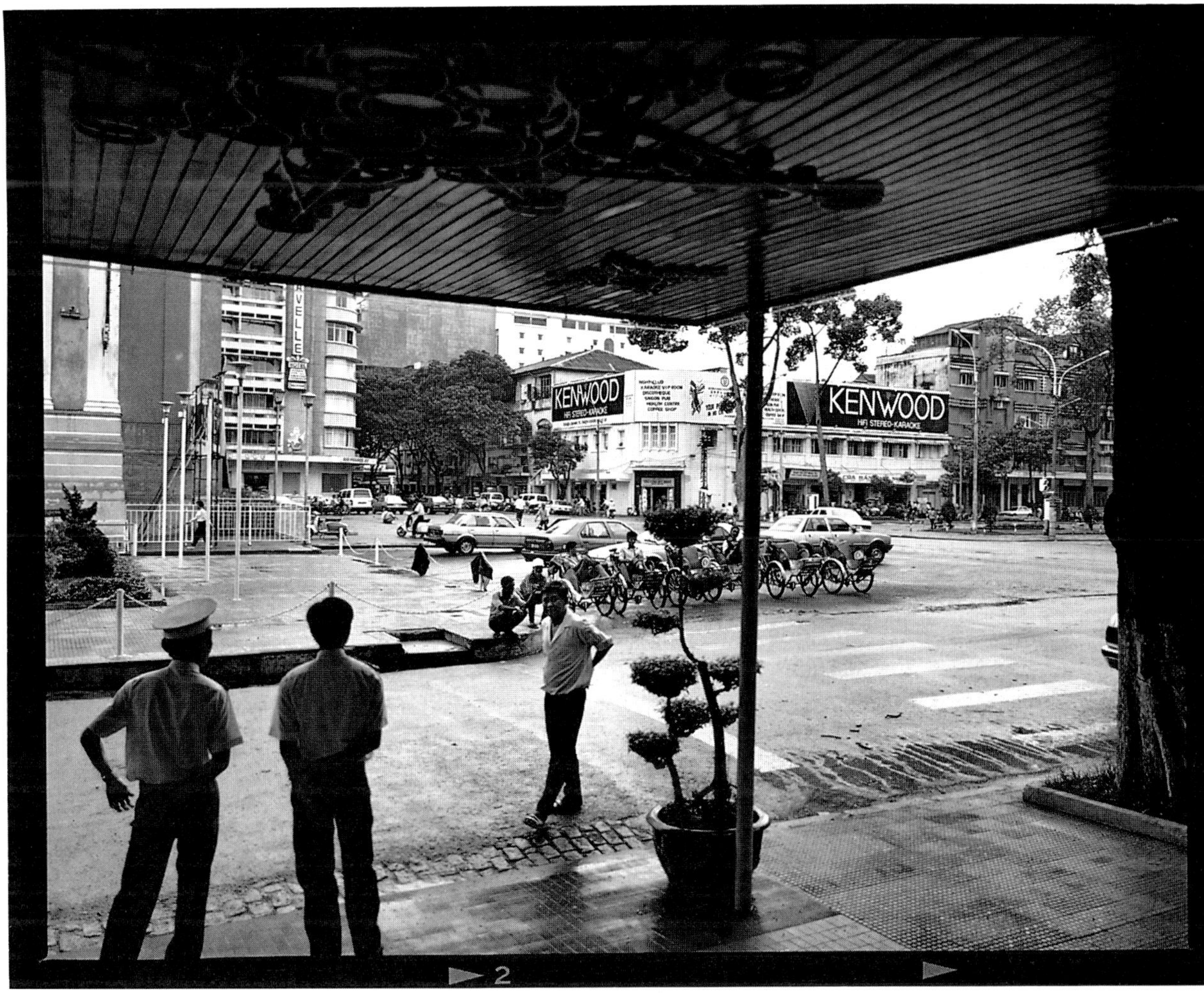

Hô Chi Minh City from the Hotel Continental.

their gazes more distant. The young woman steering them might be the daughter of the former bar hostess. The latter is doubtless spokesperson for Vietnam Tourism – the official travel agency – or else works for one of the marvellous 'business centres' which have sprung up all over the country since the opening-up to capitalism in 1986 – *perestroika* Vietnamese-style, known here as *doi moi* (renovation). So now there are US veterans walking around the city, with raw nostalgia and naive curiosity. For them too, it's been twenty years.

To find Saigon so nearly 'as ever' is most disturbing. It is true that, over the past three years (1989–92), Vietnam has undertaken a journey back in time. As if it were coming to meet us. Saigon is no longer the big, broken city of the years 'after the fall', a surly and harsh communist metropolis – a look it took on reluctantly after the nationalization of shops, restaurants and businesses emptied the streets and brought the shutters down on confiscated stores all over. They turned out the lights, froze the bank accounts and proclaimed virtue and a radiant future while dressing the women in boilersuit blue. That was long ago. This brand of coerced communism is visibly dissolving in the disco hustle which is giving the former capital back its reputation as a city of sin and dizzying mayhem. New watchwords in synch with the times – *fax, market, managers, business, niche, joint venture* – proliferate in place of the old Leninist slogans. Saigon is becoming efficient and cynical, playful and ungovernable. Just like it used to be.

This sort of transformation is not unique. The end of communism, 'post-communism' as we now call it, is stimulating the same auspicious and 'odious' fermentation nearly everywhere. In the ex-Soviet Union and Central Europe, between 1989 and 1991, we learned to recognize the symptoms. Are they so heartening? Not necessarily. Just after the fall of the Berlin Wall, we were all said to be 'enthused' by 'the spirit of freedom' and 'triumph of democracy'. People wrote books too fast, and spoke too soon. In the meantime, there was necessarily to be a long stretch of history which was not necessarily pleasant. Nor was the outcome decided in advance. The 'post communism' which was announced in Saigon could not have the same sense, content or flavour as in Warsaw, Bucharest, or St Petersburg.

This is Vietnam.

Thirty years of fire and ashes, 1,027,085 deaths on the communist side and

254,257 for the South; 56,869 American troops killed and at least 500,000 of the civilian population (of which 430,000 were South Vietnamese). A huge area of forests and rice fields incinerated by napalm and defoliants, $150 billion spent on the war and 7,800,000 tonnes of bombs dropped on former Indochina – twice the amount used in the whole of the Second World War. Then seventeen years of impassive Stalinism, with Saigon invaded by uncouth *bo doi* (North Vietnamese soldiers). Finally, the unforeseeable aftermath of families setting out nightly from southern beaches for exile and disaster in the China Sea. A miscarriage of history (not invented by the CIA this time) awakened Western consciences with a great fanfare. It came soon after Solzhenitsyn started a devastating blaze in European thought. Thus was Vietnam, for one or two generations, far more than a Third World country. Incarnation of the colonialist fiasco, protagonist in a Thirty Years War, cannon fodder, field of destruction wrought by 'American imperialism', Vietnam *immediately* became a textbook case of Stalinism, a disturbing affair of 'boat people'. The bloody and emblematic countenance of a whole era, finally, the swindled heir of the 1970s.

Vietnam. People of our generation began their adult lives with that single word on their lips. Everywhere, in Europe as in America, there was a 'Vietnam generation'. Does it remember? Student agitation in the mid 1960s, the intoxicated rage of grassroots political groups, countless demonstrations, banners, *Power to the People* . . . a lot of words.

Today, it's worth reading North Vietnamese writers, in translation. Their disenchantment resembles our own. Except that they paid the price of their convictions. 'This war was not simply a struggle against aggression,' murmurs Duong Thu Huong's hero in *Untitled Novel.* 'It was also a resurrection. Vietnam was the Chosen One of History. After the war, our fatherland would become humanity's paradise, our people would have a place apart, we would become honoured, respected. . . . We believed and so held back the tears of weakness. Ten years passed. Nobody talked about it any more.'

In another book, the writer of the preface to Pham Thi Hoâi's *The Crystal Messenger* responds: 'A century of violence comes to a close with a wound: Vietnam. Perhaps an era of peace is beginning in Europe. If it had to be a peace of cemeteries, one of the largest would bear the name: Vietnam.'

Vietnam!

To this emotion, which overwhelms us from day one, we append another. It was here that many were born to journalism. In Saigon they confronted the ambiguities of bearing witness writ large, the anxiety that goes with the job, the reporter's troubled solitude which subsequently distanced him from militant solidarities. As if he were in exile. There were so many polemics, later on, concerning the 'errors' of so-and-so and the 'blindness' or 'treachery' of somebody else, that little was said about those who were silent. The cautious, the better-informed, who floundered more modestly in doubt and had nothing to 'confess'. I was one of them.

When reporters came back from Saigon in those days, they were too sullied by the event to have well-defined ideas. The evidence they brought back was impressionistic, incongruous, too contradictory to fuel the boiler of anti-war demonstrations. The militant conscience was ruthlessly clear: Good, Evil, White, Black. Hopeless conversations ensued with resolute defenders of the 'Vietnamese cause', ardent readers of *Le Monde* and intransigents who toed the 'line', or, just as easily, with the admirers of Cardinal Spellmann, who were anxious to save the Christian West from Asian barbarity and the 'domino' threat. Both sides absurdly simplified, neither was right. But what use is being right when you're alone?

The times, I remember, preferred theories to evidence. Reporters were those who argued and quibbled rather than 'struggled'. Vietnam made them – made us – innately suspect, prissy abstentionists. I draw from these recollections no sense of superiority whatever nor the least retrospective glory. My principal memory of the period is the exhausting discomfort. Recurrent confusion, stubborn but pathetic loneliness, exorcised by tribal incantations: '*Remember when . . .*'

Did we think of writing that we were not absolutely wrong to doubt? With the benefit of hindsight, the misunderstanding seems all too simple. Outwardly, we acted as if we were unaware of the reported rigidity of North Vietnamese Stalinism. We preferred to stick to the heroism of the 'national' struggle. In South Vietnam, on the other hand, the interested parties all employed the same language: the regime imposed by the North would be dim-witted and brutal. And they were just as silently hostile to their burdensome ally, America. They wanted

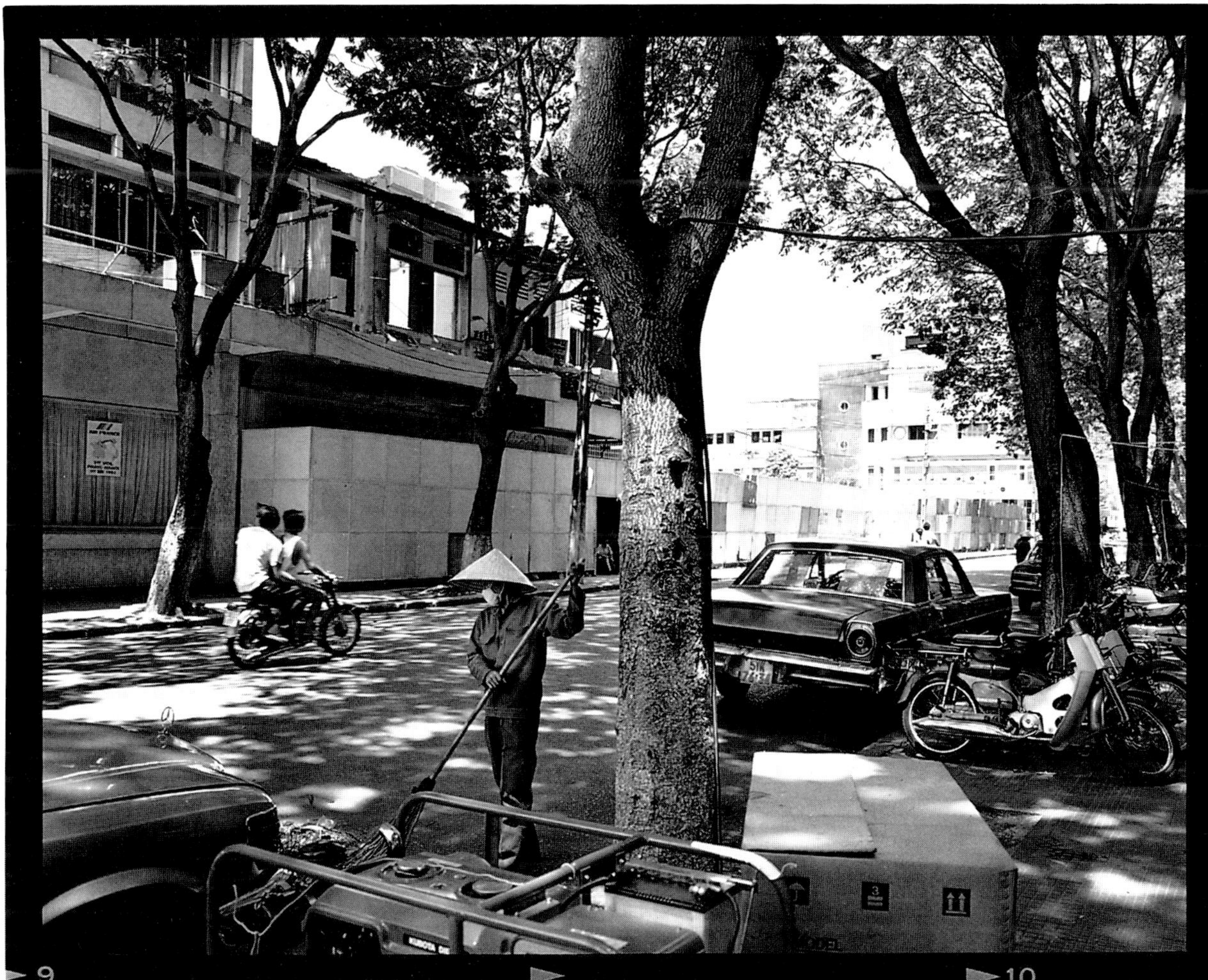

Down to the river along Tu Do Street …

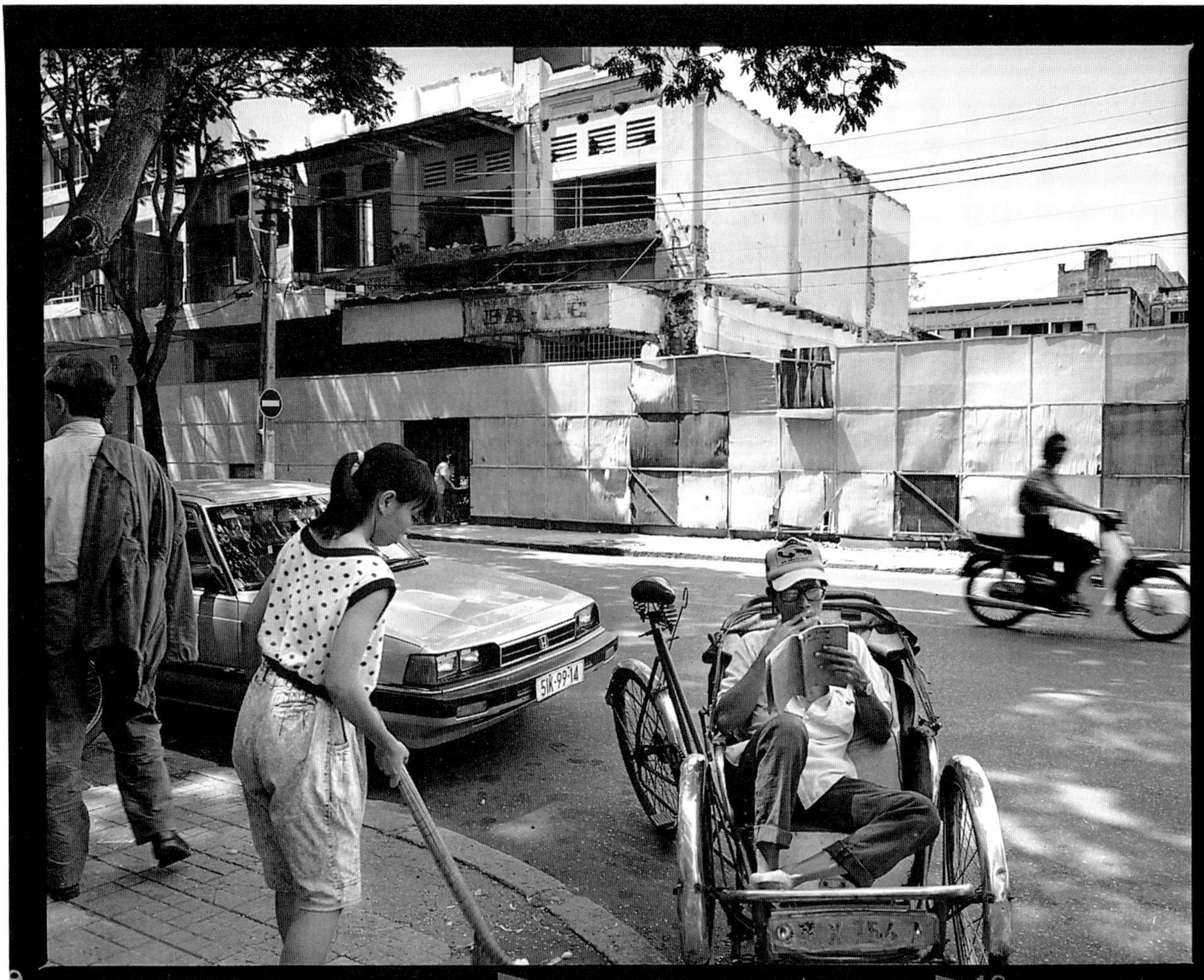

... watch out for pickpockets, they're everywhere.

independence and dignity, but without communism. In 1972, I recall having entitled an article, 'A Single Clear Idea in Saigon: The Stubborn Refusal of Communism'. Then having described at length, the following day, the corruption in the South Vietnamese regime. Two faces, one story. Was the paradox which we brought back too complicated for the time? Undoubtedly. I still think of these crackpot commitments with a sense of anger. '*Je hais l'événement,*' Paul Valéry confessed. The era itself turned away from reality. A detail: the Hô Chi Minh Trail, which today the communists proudly show off to tourists, used to be considered an invention of 'imperialist propaganda'. It was never mentioned except in quotation marks: the 'so-called Hô Chi Minh Trail'. Extraordinary!

Twenty years later. As soon as we put down our bags, we dash around the streets as if hurrying to a meeting. Surprise! The soup sellers, American cigarette and dried fish dealers are taking over the pavements again. On Tu Do Street (formerly Catinat Street), now called Dông Khoï Street ('Street of the General Insurrection'), they are once more selling old Zippo lighters bearing the insignia of the American First Cav (the First Airborne Division), 'Rambo' caps, pornographic videos, wristwatches from the former Soviet Red Army, late model hi-fis and T-shirts with the likeness of Hô Chi Minh.

In Vietnam they could always 'recycle' anything and trade in everything – ideas, suffering, empty promises. There was always a taker. The Japanese, French, Americans, Russians, Polish and Chinese: all came here to make war or build empires. Millions from Milwaukee to Okinawa carry with them a nostalgia specific to Saigon. These sedimentary strata of regret are salvaged by Saigon as little trinkets, out-of-date badges or tattered books: Russian–Vietnamese dictionaries, old issues of *Playboy*, monographs from the French School of East Asia.

Near the Majestic Hotel, five-year-old beggars selling cigarettes or the *Bangkok Post* pester us as in days gone by, jabbering a few words in twenty-five languages. On the Saigon River wharf prostitutes powdered white with painted lips – another old story reemerging – still have the same husky voices. Lying in canvas armchairs, whispering, 'Hey, darling! You're number one.'

It's said that Saigon has as many prostitutes today as before 1975. It's not true. But the times have grown more cynical. Or more demanding. The Taiwanese and Hong Kong Chinese, rich neighbours in 1992, who come to do

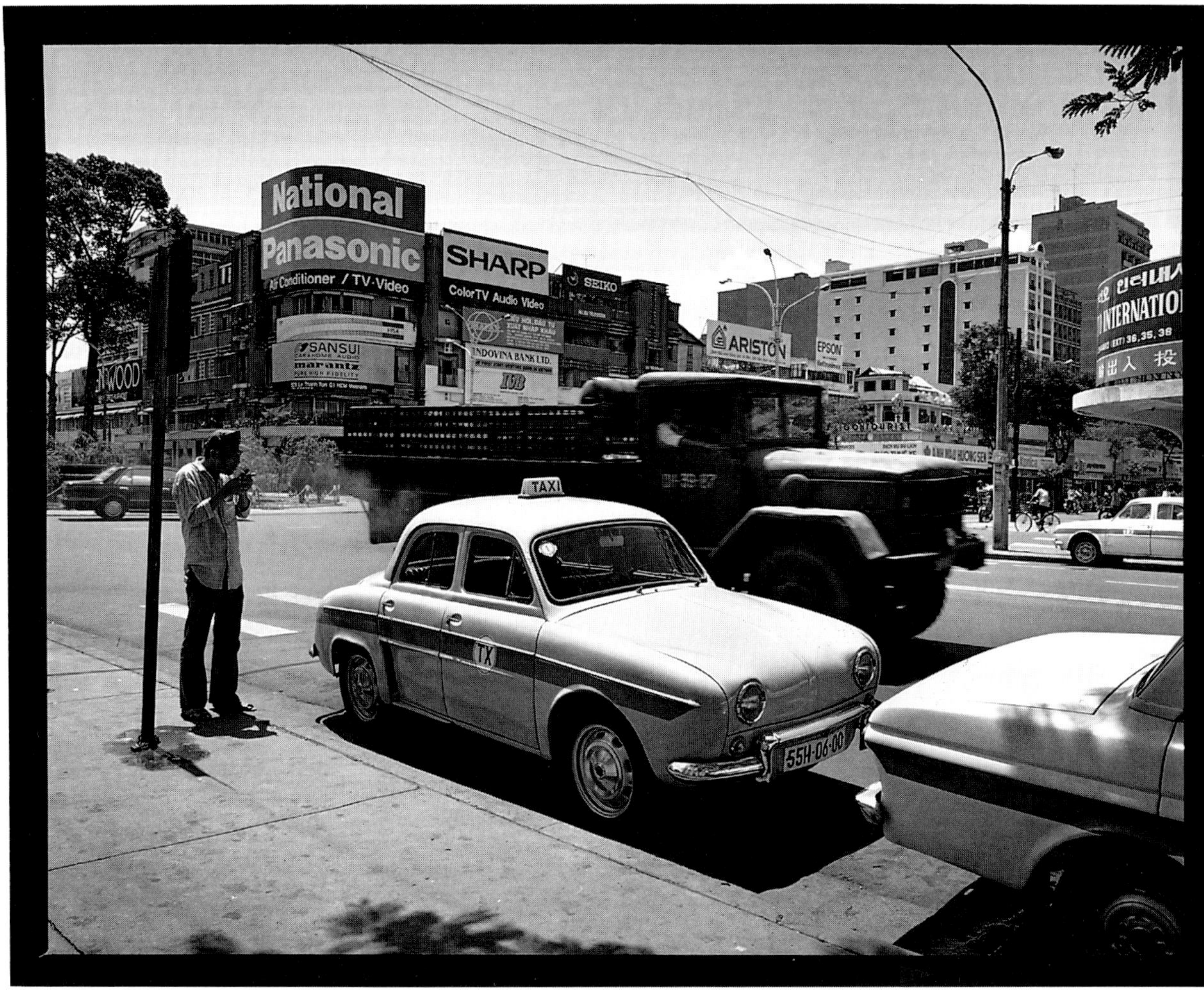

GMCs, Renault Dauphines and even 4CVs … eternal Saigon.

business or to 'do Vietnam', neglect the bar hostesses and taxi girls. They are more demanding than those exhausted GIs overcome by six months of abstinence at Holloway Camp or Phu Bai. The Chinese want maidenheads, and lay their money down: five hundred dollars in hard cash. To deflower a virgin is a token of good luck for the superstitious. If everything is coming back 'like it was' in Vietnam, then it could be even worse. Thirty years of slaughter and proletarian inflexibility to go back to that?

The former boat people, who fled the communist paradise by the tens of thousands, have been returning since 1986–87. But as tourists. They are called *Vietkieus* (overseas Vietnamese). Naively curious, with vulgar manners, they are *nouveaux riches*. A cooler, corpulent species of yellow American in Yankee dress, whose children, showing off their Nikes, no longer speak Vietnamese. Living in Los Angeles or Houston, in Australia or France, they are the new 'American uncles', dashing around on group tickets to exorcise nostalgia or set up joint ventures with communist party members – their former torturers. You meet them in the lobby of the Majestic or on the beaches of Cap St Jacques. They've got Levis, camcorders and Vuitton bags. They leave a trail of greed and envy in their wake. Their success is met with the sarcastic query: are they Vietnamese – or Chinese from Cholon?*

Pasteur Street leads to the big esplanade, Cong Viên Thông Nhât, which opens onto the rear of the cathedral. We go for a walk. It is an understatement to say we are heartsick. Saigon's customary disorder, the odour of hot soups and grilled shrimp, the occasional whiff of a joint. Beneath the trees across from the Ministry of Foreign Affairs, jarringly out of place in a city on parole, is a sizeable group of men. Mostly elderly, sitting in the grass, leaning on bikes or standing, they congregate in lively little groups. Some sort of demonstration? A strike? In fact, this gathering is an everyday ritual which has become part of the landscape. All these men belonged to the former South Vietnamese army or to the pro-American administration which the communists called the 'puppet government'. They served time in reeducation camps before being amnestied. Forbidden to

*Cholon is Saigon's Chinatown. (Tr.)

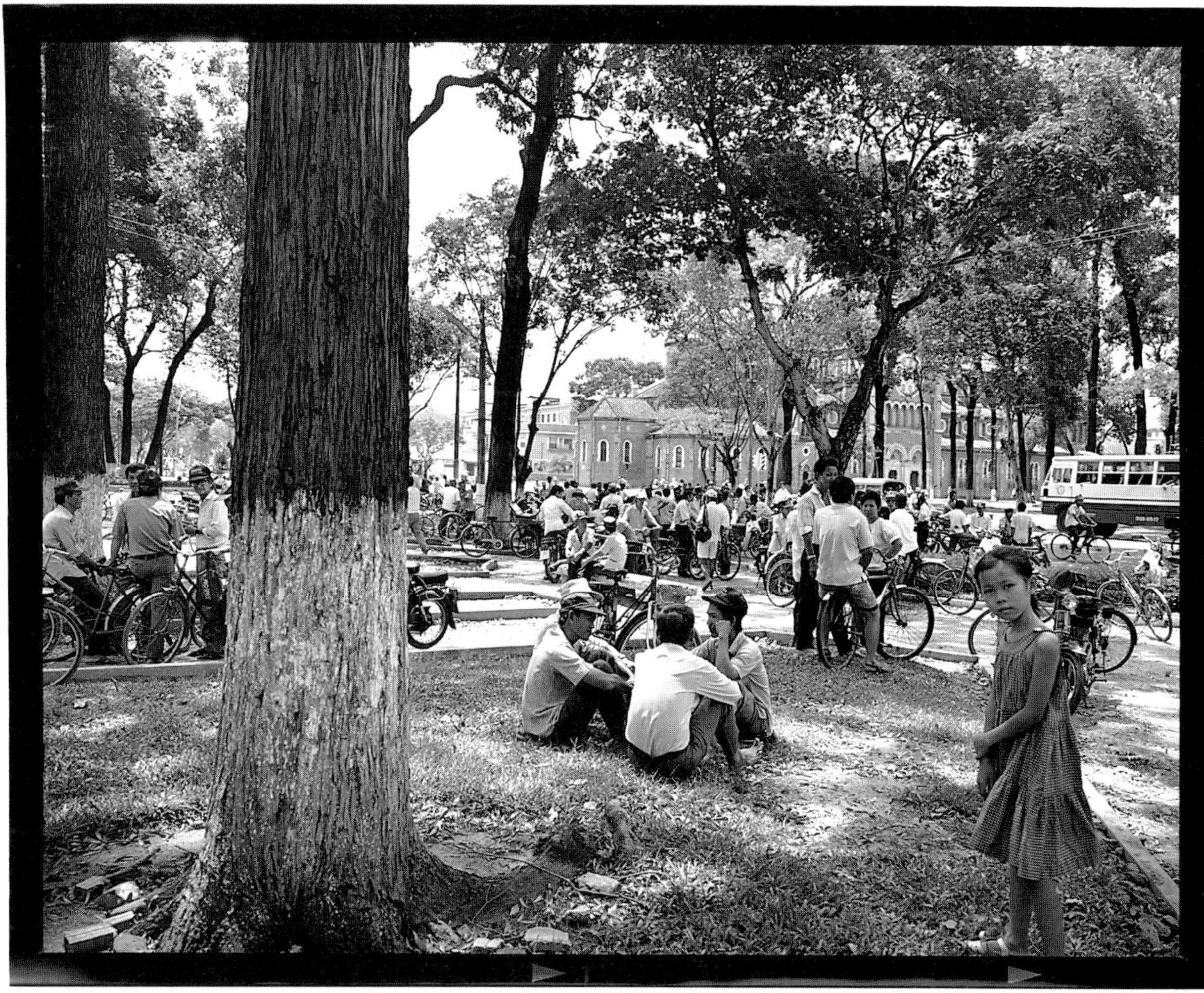

They are waiting for American visas, day after day …

work, prevented from or indifferent to rehabilitation, they float in a state of non-existence which has made them old. For years they lived in the vague hope of a visa for America, Australia or France. They were told: 'Come back tomorrow.' Thus they took to gathering in front of the Ministry of Foreign Affairs.

Any hope of getting a visa has vanished but the habit remains. So here are the dead souls of Vietnam, the inoffensive ghosts of 'the time before', the puppets of downtown Saigon who congregate beneath the acacias to rehash the same stories of escapes, being on the lam, failed getaways by boat, clandestine lives. For whom the Vietnamese have invented a mocking yet compassionate term: *Ho don gio* – literally, 'Those who await the wind'.

But what wind? When talking to foreigners, people of the South refuse to choose between two expressions: the 'fall of Saigon' or 'the liberation of Hô Chi Minh City'. They say, 'before 1975' to designate the vague period dating more or less from the 1954 Geneva Treaty to the exodus, in April 1975, of Huey helicopters from the roof of the US Embassy in Saigon.

Before 1975 . . .

All around us thousands of boys and girls turn giddily, as they do every night in Saigon, three to a Honda, two to a bicycle. An exuberant, pathetic whirl: a frenzy of gilded youth but also flies buzzing against the sides of a jar. Right and left Hondas skim past, ridden by girls no less, wearing elbow-length gloves, sputtering from one red light to the next. Sometimes we nudge each other. Mustn't give in – too much – to Asian nostalgia in 'the old boys of Indo' vein or like some Pulitzer Prize winner 'who covered Kontumin 1972'. Mustn't exaggerate the dreamy pleasure of setting down your bags in the Continental Hotel (reopened 1989). Mustn't overdo the strolls along Pasteur Street, scanning the ochre façades for the old Agence France Presse. A fresh eye will be needed to measure the fate of this triumphant land again become – seventeen years after its victory – a beggar of the far east.

Will we be able to manage it all?

It is pitch black now. On the pavements of shopping streets Japanese-made generators are brought out. The Triang hydroelectric dam, constructed near Biên Hoa with Soviet aid, is insufficient when the rains stop. Saigon is deprived of electricity two days a week. In front of each store, the generators purr as though thumbing their noses at communist incompetence. Groping along, we step over electric wires in the yellowish light of the display windows. We stroll aimlessly. Sometimes we enter one of the stores where, just as in the past, they sell lengths of Dalat silk and lacquered furniture. The abiding scenario: Grandmother, teeth red from betel, is in the back of the store; the daughter sets aside a Hong Kong photo-novel; the owner, with pudgy hands, mumbles stories about her sons in Virginia, houses expropriated, shops on Dông Khoï Street confiscated for the benefit of communist police, and of corrupt 'BK' (North Vietnamese). All in soft, cautious French which of itself is expressive of the past.

The melancholy of the first evening.

Late at night, in the Bamboo Bar of the Continental Palace, an escapee from the reeducation camps offers us Chinese beer and one tragic tale after another, smiling from ear to ear. His fourteen escapes, thirteen years of clandestine existence in Saigon, his wife gone to Virginia. Then he goes to the piano and sings us all the verses from an old hit by Adamo: '*Tombe la neige, tu ne viendras pas ce soir..*'. Across from the bar, on top of a building on Le Loi Avenue, a huge, brand-new sign, illuminated by spotlights, punctures the night. Suggesting a programme for an 'escape from communism': *Kenwood Hifi Stereo-Night Club-Karaoke VIP Room-Discotheque-Saigon Pub-Health Center-Coffee Shop.*

STREET CORNER

You hear the same thing everywhere: 'Saigon is coming back to life,' and 'The people buckled under for fifteen years, now they're fighting back,' and 'Trade is picking up again.'

Inadequate expressions for a world once more in flux, determined, inventive, voluble: witness the barely remunerative street hustle, the thousands of squatting street traders who, a half century ago, were already fascinating visitors to *Indochine*. Certainly it has the vitality proper to Asia in general, and offers a spectacle similar to those in Hong Kong, Chiang Mai or Vientiane. But Vietnam carries to the limit this casual, do-it-yourself audacity, this 'natural' proclivity which bided its time behind pompous, well-worn catechisms, and triumphed in the end over calculated shortages and murderous economic planning. Saigon, like Athens in ancient times, was able to 'conquer the barbaric conqueror' with the art of bargaining or compromise, the intuitive science of speculation and wrangling. This is the Vietnam where they squat down, nibble and chatter while haggling over wares and musing philosophically on the times and customers as both pass by. Warriors from the North, ascetic *bo doi* and moralizing commissars, are becoming embroiled body and soul in this profuse effervescence. They have clearly forgotten the advice Hô Chi Minh gave the Vietminh guerrillas as early as 1954: 'You are going to see the city after eight years in the jungle. Be not tempted by the beautiful things there. You have vanquished through your simplicity, preserve these qualities.'

Are these 'beautiful things' just Saigonese local colour? Not merely. Here the picturesque is in essence political.

Spring 1992: the South utterly triumphs over the North. How to square politics with reality and draw the obvious consequences will come later. (It will indeed be necessary to redistribute power and 'decolonize' the South.) Today, business is winning over arms; a certain propensity for shrewd realism is getting

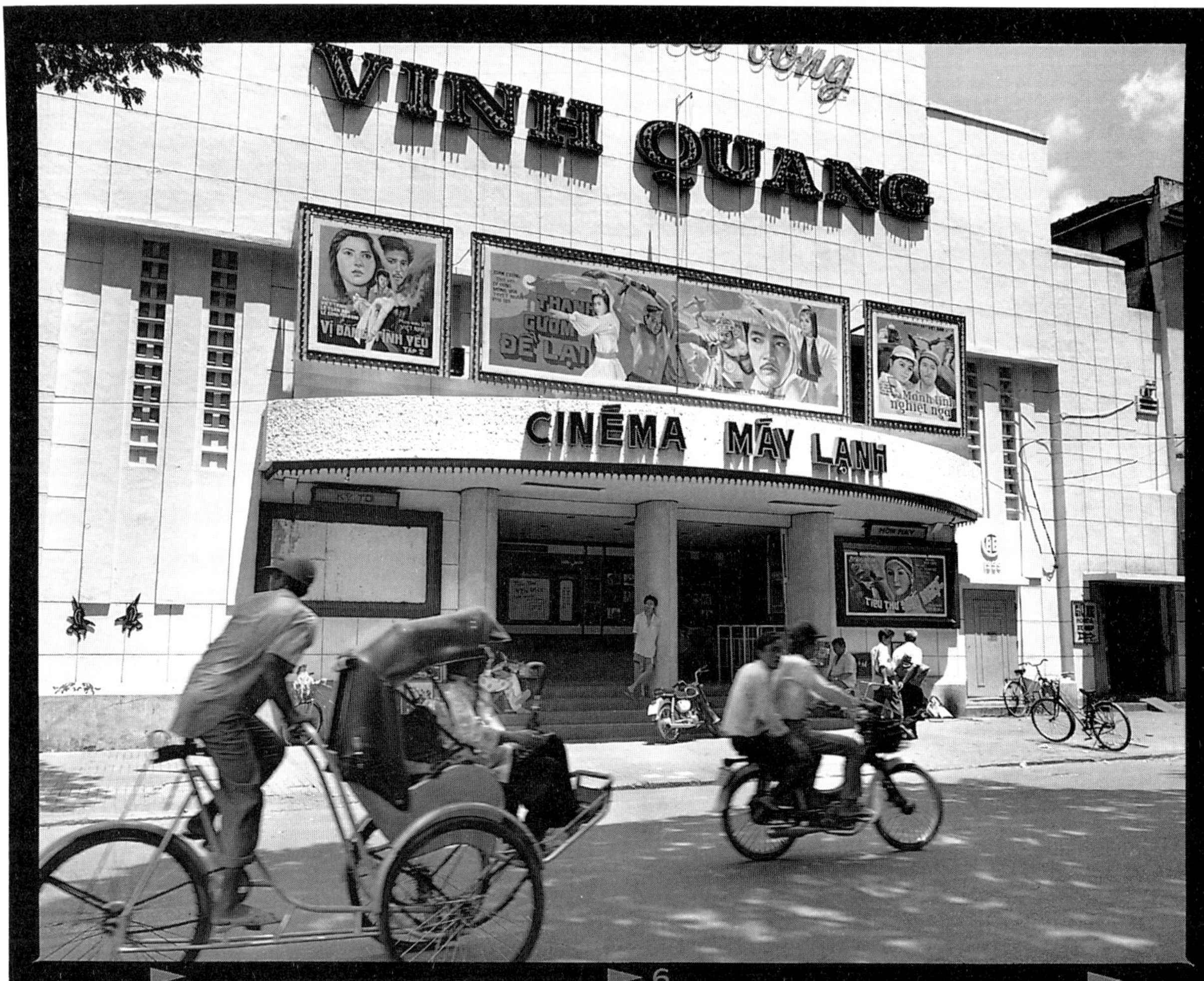

Pasteur Street, opposite the cinema …

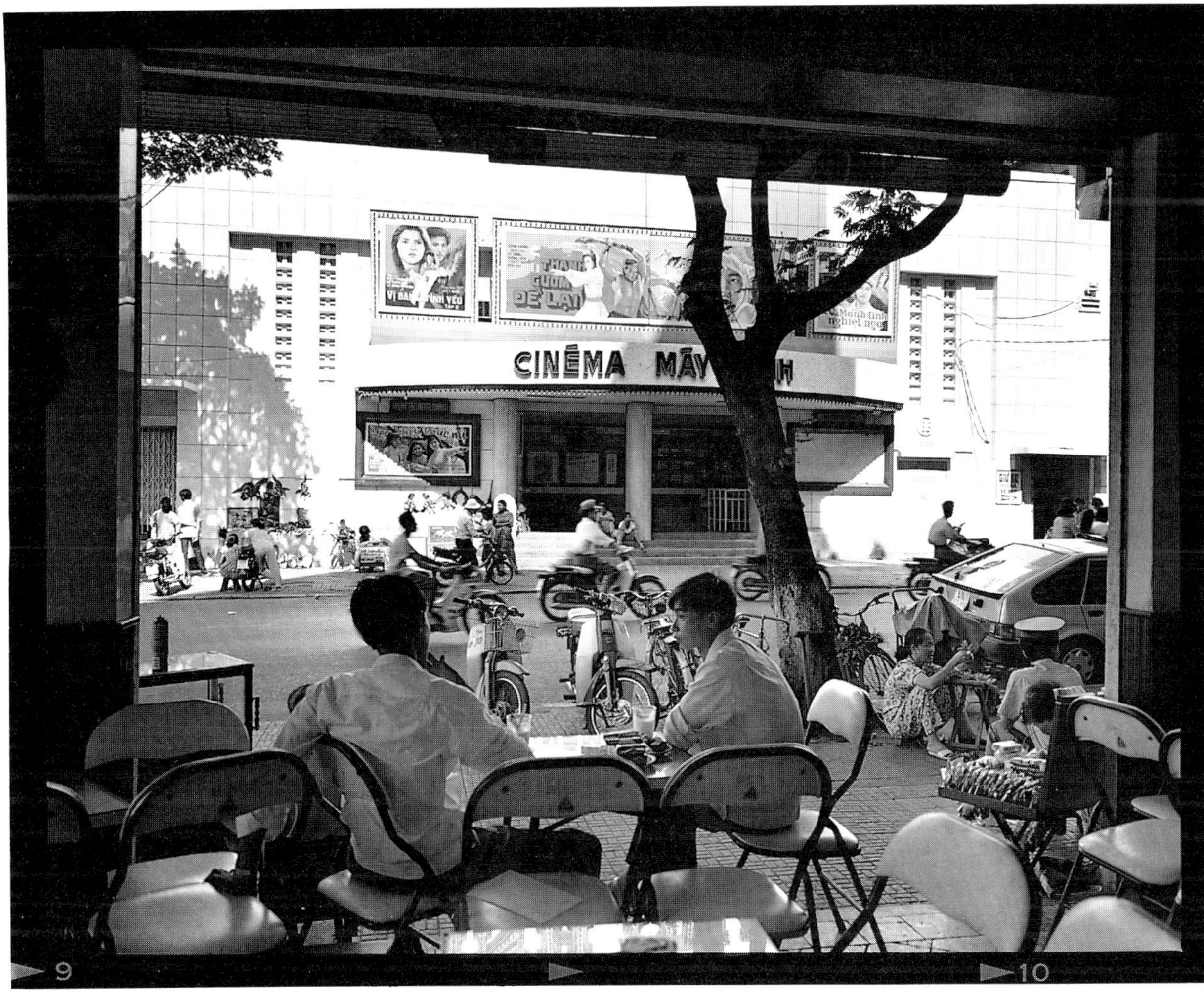

… *a terrace* à la française.

the better of militant theories and poverty. The somewhat Neapolitan South Vietnam is winning the peace just as irresistibly as the still-Prussian North won the war. This involves more than the downfall of Marxism. Mysterious substances and invisible bacteria have been at work, enzymes patiently eating away the martial armour.

Nothing more troubling – nor more visual – than this victory. But how do you grasp something so elusive? How do you describe the alchemy of something so infinitesimal? Raymond and I constantly come back to stroll the streets and wharfs of Saigon, lingering in the crowd, arms dangling, each time stumbling across new surprises. Their overabundance is perplexing. Just as he would have done twenty years ago, Raymond murmurs: 'Anyone who discovers Asia by way of Vietnam is liable to be disappointed everywhere else.' Sometimes he lowers his big 6 × 9 camera. Frustrated and discouraged. How do you photograph all that?

We take up position at the Kem Bach Dang café. The place is ideal for careful observation. From our corner terrace we take in several dozen metres of sidewalk, a short stretch of what was formerly Charner Boulevard, and the entrance to a municipal market (one of more than a hundred in Saigon).

The café is laid out with a terrace *à la française*. Above the counter a pale green plastic vine climbs the black lacquer panels inlaid with mother-of-pearl birds. An aquarium contains fat, phosphorescent fish; two myna birds in a cage and a doughnut-maker complete the altogether well-defined world of the neat and tidy cashier.

On the pavement right beside our table, several roving merchants are competing side by side. A 'recharger of disposable lighters' stands behind a painted wooden stand with a set of screwdrivers, eyebrow tweezers and bottles of gas. In two or three movements he refills the Bics or Crickets which nobody thinks of throwing away. To his right, his well-to-do neighbour is setting out, on one little stool, bunches of mint and powdered spices on pieces of newspaper. Beside her squats a woman, elbows on knees and palms in the air, offering passersby a tableful of American cigarettes, crushed peanuts and boiled quail eggs.

Between two acacia trees on Pasteur Street a little girl swings musical key chains, chanting a kind of slogan; an old man in shorts, wearing a Kubota cap, brandishes three wads of lottery tickets; a peasant woman in black pyjamas holds on her shoulder a heavy litter full of peeled shrimp and fried squid. A soup seller (4,000 dongs the platter) pokes at the embers of a brazier.* In the corner of the first building, a man and his daughter turn the handle of a sugar-cane press: 500 dongs per glass. A little further on, inside a makeshift hut an adolescent girl rents pirated videos, carefully noting her clients' names in a school notebook. She sticks out the tip of her tongue, lining up letters and numbers: 2,000 dongs for twenty-four hours, your choice of old Russian and French films, kung-fu, light romance from Taiwan, 'B' westerns or rock 'n' roll videos. At the foot of the hut four old men sitting on their heels are playing mah jong, imperturbable in the commotion.

Is it real or not – this old detachment and imperceptible casualness, expressed in each gesture and the relentless pavement activity? As if a playful disposition effaced the harshness of things and the severity of drudgery. Saigon, you could say, *plays* at commerce, at work, perhaps at living. A smile comes easily. Even pickpockets, escorting us along Dông Khoï Street, are never completely 'hard core'; a glint of irony dances in their eyes, soliciting our complicity beforehand, so ingenuous as to slightly absolve them. Nothing is serious, the city whispers in your ear, things remain frivolous and, no matter what they say, love and death are not such solemn sport. This is how, in times past, South Vietnam lived through the war. Here surely lies a part of its secret. A part of the immediate charm which wells up from this street corner.

And we haven't yet tallied the more ephemeral merchants soliciting us. Vendors of shellfish, coconuts, postcards, stamp albums, mangoes, old 100-piastre bills and back numbers of newspapers; four-year-old boys hawking communist insignia pins and packages of chewing gum; little girls begging for a smile; grandmothers brandishing dried hippocampus renowned for its aphrodisiac properties; real or phony blind people sending a child out to beg; and young women wearing too much makeup who come and go on the street, leaning heavily on their charms.

Nor have we counted, to our left along Le Loi Avenue, the lavish shop

*At the beginning of 1992, £1 = 19,280 dongs; $1 = 11,290 dongs. (Tr.)

windows of *real* stores – prosperous and respected – whose saleswomen, standing to attention in their long tunic dresses, assiduously bring in customers from morning to night. Television sets in boxes, cameras in showcases, maps or wood sculptures reproducing ad infinitum the same kneeling nude, hands on thighs, head thrown back with pointed breasts like 130 mm shells, the same stag bellowing against a background of pagodas in *trompe l'œil* and the same eagle with outstretched claws. Not to mention the unbelievable procession along the boulevard, nor the overloaded two-wheelers precariously bearing Yamaha electric organs and Chinese furniture, blocks of ice wrapped in newspaper and assorted women's shoes in plastic bags.

The value of this inventory lies not only in its comic appeal. Most of this merchandise is illegal under communist trade regulations, that is to say, it is smuggled or brought in by means of bribes. Each item has a crooked story behind it, a deal or a scam, a touch of corruption. Take the eight Honda 70s parked in the only available space in front of our table. These motorbikes, which gave Saigon its pre-communist look, were originally imported clandestinely by sailors on Vietnamese cargo ships landing in Korea, Singapore or Japan. First, used Hondas found buyers among communist party family members and well-off police; then came the new models, which sell today for $2,000 each (payable in golden taels). You rub your eyes in disbelief.

Honda City!

This 'tidal wave of capitalism' spreading across Vietnam does not apply only to small trade. From dance halls to restaurants, from electronics to the hotel business, hundreds of larger firms – marginally legal – have opened and relegated state stores to the status of subsidized museums. Thus the hotels – all nationalized – find themselves in tough competition with what are called 'mini hotels', most often converted old villas, where prices are low, service enthusiastic and management less concerned with 'the women who go upstairs'.

It wouldn't take much for us to continue our inventory until evening. Raymond discreetly photographs our neighbours on the café terrace. Two well-off *Vietkieus,* mother and son: she, plump in a green blouse with sunglasses sticking out of her pocket, he in fitted jeans, a yellow leather flight bag and Nikon camera slung across his shoulder. Both a bit distant with the waitress, to some

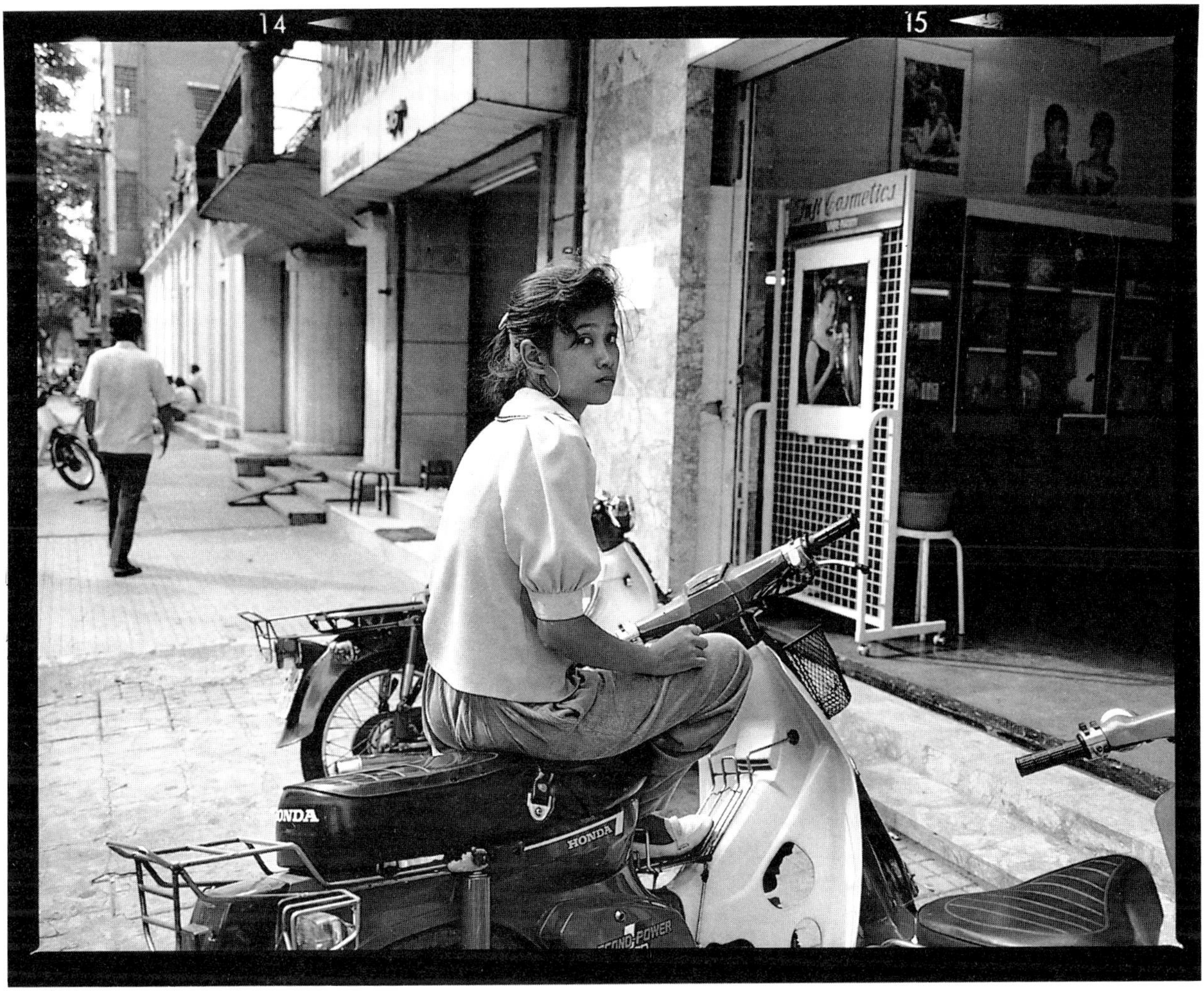

Looking back at the foreigners … she's too young to remember the war.

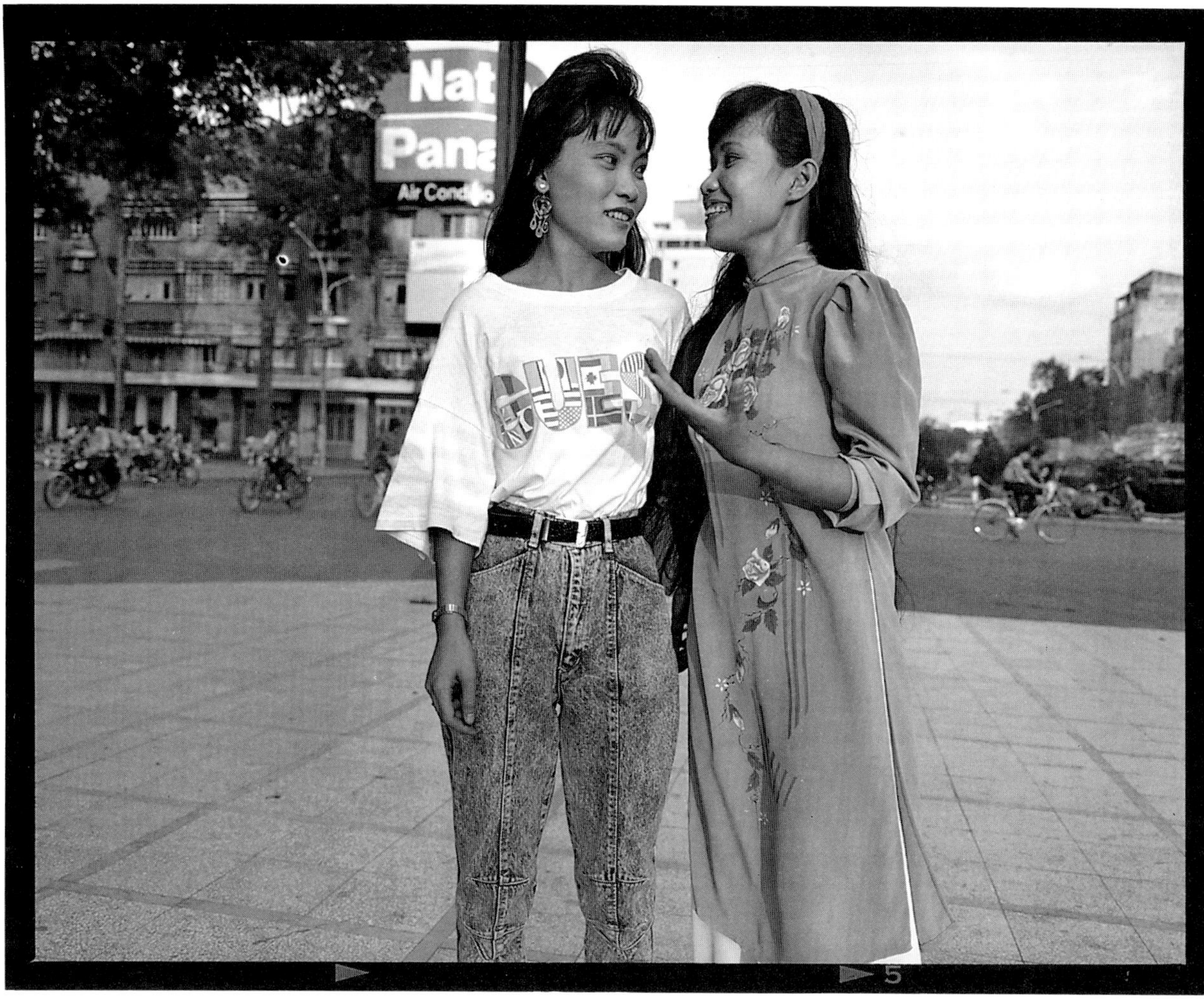

The new generation.

extent foreigners in their own land. Just beside them, two young students with short hair and painted fingernails eat ice cream and bat their eyelashes each time Raymond gets them in his viewfinder.

On the pavement across the street, the Vinh Quang Cinema is showing a sentimental Vietnamese film and a kung-fu film from Hong Kong. The *Saigon Times* (controlled by the Communist Party) criticized one of these films just this morning as being unduly interested in 'the luxurious and dissolute life of the new playboys'. The newspaper concluded with a prudish and empty flourish: 'They say our films have plenty of love. But it is a petty kind of love. No film talks about the love that really matters'.

In reality, the Vinh Quang cinema on Pasteur Street is heroically resisting new competition from the video bar which has opened right next door in the 1930s-style former Panhard Automobiles Building. Over the past few years, hundreds, perhaps thousands of video bars have appeared. Young people gather in these places and drink Coca-Cola (for 8,000 dongs a glass), hypnotized by flickering videos of Michael Jackson, copied so often they are barely watchable, or by 1960s oldies reorchestrated by *Vietkieu* singers, lip-synched on the streets of Paris or the beaches of Los Angeles. Glimpses of foreign paradises, which must be real since they're on the screen.

In front of the video bar, four policemen are sitting on the curb. They have visibly renounced the fight against subversion. Blue and grey shirts, green trousers, red-bordered caps and badges with name, number and photo pinned to their chests. They mop their necks with handkerchieves and carry on furious conversations punctuated by peals of laughter. To be a cop in Hô Chi Minh City. . . .

But how suddenly are we prey to the return of more ambiguous feelings. It takes almost nothing. A group of Western tourists pass by along the pavement, unwittingly hideous in fluorescent shorts, caps, sweaty tank tops, and belt bags around their waists. To see them ponderously pursuing the 'picturesque' in Hô Chi Minh City, waxing ecstatic over the least sign of squalor and counting their devalued dongs like they were a bonanza, plunges us immediately into an old argument. There is nothing like the tourist's self-parodying, arrogant obscenity to arouse something like scruples.

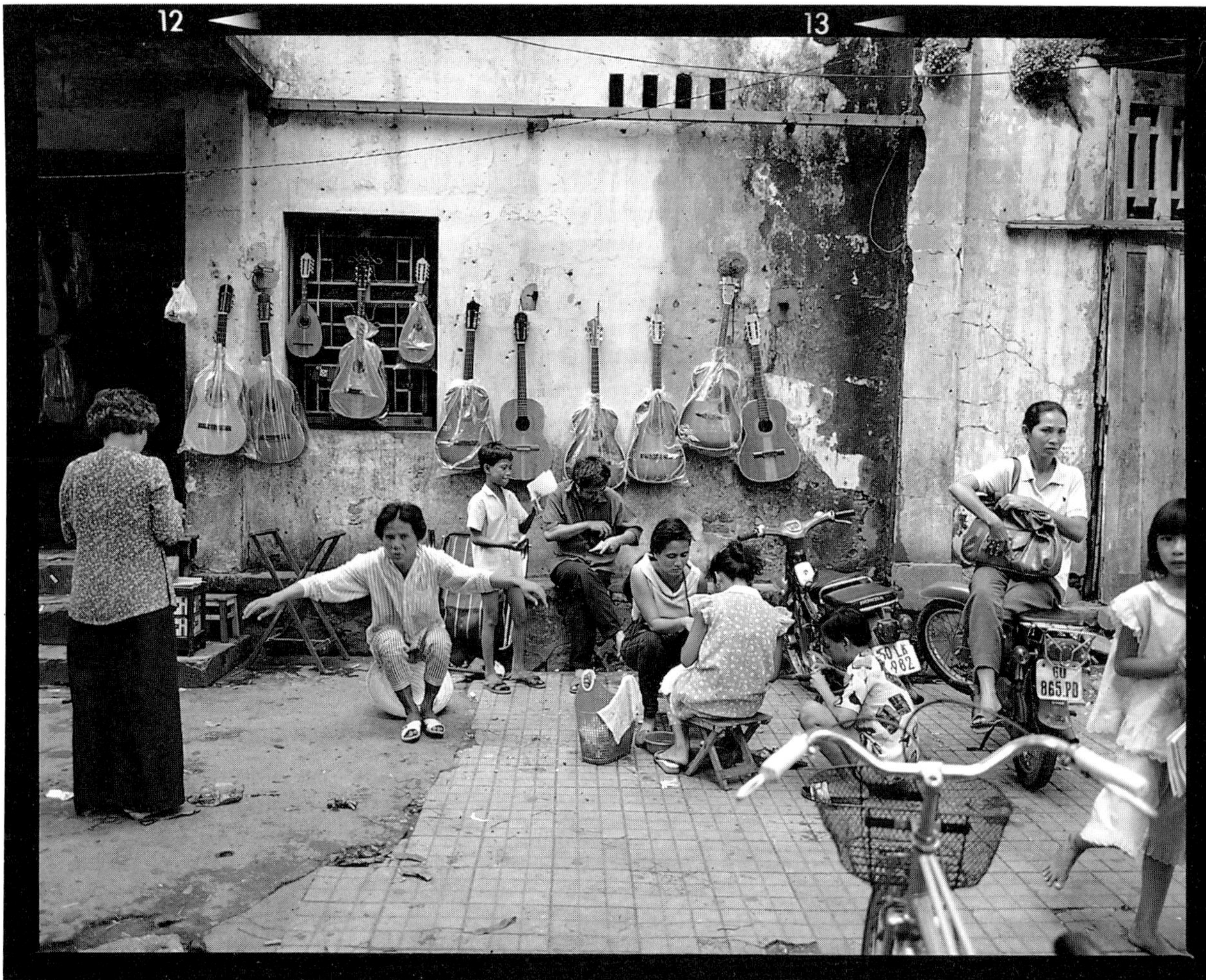

Little Paris … Naples … Pasteur Street.

Isn't what we see as 'local colour' merely the energy of despair? Will we in turn be astounded to discover that the other is so 'different', and embroider with adjectives the destitution of streets 'so much more lively' than our own? The only answer is the obvious one: we must pay attention to details, try to be accurate.

In Saigon, as elsewhere, the truth is born of several approximations holding together, it is at least double- or triple-faceted, complicated and ambiguous. All the people around the Kem Bach Dang café, resourceful street traders, tireless kids, soup sellers, 'victors over communism', are *also* inhabitants of a country which is among the poorest of the poor. Their vitality is that of the penny chase, a leap from destitution, with nothing very picturesque about it. In addition, each of them has to pay off the *công an khu vuc* (local policeman) to be allowed to do business on the pavement. A ransom which the collapsing system, unable to put an end to individual initiative, demands of it. To put it plainly: running a soup cart costs 300,000 dongs per month. As for the 'charming' cyclopeds which follow the foreigner at every step, they are often pedalled by engineers, unemployed doctors or needy teachers for 100,000 dongs per month.

In bankrupt Vietnam, the commercial inclination, this Saigonese art of living, turns into a panicky obsession. The collapse of state factories and businesses brings out more small traders than the pavements can hold. The Vietnamese have invented an expression which evokes this feverish activity rising from the ashes of communism: *Tram nguoi van, Van nguoi Mua*. Thanks to the sonority of the language, it sings – only sadly, like an aphorism: *Once there were ten million buyers for a hundred sellers. Now it's the other way round.*

THE XUÂN LÔC HIGHWAY

Xuân Lôc, sixty kilometres from Saigon.

At mortar range from this village surrounded by rubber tree plantations, Michel Laurent, a photographer for Gamma, was killed on 27 April, 1975, by a burst of gunfire from a communist soldier's AK-47. It was three days before the fall of Saigon. With Christian Hoche of *Le Figaro*, he was covering the final battle fought by South Vietnamese General Le Minh Dao's 18th Infantry Division. In the midst of the fighting, a television crew from Antenne 2 was falling back. From a distance, helpless, its cameraman filmed the scene from behind a car. I clearly remember the images broadcast at the time. Michel is running the length of the trench; in the foreground a young Southern recruit in a black uniform is firing his M-1 at the VC soldiers – then the image blurs.

In Paris the disappearance – and probable death – of Christian Hoche and Michel Laurent was announced on the same day. In fact, Hoche was only wounded. Captured by the communists, beaten up and dragged off into the forest, he was not freed until ten days later, thanks to stubborn negotiations conducted in the jungle by Jean Pouget. A French Embassy representative subsequently came to identify a body hastily buried by the highway between Biên Hoa and Xuân Lôc – it was Michel Laurent. Michel was a friend of ours.

Seventeen years later, we are standing before the headquarters of the People's Committee of Xuân Lôc, a one-storey affair with plywood notice boards, some men squatting on the wooden porch and a big, scarlet flame-tree, in the shade of which our chauffeur has parked the car. The 'comrade-in-charge' of the People's Committee brings us into his office. Glasses of tea are served. The comrade is wearing a dark shirt and a pair of old trousers without a belt. With a table loaded down with dog-eared school books, his office resembles a union branch office from the 1960s. The décor is spartan, the atmosphere strangely clammy, stuffy. The comrade regards us warily. It is probably the first time he has

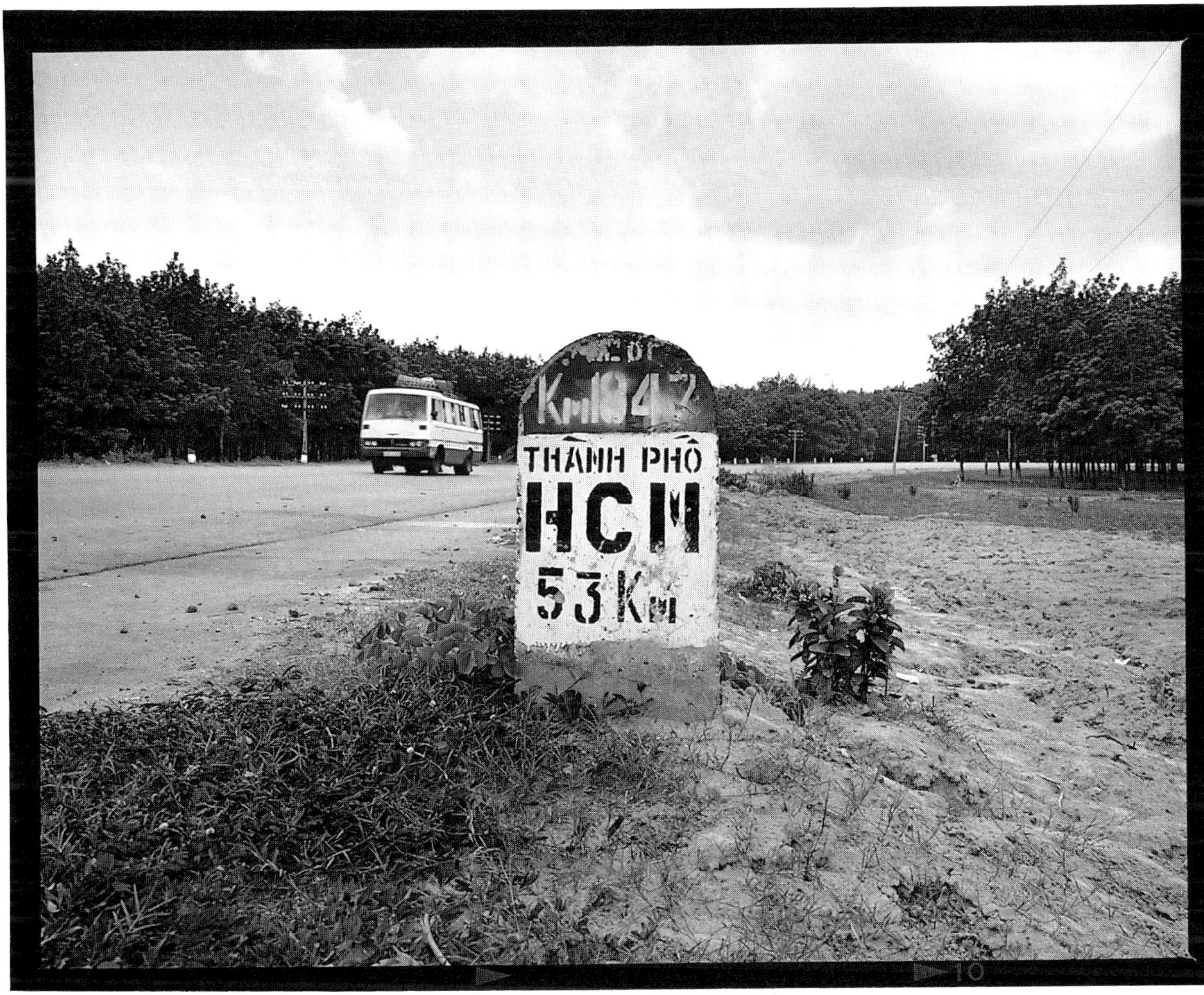

The spot where Michel Laurent died, 27 April 1975.

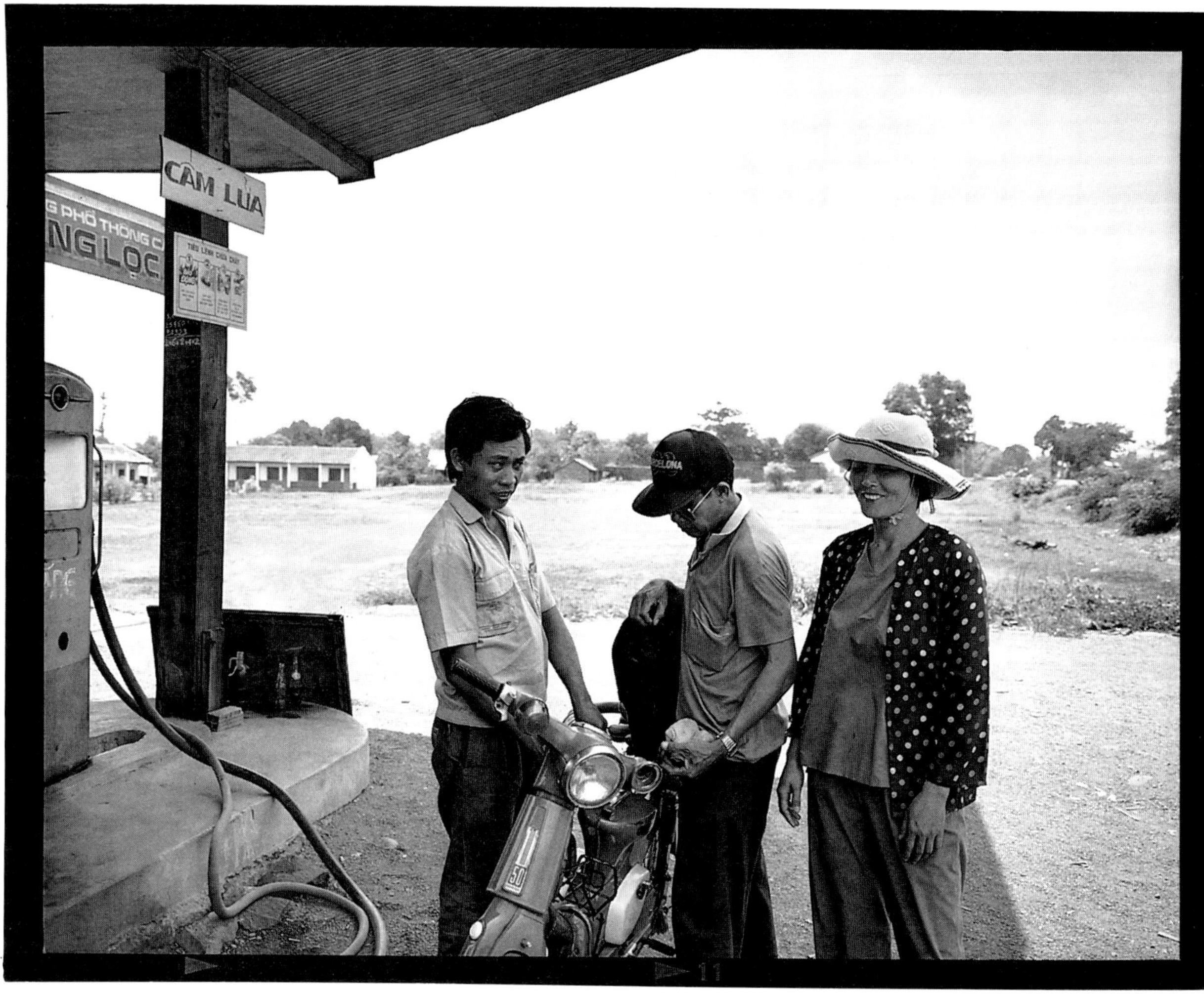

Right next to a school and a service station.

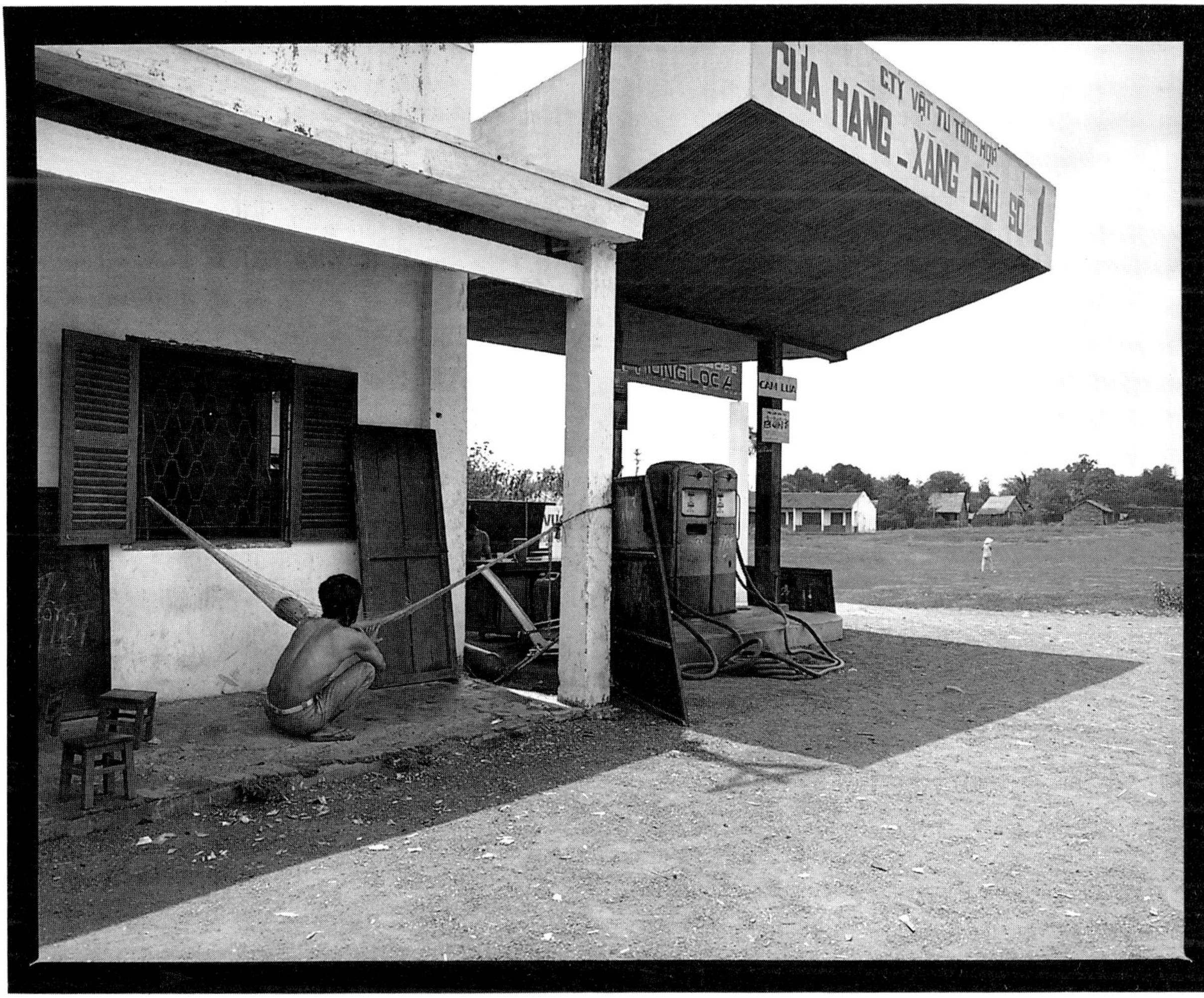

It was the last day of the war ... he was twenty-eight.

met Western journalists. We sense his reticence. We are not here, though, for an interview or to inquire into the decollectivization of rice paddies. We are simply asking permission to travel freely in the province, to ask questions of people and to stop along the highway to locate the exact spot where Michel died. We are here to see him in order to cover ourselves.

It is ten o'clock in the morning.

We left Saigon two hours earlier in an air-conditioned Renault R21, rented for $50 from Vietnam Tourism. In addition to a chauffeur, resolutely silent behind fake Ray Bans, we were accompanied by a 'private' interpreter: the equally taciturn Mme D. Both were perfectly aware of what we wanted to do and had made no comment whatever. The chauffeur listened to sentimental and nostalgic love songs on *Vietkieu* cassettes. Raymond and I weren't talking much either. Along the former 'Mandarin highway', which leads to Phan Rang, we saw a host of old and patched-up Russian and East German trucks, former US Army GMCs (42,000 abandoned in 1975), motorbikes, cyclists and convoys of ox-drawn wagons. The sputtering, backfiring hubbub of all these lopsided vehicles bears witness to a statistical fact: since 1962 the population of Vietnam has grown by twenty million. In twenty years.

Our car, very *nomenklatura* with its tinted windows and cocky chrome trim, was the only one of its kind. Several kilometres outside the city, a low cement wall divides the highway into two lanes. The wall was built in 1972. At the time, Saigon feared planes landing along this lovely straight line bordering the US bases of Biên Hoa and Long Binh. North Vietnamese planes? Mutinous ARVN (South Vietnamese)? Both could be envisaged. Twenty years later the wall is still there. By contrast, of the monumental bases from the late 1960s of which General Westmoreland was so proud, nothing remains. At Long Binh, a great sandy wasteland scattered with bushes has replaced the base's huts, bunkers, watch-towers and asphalt runways. Nothing else. Not a chunk of cement nor a scrap of iron.

At Xuân Lôc, the head of the People's Committee speaks not a word of English. Nor French. He listens silently to Mme D.'s explanations in Vietnamese. His frown gives us little hope. However, against all expectations, the face of the 'comrade-in-charge' suddenly relaxes. He turns to us, congratulates us and solemnly accords us official authorization to go where we like and to question the villagers. Do we appreciate the favour? We raise our glasses. He insists: perhaps we will find some people who remember our friend. He wishes us luck. What happened? We didn't understand a word of what Mme D. told him. No matter!

We get back in the Renault, whose air conditioning is still humming. The driver is reading, leaning on the steering wheel, indifferent to our negotiations. Then something happens. Just outside the Popular Committee compound, the driver removes his fake sunglasses and seeks our gaze in the rear-view mirror. After having not said a word all morning, he launches into a profuse and astonishingly precise speech. He remembers our story and the death of the French journalist in 1975. And with good reason! At the time he was an aviation officer with the ARVN, piloting an F-5 fighter-bomber. He took part in the rear-guard action between Biên Hoa and Xuân Lôc, bombarding the communist positions. General Le Minh Dao had constructed a long anti-tank ditch which cut the highway in the region near Dau Giay. Then he ordered the air force to drop two huge CBU bombs six kilometres northwest of Xuân Lôc, and the F-5 fighter pilots to do the impossible. The CBU 55Bs were known as 'fuel air explosive' bombs, devices weighing 7,000 kilos that the Americans called 'daisy cutters' – normally used to clear jungle areas, not against armies. Dropped by parachute, they consumed oxygen from the air within several hundred metres and killed by asphyxiation. The North Vietnamese 341st Division paid the price. It was 15 April. Several days before the death of Michel, at the same spot. As he talks, the driver grows excited and hits the steering wheel:

'In my F-5 I machine-gunned anything that moved in communist territory. By God! I can still see them running through the rice paddies.'

He adds a piece of news: the same General Le Minh Dao, considered a 'war criminal' by the communists on account of the two CBU bombs dropped on Xuân Lôc, has been freed after seventeen years in a prison camp. The same week we arrived in Saigon.

While we backtrack to Biên Hoa, Mme D. gets involved. She – who we had suspected had been detailed to keep an eye on us, who had maintained an attitude of laconic prudence, responding to our questions with monosyllables – now mutters in a completely unfamiliar enthusiastic tone:

'You know what I told that character from the People's Committee?'

What had really happened was that Mme D. had laid on a thick coat of false courtesy, repressing her silk-stocking, Saigonese disgust for this yokel from the North, this illiterate 'commie' with dirty fingernails. The distaste of people from the South for the 'stupid conquerors' from Tonkin is expressed clearly and without constraint in Saigon. Thanks to our articles, she assured him, western tourists would soon be arriving in great numbers at Xuân Lôc, bringing hard currency, etc. Or something like that. Some such bullshit which the 'comrade-in-charge' took for real. 'A cretin,' adds Mme D.

We are reflected in the mirror. It is one of those moments when, unexpectedly, the veil falls, silence is broken, the fog of reticence lifts.

Suddenly Mme D. is telling us about herself. Her Catholic family, who came from the North during the great exodus of 1954; her father, who worked for the 'puppet' government; their failed clandestine departure, in 1982, when the captain absconded with the boat people's money ($500 from each of three hundred passengers); their arrest by the *bo doi* and their six months in reeducation camp, etc. They only did six months because they bribed their jailers. The usual sentence was two years.

We weren't expecting such openness. Vietnam is such a great sorrow, so long suppressed, that sometimes it explodes without warning.

Nearing the presumed location, we scrutinize the twists of the highway and the contours of the countryside, thinking of the images on Antenne 2. Cyclists stop and watch us, a hand on their saddle. Peasants approach the car and offer coconuts and miniature green bananas. Mme D. bravely ventures onto the little paths to question some of the locals who appear in their doorways. Nobody seems surprised by her questions. We are looking for a slender thread, a distant memory.

It is not so easy. Many of the people we question weren't living here in 1975. Some come from the North, others from Huê. There was a constant exodus in wartime Vietnam. Little by little, in spite of all this, the testimonies become less vague. Someone heard his parents talk about a journalist who was killed, another suggests we stop by the school in Hung Lôc. Finally we find the precise spot. A marker indicates HCM (Hô Chi Minh City): 53 km. A long straight line, slightly downhill, ending in a bend to the right: exactly like the image on Antenne 2.

We get out of the car. The countryside is wooded, dotted with small, cramped-looking, painted concrete houses. Raymond photographs the vehicles which pass along the tarmac: high-seated tractors manufactured with old GMC chassis, bicycles equipped with huge batteries and radios attached with rubber bands, wheezing trucks transporting dead pigs in big wicker baskets.

We look along the side of the road. A red dust stains the asphalt. There it is.

I don't know what we came to do at this stretch of highway. Nor does Raymond. Nevertheless, ever since we thought of coming back to Vietnam, we knew there would be this stop to make and this ditch. Reporters didn't sign petitions but seventy-three of them were killed in the war. Michel was the last.

A man wearing a cap approaches us. He clearly wants to talk. He gives his name at the outset: Anh Thang, which means 'Victory'. He is thirty-seven years old and has always lived here. With a furtive gesture he points to his house, to the left of the highway. All the others roundabout were constructed after 1975 by people from Huê come to 'seek an easier life'. The region was called Bau Ca before 1975; now it is Hung Lôc.

Does he remember?

He nods and is silent.

From the beginning, Raymond photographs him in extreme close-up but he pretends not to notice. Ordinarily, Raymond frames his subjects from a distance. His assertiveness here doesn't really surprise me. I already know why he is choosing tight shots. When we get back into the car, we are both thinking the same thing. The man we were just talking to resembled, in every feature, the young Southern soldier who is seen shooting an M-1 in the images on Antenne 2. In addition, the dates and his age correspond. The boy was about twenty at the time. It is him.

The car starts up again. Briefly we talk about Michel, the cigars he smoked, his naive, cherubic face framed by curls.

Then not a word till Saigon.

THE KILLING FIELDS

Nguyên T.V. falls into our arms. He is a colleague. Before 1975 he was the 'stringer' for a BBC journalist. At the time, every journalist posted to Vietnam had one. Assistant, interpreter, translator of the Vietnamese press, the stringer often became a friend. Living through a war side by side, facing fears together, favours friendships which are rarely superficial. The film *The Killing Fields* depicts them accurately enough. Today just the word *stringer* evokes in each of us memories which itch under our skin like so many splinters.

After the war, journalists left but stringers remained. *We're on our way – take care.* When a bandage is suddenly ripped off, a bit of skin comes with it. We didn't notice at the time. We all of us left behind a face, profile, name and certain way of bitching when things weren't going well. Vietnam was no longer our business. It remained theirs. There were long silences which lasted years. Some innocuous letters, several more urgent messages transmitted through elaborate channels. Reunified Vietnam slipped out the door and moved into the foggy past.

Like so many, Nguyên T.V. found himself alone in Saigon, renamed Hô Chi Minh City. The BBC journalist for whom he worked didn't have time to pay him before being expelled. Nguyên T.V. no longer had either work or money. As a former collaborator with the 'imperialist press', he was categorized as one of 'enemies of the people' to be reeducated. He was quickly arrested and sent to a prison camp, near Nha Trang. After four years, provided with a false voting card, he managed to escape, mixing in with a group of families visiting the prisoners. He was captured. He escaped again. Recaptured, escaped once more. Several attempted departures by boat failed; he was arrested, escaped again. Like many others.

And, like others, he succeeded in living clandestinely in Hô Chi Minh City. At night he slept aboard boats anchored on the river. By day he survived with the help of little jobs: pedicab driver, newspaper seller, money changer on the black

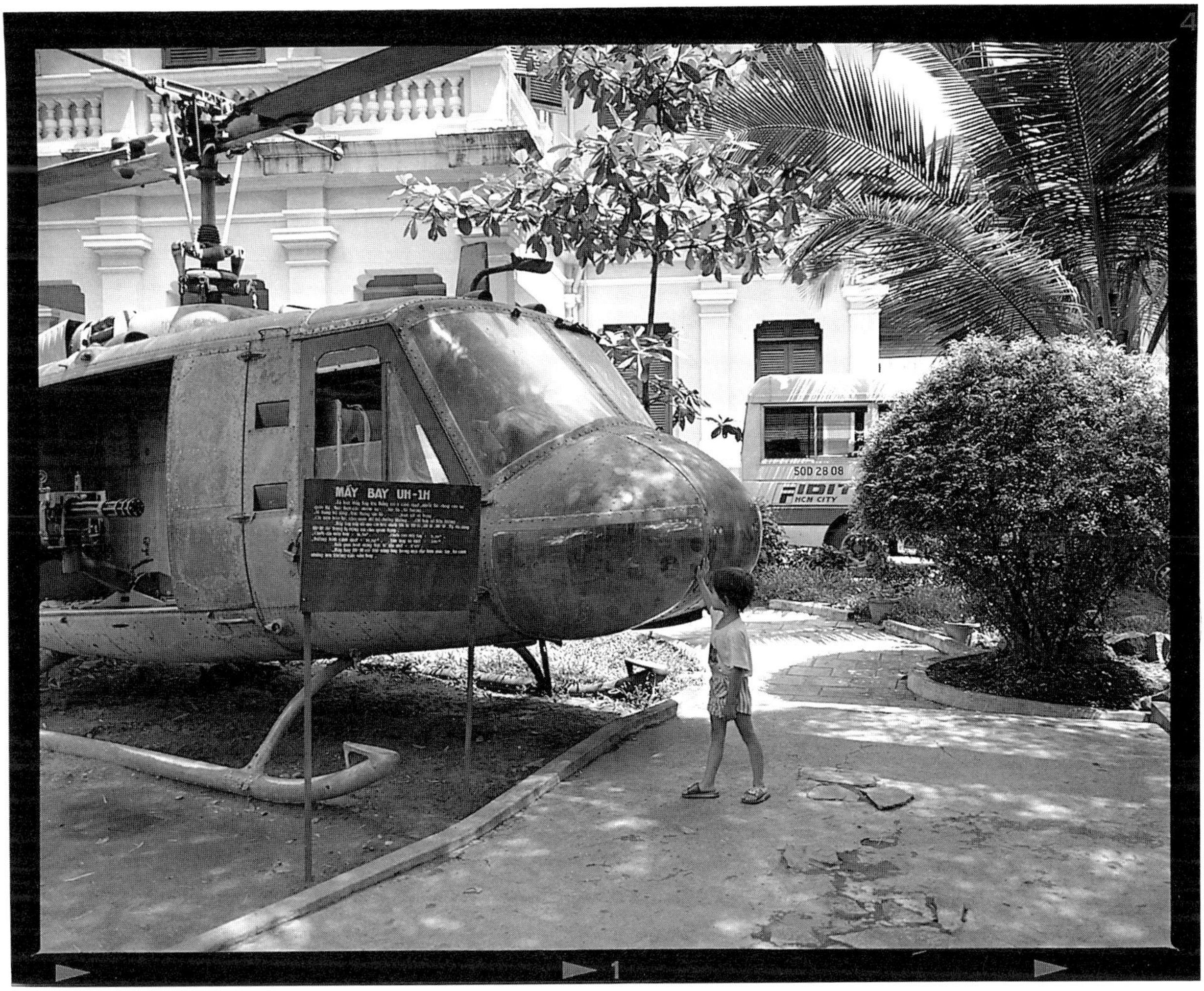

Playing the tourist at the War Museum …

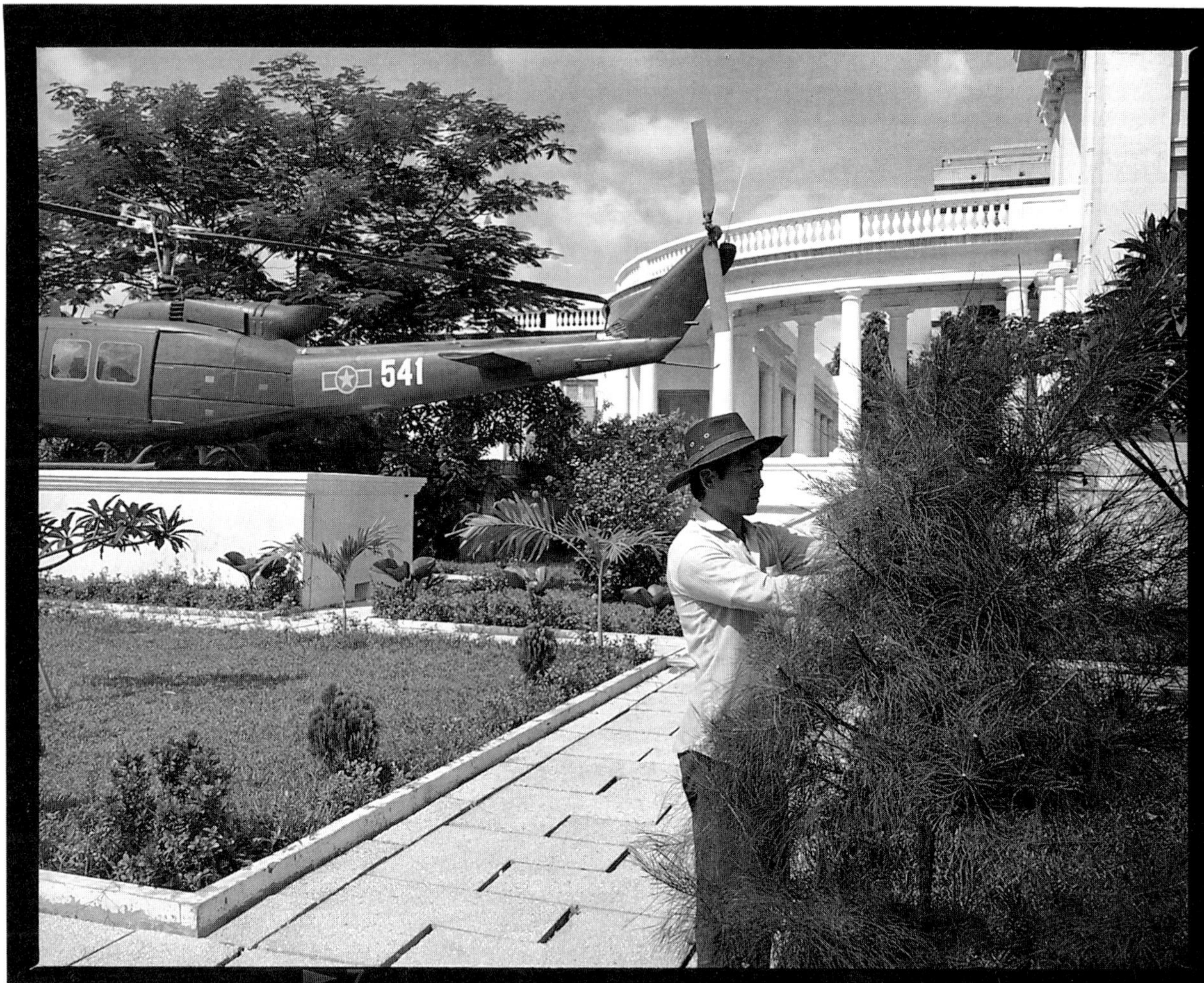

... in the parks ...

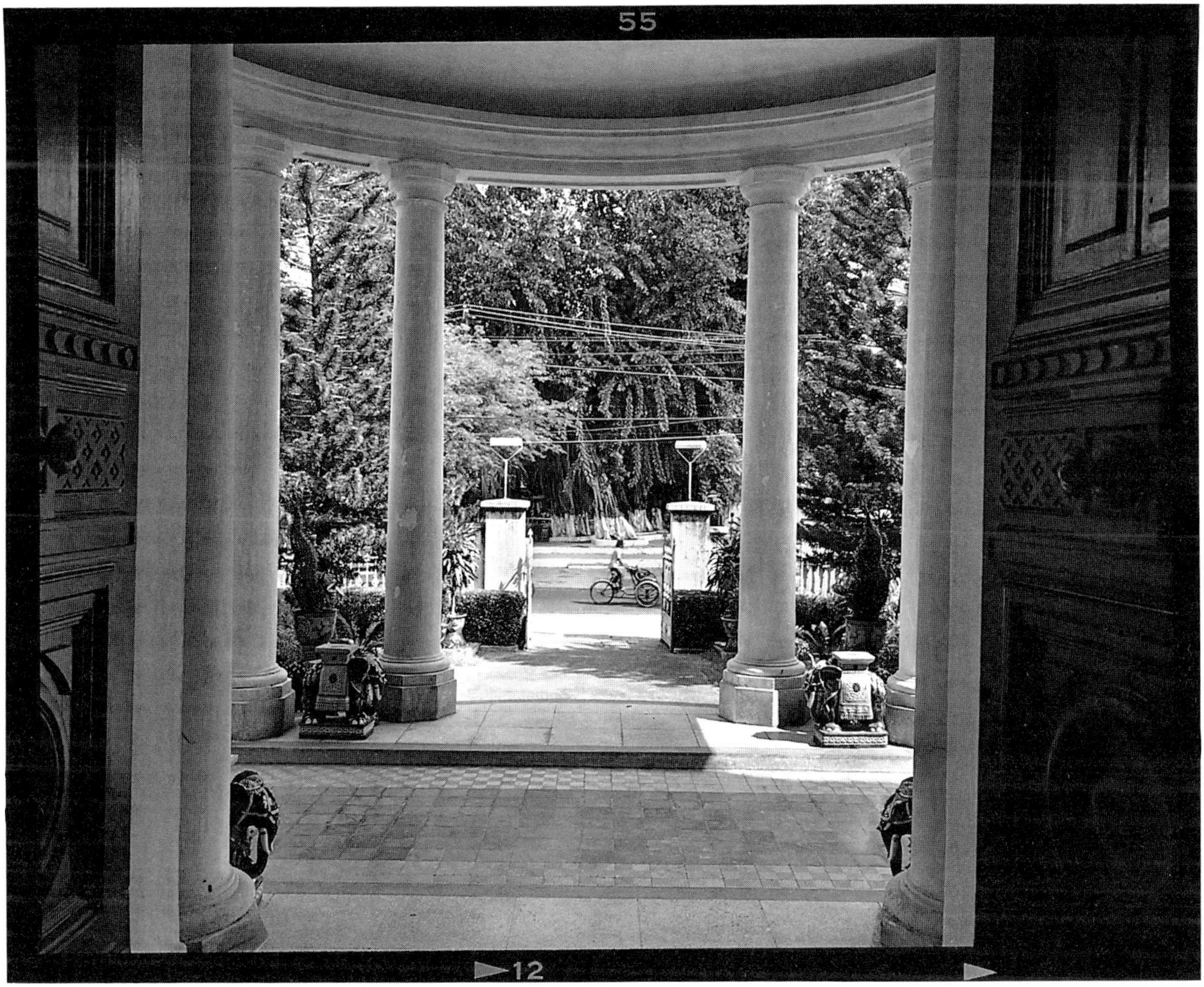

. . . and in the former colonial mansions.

market. Eleven years passed – yes, eleven. On his transistor radio he continued to listen to the news bulletins of the BBC World Service. Several times he heard 'his' journalist, who was now covering other stories, other wars, employing other stringers. Then came one day in 1986. As he was walking along Dông Khoï Street, he couldn't believe his eyes. On the pavement across the street he recognized the BBC reporter, come back to Saigon on account of the proclaimed 'opening-up'. His old chief. His English friend. He recounts the day as if reciting a fable.

'It was too risky for me to go across the street to see him. So I followed him at a distance. After a while I succeeded in approaching him discreetly. He couldn't get over it, he stared wide-eyed. I couldn't talk long. I quickly asked for my money. I needed some, I was dying of hunger. The fellow was devastated. Patting his pockets, he said he didn't have any on him. I had only to get in touch with him, that very evening, at the Caravelle Hotel, room 505. I didn't even have the time to reply, there were cops around. I continued on my way without turning back. In reality, he should have realized that it was absolutely impossible for me to contact him at the Caravelle. We were watched, still more the big hotels. So ... I never saw him again. Several weeks later, listening to the BBC, I recognized his voice. He told the story of our failed reunion. He seemed moved. He said that the meeting had upset him, things like that.'

Before leaving Saigon, I pay a visit to Dinh's parents, near Nguyên Tung Truc Street. I bring some letters and dollars which Dinh gave me in Paris. Dinh was my stringer twenty years ago. His story is identical to Nguyên T.V.'s: risky escapes, attempts to flee by boat, more or less clandestine survival in Hô Chi Minh City.

Over a period of twenty years Dinh wrote to me from time to time. Perhaps two letters a year, typewritten on onion skin paper and entrusted to reliable 'pigeons'. Each letter marked his descent toward resigned and derisive anguish, the only sort Vietnamese allow themselves. As much appeals for help as signals of disillusionment. Faced with the communists, Dinh, whom I had known as anti-American and nationalist, but also horrified by the blindness of those he called western *intellos*, maintained an unequivocal hostility. He shut himself off in interior exile and exaggerated, with sarcastic dread: 'You will see. If the commies lose the match, there'll be a bloodbath here. The people of the South have too many scores to settle. And I won't be the last in line.'

In October 1991, Dinh finally obtained the visa he was waiting for. He arrived in Paris beneath an autumn drizzle. It was the first time he had left his country – to discover Europe, France, winter weather. We had not seen each other for nineteen years. I recollect a strange dinner, at Odéon, with some uncomfortable silences. Several days after his arrival and obligatory visit to the immigration centre in Créteil, Dinh was finding his way around the metro with no trouble. He had found some unskilled work in the suburbs. He had few illusions about the future. Dinh was over forty. He knew that France was not a paradise for all.

At the time, I was preparing my return to Vietnam. In a word, our paths crossed.

WAR CORRESPONDENT?

In Paris, Dinh reminded me of a few shared memories. They are not all proud ones.

PLEIKU, 1972, MAY 13 (NOTES)

A detail, a simple detail has been bothering me since yesterday. A behind-the-scenes event which I didn't talk about in my articles. It happened in late afternoon on the landing strip at Kontum, eighty kilometres from here. Before going on, a few explanations are in order. Dinh is my stringer. A former student and now freelance photographer for AFP, he travels with me, serving as interpreter, guide, adviser. In exchange, I pay all his expenses. We've often been scared to death together.

For several days he and I have been wandering through the débâcle. On the forty-third day of the communist offensive, the fronts are crumbling everywhere. Especially here, in the highlands, where the situation has completely changed since last year. We make our way among soldiers in disorderly retreat, refugees loaded with bundles of clothes, and hordes of kids. We pass indescribable crowds, with islands of tranquillity here and there: a cheap restaurant run by a fatalist, a Montagnard village which remains quiet and calm in the mayhem.

Mayhem? In the highlands nearly all the ARVN bases protecting Kontum and Pleiku have fallen: Dak Tô, Pleikleng, Yankee, Charlie, Bravo, Lima, Ngotrang, Benhet (retaken May 10).... More seriously still, the Tan Canh fortress was overrun on 24 April at 6 o'clock in the morning by communist tanks. One of three American advisers who escaped (there were nine), Colonel Terry McClain, told me about that incredible morning: 'Christ! First you heard their motors in the night before seeing them. The tanks were rolling along the highway with their headlights on like it was the Los Angeles freeway. It was impossible! Mathematically, those T-54s couldn't be there. They were supposed to have been destroyed a long time ago.'

Badly injured, McClain was picked up by a Huey and taken to Pleiku, more dead than alive.

In this madness, thanks to Dinh – uniquely thanks to him – I was able to interview some of the ARVN soldiers in headlong retreat. Especially Rangers of the 2nd Regiment of the 23rd Brigade. They had come some kilometres at the double, without drinking or eating. They were aimlessly roaming the streets of Kontum, most of whose inhabitants had already fled south. You didn't want to make fun of these terrified deserters, youngsters with trembling hands, infantrymen abandoned by their commanders. We perfected an interview technique: Dinh went up to a soldier, offering a cigarette. Little by little he relaxed. We were set up at the edge of a pavement and right away he started to talk, rapidly and continuously, not stopping to catch his breath. I based my article yesterday on all these accounts of the flight, which contrasted with the trimphant speech that Richard Nixon had just made in Washington, which we listened to here on transistor radio. While talking to us, the soldiers were constantly, fearfully scanning the surrounding area; they jumped at the sound of every shell.

True, Kontum has got to give way. Only one outpost seems solid – November, three kilometres to the north. The orphanage has just been evacuated. Above the city is a confused whirl of B-52s, Skyraiders, F-5s and Cobras. It is difficult to evaluate the imminence of danger from the perspective of the crowd, far from a bunker or communications post. People in the city who have not left yet are frightened. Seats on the ARVN helicopters are already going for a lot of money. The pilots are taking advantage of the windfall, evacuating the well-off for a hefty sum, even if it means dropping their resupply missions. Dinh and I were so busy reporting that we weren't thinking about our own evacuation. Christ, but you hang on to a good story!

Toward five o'clock we hit a problem. We have to get to Pleiku in order to transmit. We go see the American advisers. In the bunker where they are dug in we find half a dozen journalists, mostly Americans. The cafeteria is still open – a surreal sight – but outside, beneath the barbed wire, soldiers are laying Claymore mines, rolling out their electric wires. The senior adviser tells us to get lost. Do we think he's able to call up a single helicopter for a handful of 'irresponsible' journalists! He is exasperated by our presence. That I can understand. But a guy from the *Washington Post* replies in the same tone: 'Do you realize that you are responsible for a number of special correspondents to major newspapers? You want them to be stuck here? Or killed?' They squabble for a while. It gets a bit embarrassing.

Finally, the senior adviser gives up. What else could he do with the *Post*, *Los Angeles Times* and *Boston Globe* on his back? We were to go wait near the airstrip. He was going to divert a Huey to take us to Pleiku. So saying, he turned on his heel and walked away.

We find ourselves flat on the ground at the edge of the runway. Night is coming on. We are surrounded by explosions, smoke, starving deserters. Nearby, Cobras land for a few minutes, just long enough to fill their tanks and rearm their rocket launchers. We can feel the heat from their engines. All around us unarmed Vietnamese soldiers in tattered combat uniforms are also waiting for a lucky break – the miracle of a chopper.

After an hour, a Huey sets down two hundred metres away. It is ours. We make a disorderly run for it. One of the pilots puts his head out and shouts at us to hurry up.

We quickly get on board, piling onto the deck. Just behind me, I catch sight of a Vietnamese deserter huddled up in the back of the machine. He has managed to slip quietly among us and, once inside, his face lights up. All this happens in a few seconds. The kid thinks he's made it. He's happy.

Just when we are about to take off, one of the pilots, turns round and spots him. He takes off his helmet and earphones, abruptly gets up from his seat to come around the cabin. He seizes the kid by the collar of his uniform and, without a word, throws him outside. None of us moves a muscle. It's not our business. We lift off and, when the Huey makes its turn, I see all the Vietnamese soldiers looking up at the sky, watching us depart.

I'm ashamed.

This is one time I feel like a tourist, a shitty VIP, ploughing through hell in lace underwear.

War correspondent? Forget it.

OPIUM OF THE PEOPLE

A Sunday in Saigon, in front of the pink brick cathedral whose bulk dominates the city centre.

It is barely seven o'clock but night has fallen. Snatches of hymns can be heard. Evening mass. The church is so full that a second congregation has formed on the square – drivers and passengers astride dozens of diagonally parked Hondas. Contemplative, leaning on the handlebars in their Sunday best, they sing hymns and psalms, whose words they make out from the confused sounds coming from within. A strange, absolutely immobile fleet of two-wheelers, somehow frozen in prayer, parked seat to seat, handlebars abutting. You guess that in a little while they'll suddenly be off again, buzzing noisily along the dark streets, playing games and running errands. The way an image on film, momentarily frozen, starts to move again.

Inside the packed church, a mixed choir is singing. Stylish women are wearing fitted *ao dai* (the traditional tunic) or white blouses, with their black hair gathered up at the back by mother-of-pearl slides. A large contingent of young people occupies the nave and side chapels. The religious fervour is as apparent here as in Moscow or Budapest, and signifies the same post-communist confusion. Or the same hope.

Churches are full as never before in South Vietnam. The flamboyant and stubborn Catholicism of the 1954 refugees implanted traditions which seventeen years of obligatory atheism have only sharpened. And the pagodas are not to be outdone. Restored and repainted, they are reopening by the roadside and have already regained lost ground. And while bonzes and priests continue to be watched and even persecuted by the regime, they are once more a force to be reckoned with.

RAILWAY STATION BLUES

Railway stations are where a city bares its soul, where anguish comes to the surface. The people you find there are without guile; they are caught in a hurry, in a sweat, in a state of worried fatigue. Railway station platforms are a backstage brought into view, a window display without artifice. In Saigon, almost unexpectedly, you find this darker side of Asiatic poverty, families weighed down by baggage that looks as if it has been hastily bundled together for an exodus. But this is also part of Saigon – vagabonds by the thousands, drug addicts, orphans and whole families who, every evening, roll themselves into a patched-up blanket right there on the street. The raw truth of railway stations.

We were no longer smiling. In the throng we are suddenly like foreign bodies, obviously gate-crashers with our compact luggage, our tickets in order and our bottles of mineral water. Doors which remain closed for others open wide for us; we receive exaggerated help, and are escorted with embarrassing solicitude. As we pass, the crowd moves back in silence, a path opens to the ticket window. We don't much like it. We would like to be different people, perhaps yellow and barefoot, in any event anonymous.

I am quite familiar with these brief, awkward moments at the entrance to railway stations in foreign lands. I have taken other trains even more filthy and improbable that this one, less dependable than this clear line on the map, drawn long ago between Saigon and Hanoi. This colonial wager of 1,738 kilometres, broken a thousand times by war, cut up and ground into mincemeat – an iron nerve laid by the French in 1938 between the two baskets of rice hanging from the Vietnam pole: the Cochin Chinese and the Tonkinese, with Amman in the narrow centre. A rough, bumpy, crooked and narrow road that the French called the Transindochinese Corridor and which, from 1954 on, was cut clear in two by the River Ben Haï, along the 17th parallel. And, in both North and South, pulverized a thousand times by bombs in twenty-one years of war.

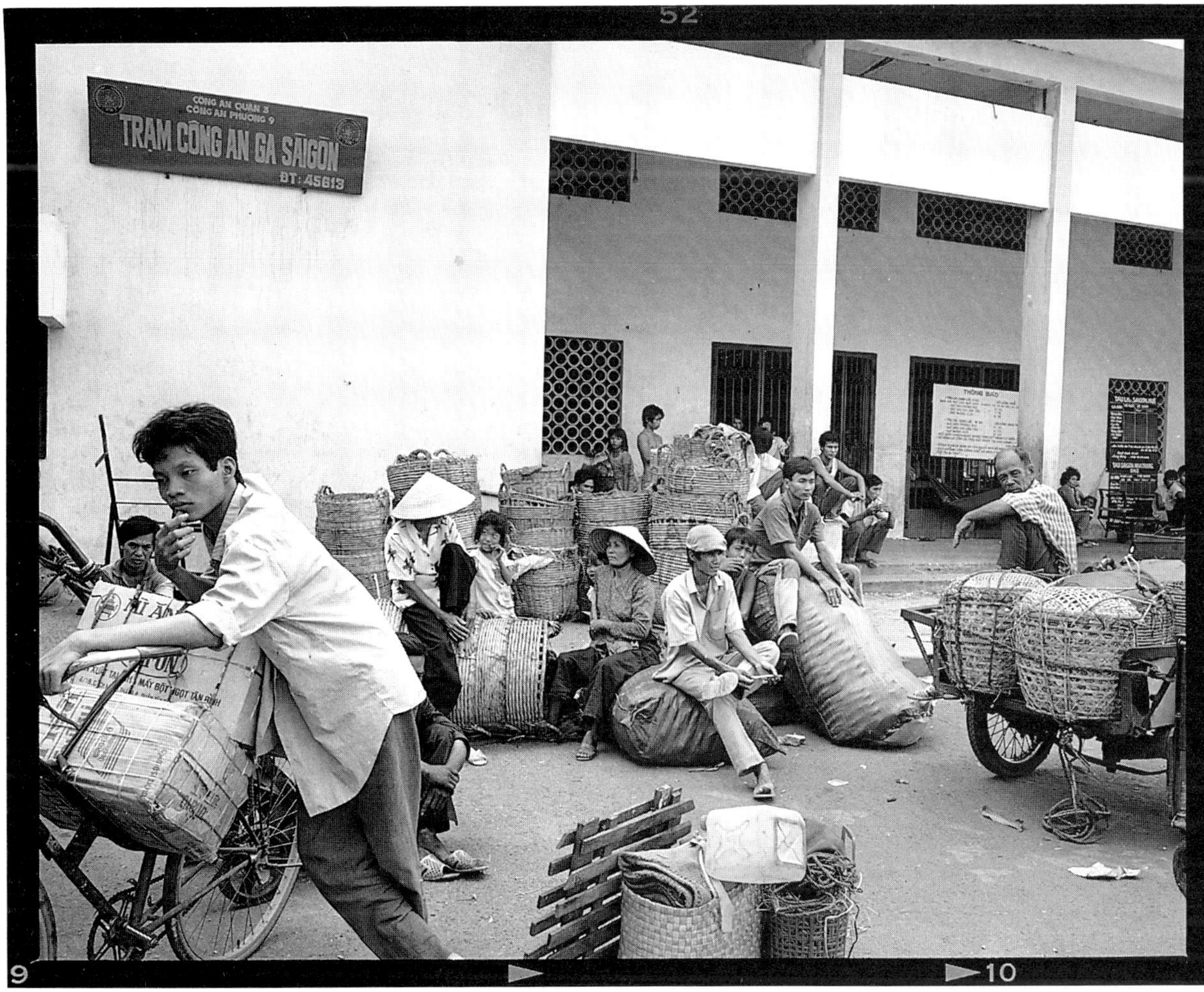

Leaving Saigon on the train to Hanoi … at last!

The Hanoi conquerors have given the name *Thong Nhat* ('Reunification') to this symbol-laden train which, having been fixed up, holds together anew the two halves of the country. They attach great importance to the train and have apparently spent considerable sums of money on it, although only enough for it to do forty-five kilometres an hour. The daily service is not just some miracle. It is a political project. As if it needed a Thirty Years War finally to reunite these two long stretches of track. Several categories of service are available. The slowest and least comfortable must be shunted off the main line periodically to let the 'express' pass. We want the 'slow' train.

We jam ourselves into the waiting room well before the time of departure. Mme D. has decided on new jeans and espadrilles, and is wearing a cap that gives her the look of a *Vietkieu* from Los Angeles. She is not much more comfortable than we are. It is the first time she has been on this 'Northern' train and no doubt it is also the first time she has been so close to the masses. Over the station's loudspeakers we listen to a Vietnamese version of *Capri c'est fini.* A banner above the ticket windows proclaims in yellow letters on a red background: 'All railway employees must work with care and devotion.' A hundred or so people scuffle at the doors to the waiting room, kept out by an inflexible *bo doi.*

Raymond roams around outside, constantly looking through his viewfinder. Not a word. We bottle up our normally voluble impatience to be off, paralyzed by silent embarrassment. Of course, Vietnamese destitution is not like the agonizing vacant gaze of poverty in Calcutta, nor even the sickly inertia of the suburbs of Bamako. No skeleton-like children nor grizzled old people in rags here. Vietnam is poor among the poor but not starving. But so what? Movements are slow, looks are long, jests are rare. The whole crowd is awash in grey dust, their faces creased by it. A worker's salary in Vietnam: 100,000 dongs per month. In Vietnam the 'Asian smile' often conceals a tear.

Finally we get on the platform and look for our carriage. But suddenly there are shouts and exclamations. Raymond, who ran off to see what was happening, returns slightly pale. In the middle of a train standing on a siding, men have opened the sliding doors of a steel freight car. Inside they have found hundreds of baboons, in wooden cages piled several metres high. Live cargo destined for Europe and forgotten, imprisoned in this oven? Illegal traffic in zoo animals?

Choice meat for China? The animals have had nothing to eat or drink for days. Most are dead. Some are still dying, their faces comatose, their eyes glazed. Especially the females, with their rigid young, slowly moving their feet like spiders.

The cages are opened one by one. The curious jostle each other. The bodies are laid out on the platform. A long line of curled up cadavers forms just under the passengers' feet. Some bodies are still moving. Death has returned to Saigon.

Raymond is deeply distraught: 'I'm not photographing that.'

BY TRAIN TO THE NORTH

Now we are travelling through the night in the swaying, creaking, lurching train, plunging through a perfumed darkness spangled with fireflies. Wet leaves smack against the windows, stippling our cheeks with raindrops. Straw huts lit by oil lamps swaying in the wind, children asleep in hammocks, a gleam of moonlight on the rice paddy. Saigon is far away. We lean out to breathe in the night. The train makes unscheduled stops in the depths of the countryside. Voices call out to each other, there are brief discussions somewhere down below the carriages, axles are checked and adjusted, then we slowly move off again. In each carriage attendants have distributed mats and pillows. Our neighbours are dozing. Could we think of sleeping? And would we be able to anyway? We have long since sweated ourselves dry, the wind has stiffened our shirts.

Little girls selling all kinds of things are waiting in ambush at every station, rushing forth out of the dark. Commotion fills the train. They drag their baskets and poles through the corridors, harangued by the passengers along the way. They brandish pieces of pineapple and chewing gum under our noses. We no longer know which town we're coming to, but it's not important.

Day breaks over the China Sea, as we near Phan Rang. The sleeping berths are folded up and the compartments are put back in order. Men and women, still heavy with sleep, besiege the toilets. The journey starts again. By now we have become full-fledged passengers on the *Thong Nhat.*

Tuy Hoa, Dieu Tri, Quang Ngaï. The stations go past; some with white-washed brick pavilions dating from the French colonial era. With one buttock – a single buttock – perched on a wooden seat, jolting about for seventeen or eighteen hours at a stretch, we sail along feeling nothing but happiness. Even though a grandmother's hammock, tied to the back of my seat, is digging into my left shoulder; even though Mme D. is stoically dying of thirst; even though my neighbour, a Tonkinese agricultural worker from the plantations of Lang Bian,

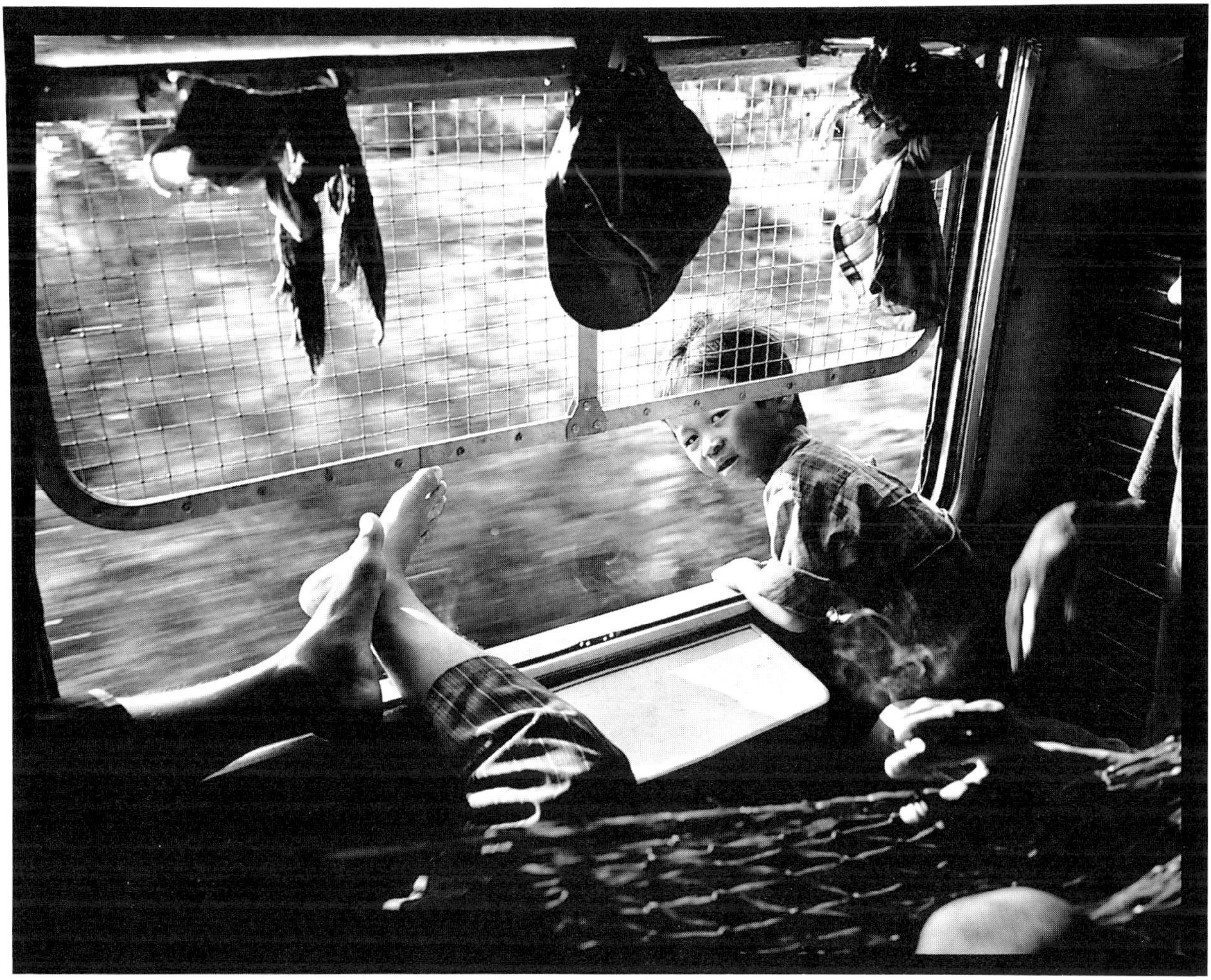

It's hot … it's a long journey …

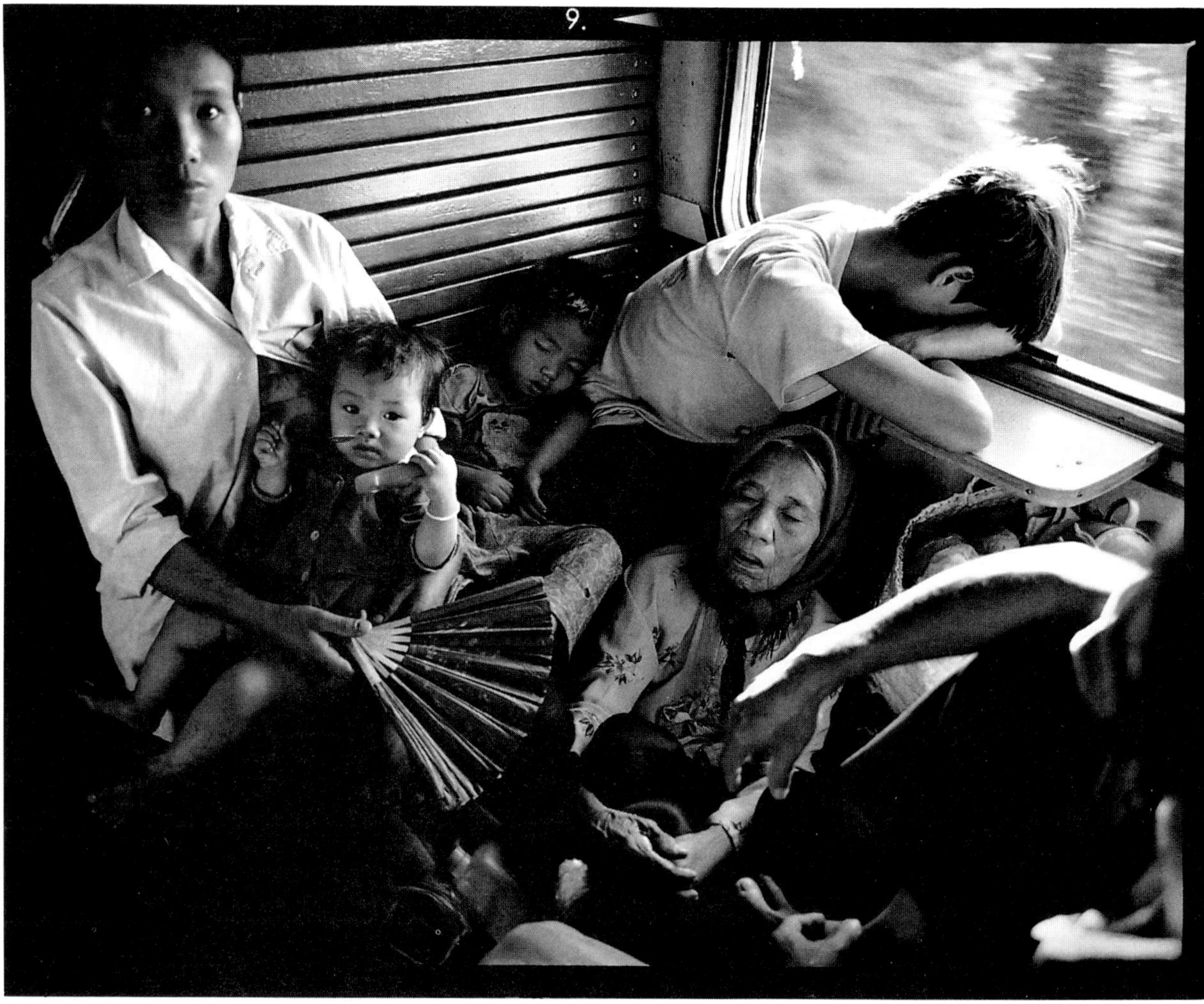

We sleep … we eat …

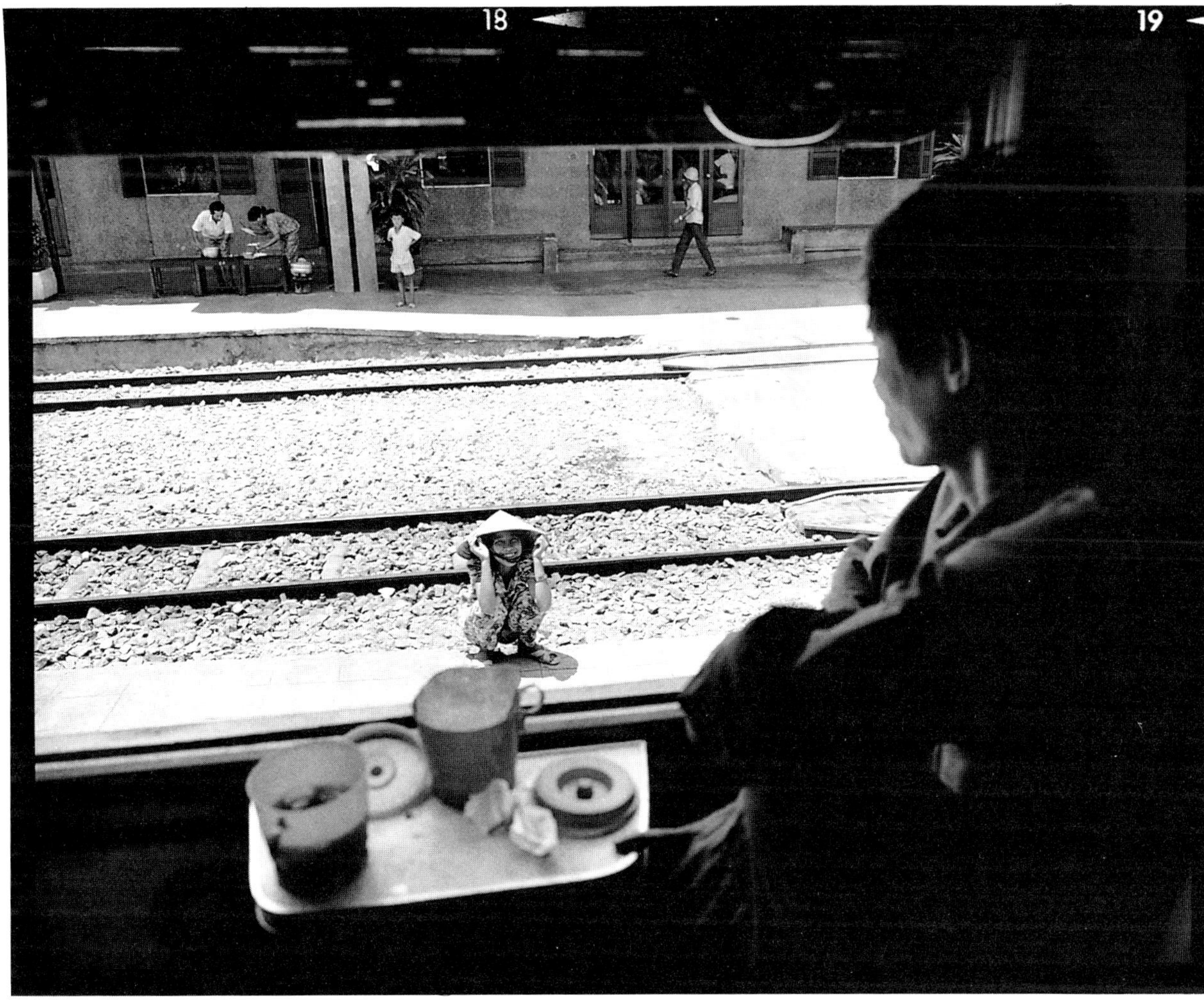

... there are long stops at the stations ...

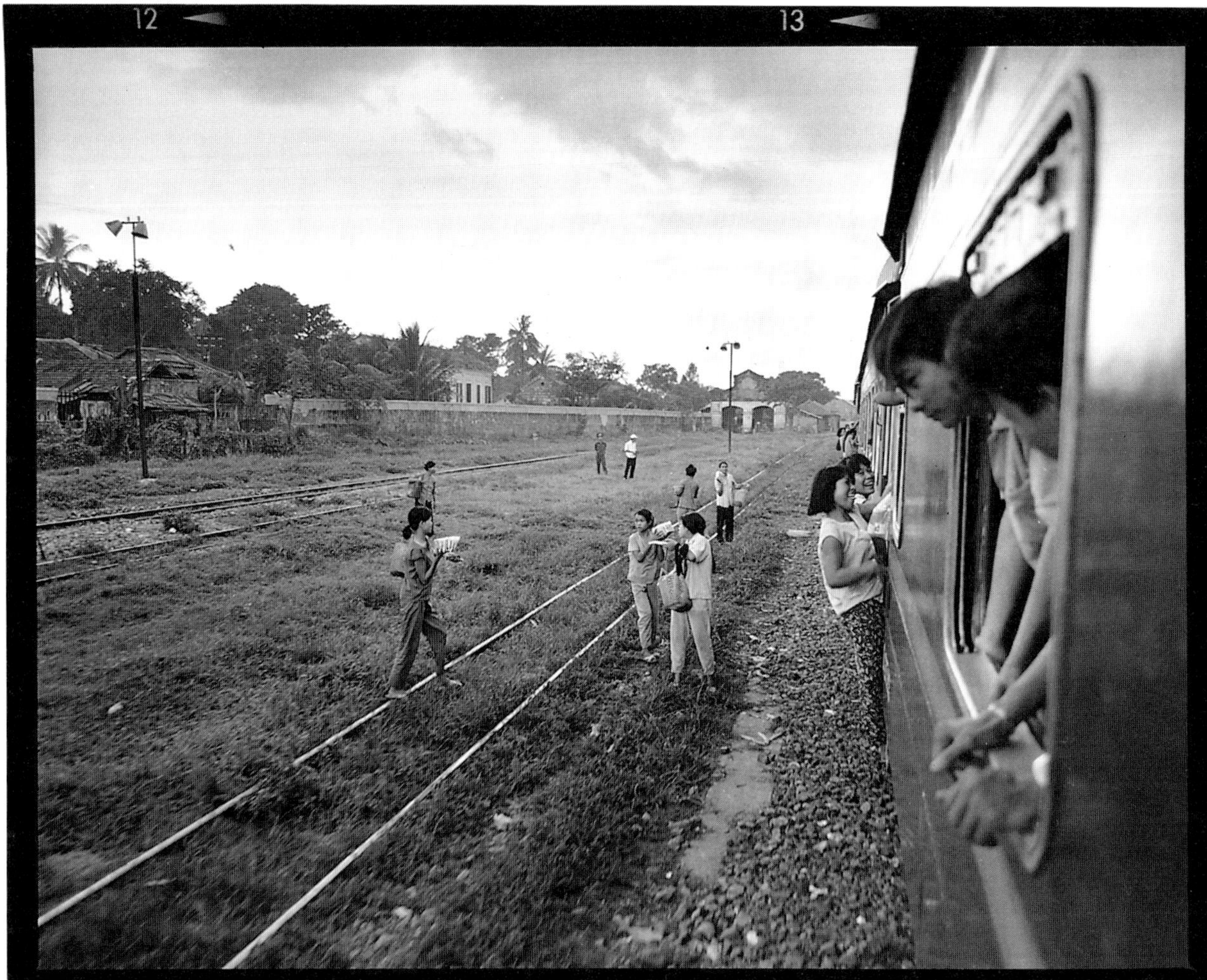

... where we're always besieged by girls selling things.

squeezes my biceps and bursts out laughing; even though it is difficult to contemplate – amidst bundles, children and illicit passengers – the most modest expedition to the toilet.

Happiness? Let's quicky get rid of any vaguely sentimental notions. By which I mean the visitor's waves of sympathy for that straightforward and clamorous humanity which we used to call 'the Vietnamese people'. (But even so, is there any people easier to like?) Let's not overemphasize, either, their gentle patience which visitors can find so gratifying. The Vietnamese people's liking for foreigners whom they are – finally! – allowed to welcome is reinforced by very temporary circumstances. Except for several streets in downtown Saigon (Dông Khoï, Le Noi, Nguyên Huê), western visitors are still far too rare for the Vietnamese either to hunt down as prey or to treat as invaders.

Forget all that. A train carriage is first of all a concentration of humanity – a mystery finally viewed at close quarters. The ordinary Vietnamese people. The majority of passengers are from the North, assigned to the South after 1975. Military personnel, civil servants, agricultural workers, they have the right to ten days' paid holiday per year. They have saved for two or three years to be able to return to the North. Several had to accept the demeaning terms of railroad employees who trade in illegal tickets. Their baggage is often reduced to a wicker basket, a canvas sack. Children and old people are wrapped together in sleep. Insignificant activities, little scenes, gossip, brief skirmishes tell the truth about a country.

For example, the announcements resounding through the train's public address system. Between two revolutionary slogans come a great many official prohibitions. It is forbidden to attach hammocks to the back of another person's seat, to sell merchandise, for three or four people to occupy seats for two, to travel without a ticket, to lean out of the train. A rational order, in short, a manner of careful organization. In practice, of course, hammocks are hung up everywhere, there are infinitely more passengers than available seats. Itinerant sellers invade the carriages by the dozen at every stop, heedless of the police who, electric billy clubs in hand, are bent on chasing them; and, with passengers riding on the roofs of the carriages, the least you can say is that they are leaning out of the train.

In short, this litany of announcements, so comically belied by the facts, gives a pretty good idea of the social system and frame of mind in which the Vietnamese have been living for the past two years. Mme D. is in heaven: 'I told you there was a contrast between what's official and what's real!' A *contrast*? In this furtive exit from communism, everyone seems careful to keep up appearances; nobody attacks the 'theory' or the 'thought' but nobody, either, gives a damn. Without any overt break with the past or painful proclamations, Vietnam is imperceptibly changing its spots. Might it be in the midst of inventing a 'model transition'? A more clever procedure than that which is driving Russians to despair – surfeited as they are with proclamations, dazed by promises, but discouraged by the general bankruptcy and the meagreness of the actual changes. Might Vietnamese post-communism, which doesn't admit to things as they are, be an Asian subtlety far removed from the declamatory naivety of the white man? Probably. Big neighbour China, fish and fowl at the same time, capitalist and communist, paved the way. Vietnam, which took thirty years not to make its mind up, will thus, for a time, be capitalist *and* communist.

Every day we are learning how better to observe the clandestine pedlars. Their baskets contain as many symbols as goods. As the train approaches a station, we see them posted on either side of the tracks, holding their baskets, trays and bundles. The assault they then make upon the carriages is an indefinitely renewable spectacle which, according to the region, considerably varies the merchandise that is paraded beneath our noses: squid and fried shrimp, hot soups, cans of beer and boiling hot tea, papayas and sliced mangoes, chicken and rice, and contraband Craven A cigarettes. These repeated assaults also mean this: here as in Saigon, private enterprise, with its combines, infinite hagglings, disorder, injustice and wealth, besieges the railway's own ponderous system of catering, with its tickets, long waits, carefully ordered schedules, stingy menus and pompous announcements.

The Northern police, inspectors, state cooks and waiters on the train are standing not only by the rules but also by a certain socialist *and* Tonkinese legitimacy, a collapsing principle of social organization. They resist every step of the way. Do they sometimes appear to slacken? Sure they do. Their resistance now finds itself undermined by 'socialist defeatism' all the more widespread because never proclaimed, and is often being rotted away by corruption pure and simple.

Corruption? It so happens that right under our noses, the private traders are negotiating 'temporary freedom of trade' with the conductor in exchange for several wads of dongs. At Quang Ngaï we see a new officer get on the train, tightly buttoned in an immaculate green uniform, accompanied by two armed soldiers. This is the highest of inspectors, some sort of 'inspector of services' come to count the passengers one by one and to stop illegal trade. At his approach, the regular inspectors rapidly disperse into other carriages the semi-legal passengers who are their personal customers. A fine example of bureaucratic swindling amidst systematic surveillance.

As for the rest, minor squabbles sometimes stir up the whole carriage. By dint of the spirit they bring into play, the impulses they arouse and the suppressed violence they suddenly awaken, these fights are miniature 'Vietnam wars'. One breaks out just after we leave Tap Cham, on the southern coast.

As usual the traders have invaded the train and are deftly fleeing from one carriage to the next as the police approach. Before moving, they conceal their baskets of merchandise amidst the passengers' baggage, under seats, in the folds of rolled-up hammocks. Under my own seat I have gracefully accepted two big shopping bags, hidden by my legs. One of the travellers, a young Northerner in a white shirt, with sunglasses on his nose, has refused to play the game. Hardly have the traders left than, on his own initiative, he places the basket he was given right in the middle of the corridor. It is immediately confiscated by the police.

Departure of the latter with their spoils and the furious return of the traders, this time accompanied by a man who appears to be their chief or protector. With their rapid precision of movement, these exits and entrances of characters seem like part of an established theatrical game, a half-serious guignol. The chief has armed himself with a bamboo bludgeon weighted at one end. The 'stool-pigeon' is assailed with recriminations and threats, seized by the collar of his shirt, shaken about in the hammock in which he is lying. He does not become overly flustered and argues back fiercely. He is a Northerner. He refuses to be an accomplice to the illegal schemes of these 'traffickers' from the South, he invokes railroad regulations, shakes his head with provocative regrets. But the chief of the traders doesn't care about any of this and brandishes his bamboo club with apparent determination. They are within a hair's breadth of a serious altercation. Which would pit a battalion of young Southern women and men experienced in the art of commerce, and a king of the jungle used to defying rules and authority, against a convinced but contemptible defender of the socialist order and the commonweal. (Who is also perhaps infuriated by the illicit profit from which he doesn't benefit.) South versus North, private enterprise versus collective management, the safety of regulation versus the perils of individual initiative, cunning versus law. The two men grapple at arm's length, amidst shrill cries from the traders and the mute wait-and-see attitude of the passengers. The police follow the scene from a distance.

Will blood flow? No. All of a sudden the crisis is defused. A 'Vietnamese' arrangement has been found. The stool-pigeon agrees to compensate the trader whose basket was confiscated, but for only a portion of its value. Thus each side is able to save face. A deal is struck. He takes out a wad of dongs and avenges the humiliation inherent in any compromise by throwing the bills at his adversary with calculated brusqueness. None of these details is insignificant, all obey a delicate distribution of reciprocal concessions. Case closed. One Vietnam war which won't happen.

Approaching railway stations, everyone carefully makes sure that the windows of the carriage are barricaded. Protective grilles are to hand for this purpose and, imitating our neighbours, we lock ourselves in like New Yorkers driving into Harlem or the Bronx. Why? No one makes a mystery of it. Pilferers, pickpockets and worse may be waiting on the platforms. Others may jump out from the track side at night. We are frankly warned against some stations, like the one in Vinh, in Hô Chi Minh's native province, 'swarming with outlaws and murderers'. Adds the conductor: 'Don't put your arms out, someone might rip off your watch.'

That's not all. On the journey between Saigon and Hanoi it appears that we risk being hit with rocks. Thrown by whom? Unruly children? Or the newly poor, exasperated by the well-to-do? Both, we are told. The whole country is being undermined by criminality all the more frightening because it is rarely – or vaguely – talked about in the official press, and thus left to the imagination. Which doesn't prevent crimes from happening – hold-ups, looting, rackets. In Saigon this violence is attributed to 'northern pillagers' and 'gangs' sweeping

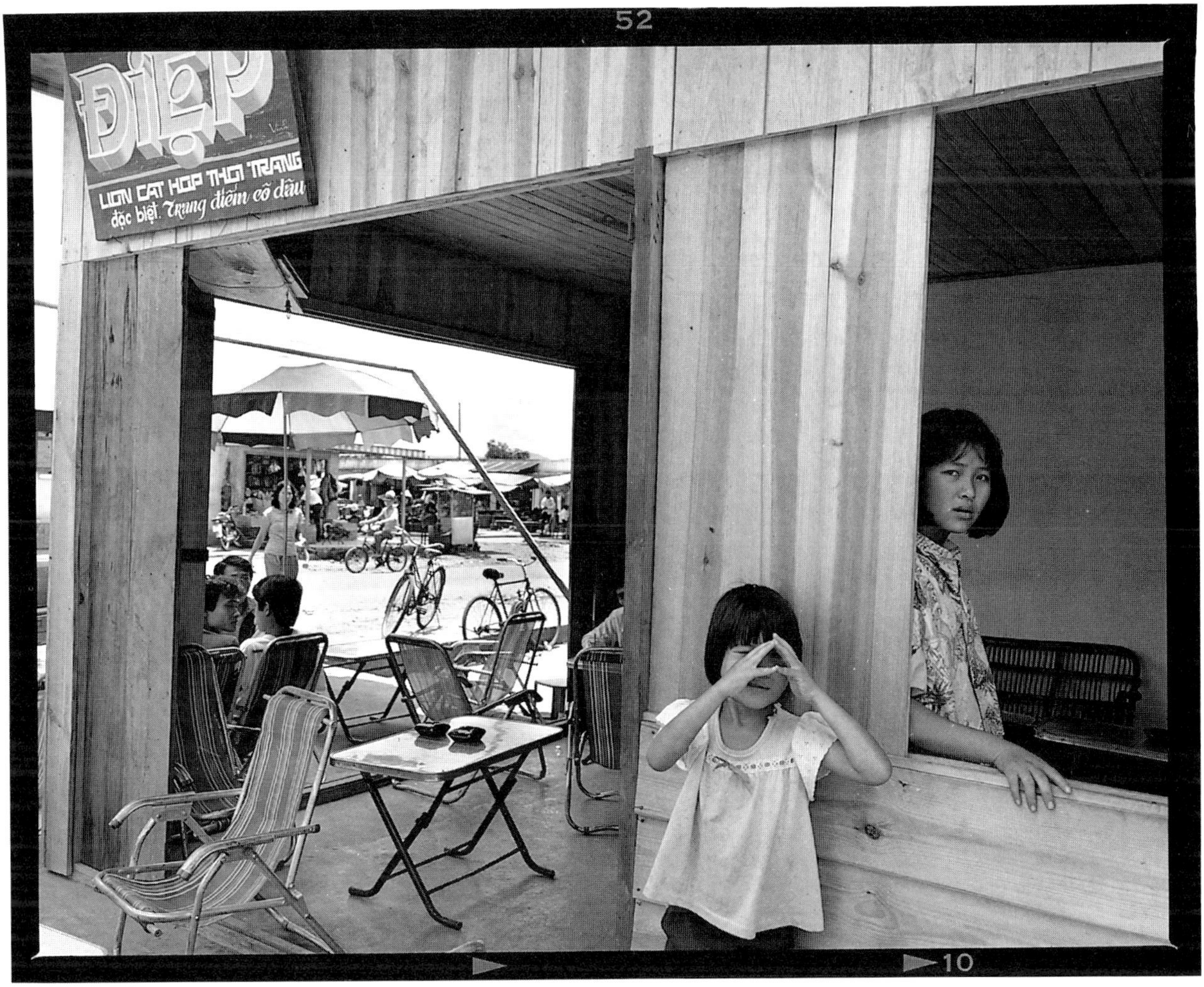

On the Dalat road …

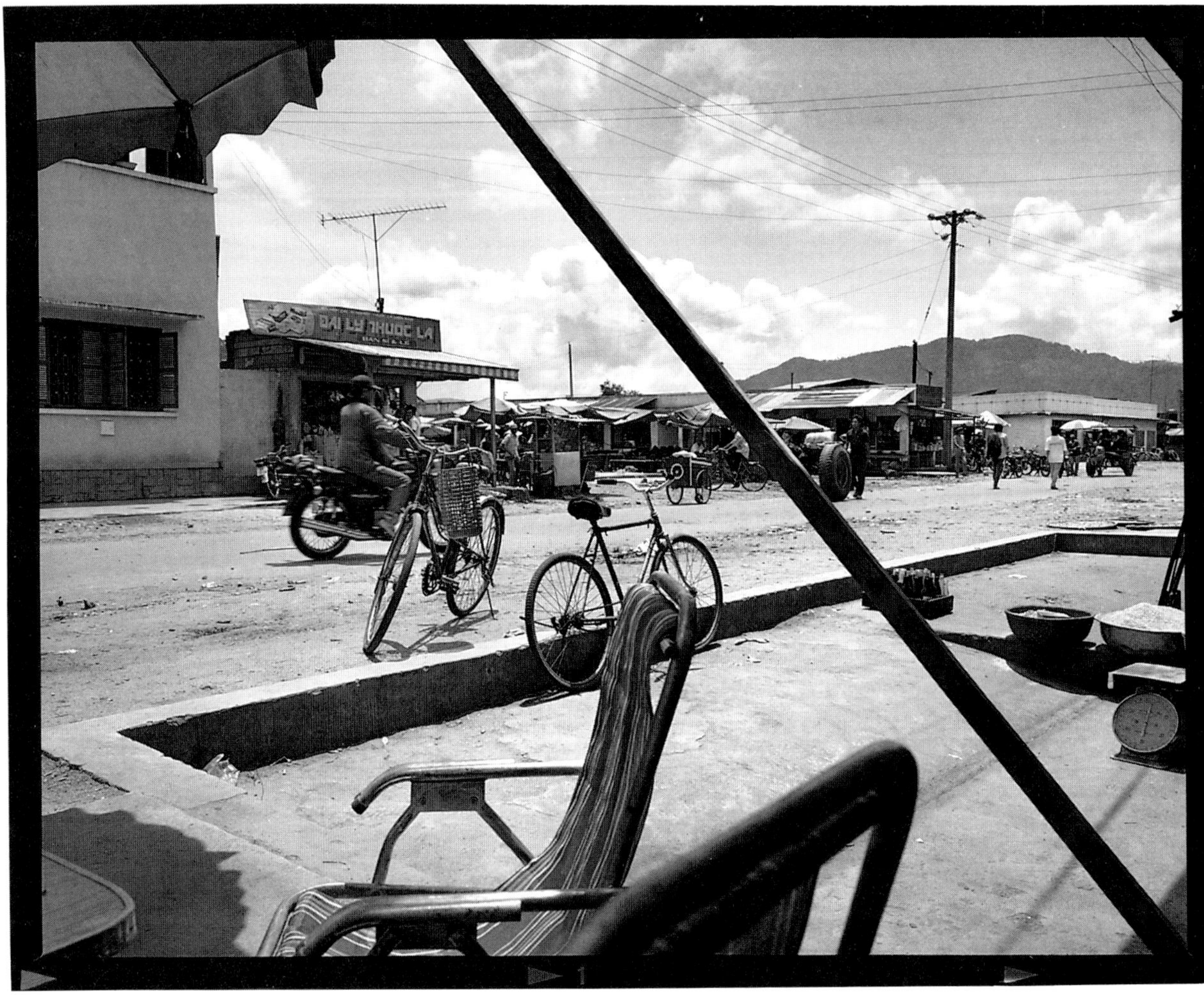

... I slowly approach ...

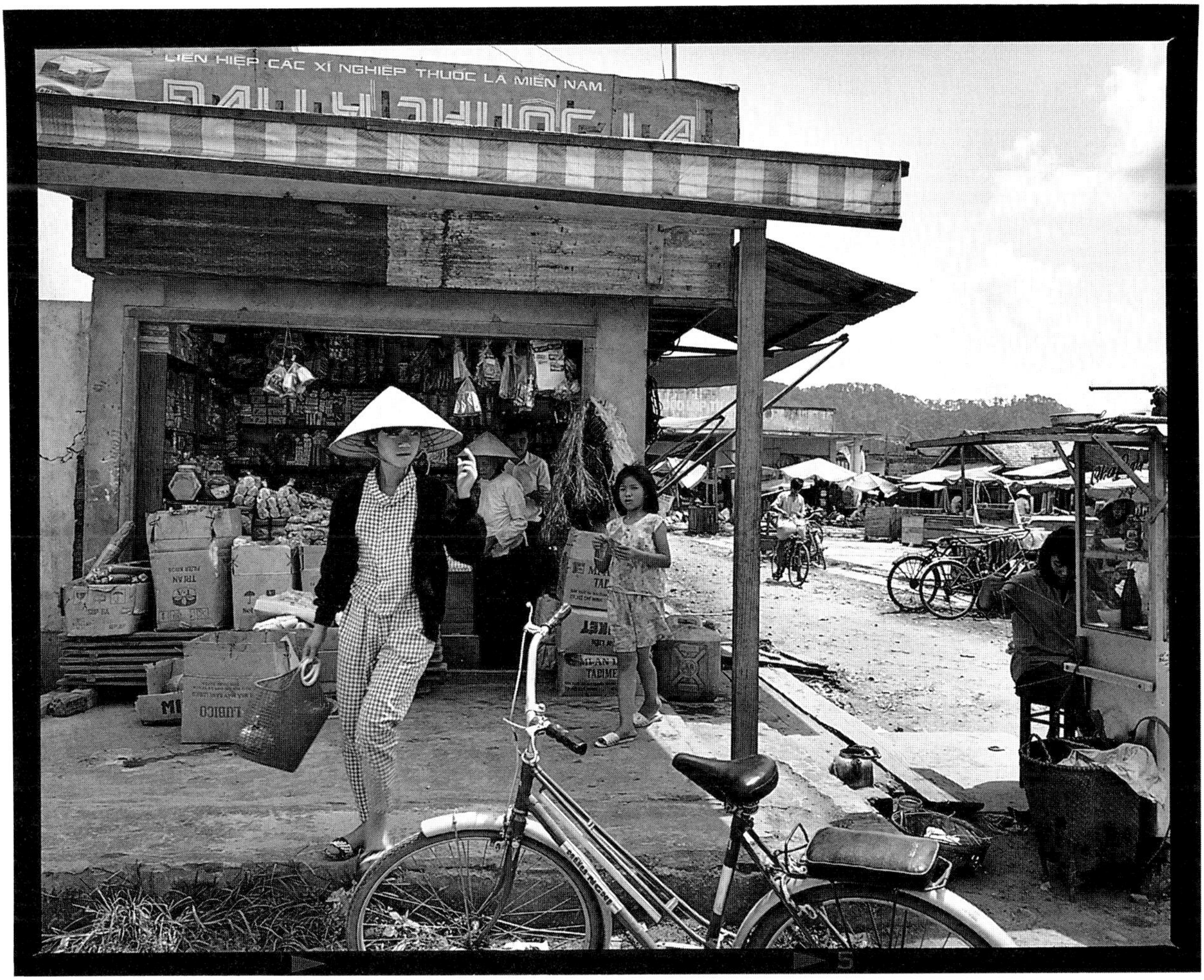

... Vietnamese men and women.

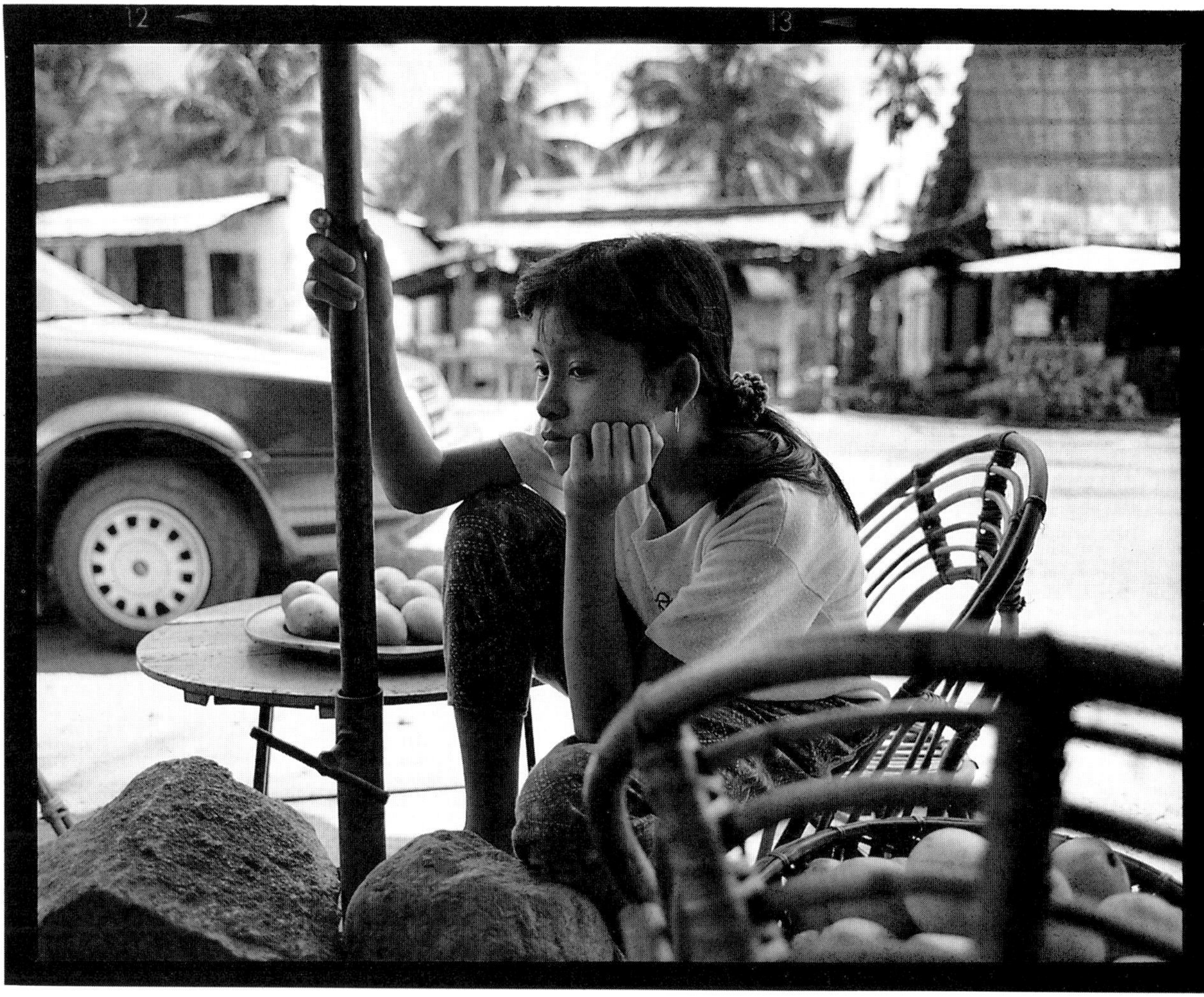

I can drink coconut juice.

down to the South like 'barbarian tribes'. But this criminality is *also* a symptom of the war's interminable aftermath and of a dissolving political system.

An obscure violence is thus waiting for us from station to station, a latent social disorder which would be difficult to conceal. Comparable disorders to aggressive disturbances which one fears in the streets of Moscow, Budapest or Leipzig, every place where the collapse of communism is giving birth to a society which is freer but harsh, unjust, and violent. A society where intolerance in retreat leaves room for the intolerable. A Vietnamese proverb which the conductor quotes for us, smiling: 'The poor become thieves, the rich learn manners.' The introduction of capitalism is also the beginning of a mercantile frenzy, a greed which already has its victims, its excluded.

Newly rediscovered 'free enterprise' is accompanied here as everywhere else by a dizzying, delirious inflation which blurs all points of reference and generates as much anguish as freedom. In 1976, the average salary was 48 dongs per month and a kilo of rice cost a half a dong. Today the same average salary is 100,000 dongs and the kilo of rice costs 2,500 dongs. So in 1976, a month's salary could buy 96 kilos of rice, against 40 kilos today. The poor, presently, are twice as poor as before.

The country is at once very poor and without shortages – save one: money.

THE CONVENT OF BIRDS

I am standing on the balcony of a large villa in Dalat one evening, in Lang Bian Province. We have travelled by car down broken highways, passed through villages frozen in empty expectation, swarming with children and yellow dogs, bordering state plantations with their gangs of northern workers. The fresh air of Dalat is recompense at the end of the road. The villa in which we are staying, and those around it, were nationalized by the communists and converted into a state hotel. One of the villas serves as reception office, kitchen and restaurant. In the others, bedrooms serve as rooms for guests, when there are any. The one we occupy remains intact – wide concrete stairways in Art Deco tiles, a monumental dining room, a profuse and neglected garden. A French colonist must have lived here in the 1950s, or else a young colonial administrator; later, a Saigonese bourgeois or a *nouveau riche* politician of the 'puppet' regime. Dalat and the surrounding plantations were created at the beginning of the century at the urging of Paul Doumer; this high-altitude town was once the preferred refuge of the French and the South Vietnamese notables who constructed their holiday homes here. In the 1920s, it was a fashionable resort, much frequented by colonial Vietnam's high society. The Emperor Bao Dai had his summer residence here. It resembled tourist resorts such as Annecy or Pau, early in the century. The whole town is evocative of decrepit opulence and broken dignity.

The décor hasn't changed a bit, save several grey concrete buildings in the market place and geometric fountains copied from ones you can find in Stavropol and Dresden. Otherwise communism wears this bourgeois architecture like a suit which is too large for it. My bedroom is enormous, with antique ceiling fans, their big, fly-specked blades constantly turning. The furniture, too, is from the 1950s: a big, low plywood bed; a Levitan dressing-table surmounted by a vertical mirror with stained silvering; several red leatherette-covered armchairs made of tubed aluminium. The walls are pale blue, roughcast plaster; in the bathroom, on raised feet, sits an imposing bathtub with yellow stains. Night has fallen upon Lake Xuân Huong where a little while ago some young women were dreamily pedalling swan-shaped paddleboats. On Duy Ton Street, several cyclists hurry by in the darkness, a dog barks, grey ponies stand immobile in the square, the wind is stirring the rose bushes and bougainvilleas.

I am alone on the terrace. I am not sleepy; the fatigue of the journey is dissolving in a slightly drunken exaltation. I will wait for morning in a bamboo armchair which creaks in the dark. This is a place which strikes some deep, human chord. It no longer seems so absurd to imagine settling in for the duration, giving it up once and for all, staying put for good. So long, old Europe – the hell with you! To be an old man immersed in brandy. To put an end to useless chatter, unresolvable questions and futile activity. To spend my days wandering between the orchid gardens on Phu Don Thien Duong Street and the bar of the old Hotel Dalat, on Tran Phu Street. Vietnam can inspire resolutions like this which vanish in the morning.

As night wears on, more and more perfumes fill the air on my terrace. Finally, daybreak surprises me. Throughout the country Dalat is reputed for its roses and poppies, its gladioli, scarlet geraniums and hibiscus. It is the only town in the country untouched by the war. To this privilege it undoubtedly owes its slightly remote nonchalance, its placidity and disdain. Here – and this is uncommon in Vietnam – no one appears concerned with the transient 'white man'. No child appears, crying *ông liên Xô* ('a Russian!'), *ông phap* ('a Frenchman!'), or *ông my* ('an American!') when he sees us, nor rushes up brandishing trinkets; no teenager casts sidelong glances, muttering, 'Dollars, dollars'. We are finally transparent, invisible, uninteresting. 'Here,' says Mme D., 'people are calm and the girls have rosy cheeks.'

On the market square, a lone former French soldier, half-derelict in rags, half-retired, ran up to us, feverishly pouring out his record of military service, down to the precise month, with a list of his postings – all in one breath in hard-to-understand French. We stopped to listen. Several passers-by immediately made a circle. We were reluctant to feel moved. Was the tremulous, theatrical nostalgia real? Were we simply wasting our time with an old lunatic looking for a handout? Difficult to say. The old man reeled off '*De-Lattre-de-Tassigny*', '*Bigeard*', and '*quatre ans de camp*', but mysteriously burst out laughing. At this point we gave up trying to distinguish between laughter and tears.

In front of the main post office, a big painted wooden sign invites customers to telephone their relatives abroad: sixteen dollars and forty cents for three minutes to France. Most booths are occupied, because Vietnam today has an immense diaspora. With which it is already organizing its existence, its everyday life and its future. For this diaspora is accessible by telephone. Big deal? Well, yes. The country is emerging from total isolation, from a 'heroic' withdrawal, secluded from 'imperialist plots' and 'bourgeois corruption', which suspended the passage of time: the calendar stood still. Reestablishing the telephone system is a return to the world, an unlocked window, the end of a 'posture'.

The external world, this great big confused ball on which live two million expatriates, is finally within voice range. In all the main post offices, from morning till night, incessant and obscure business goes on by telephone. Each city buzzes with feverish conversations, little projects, postponed meetings. A good part of the future history of Vietnam is at stake in these long distance booths – $16.40 for three minutes, no witnesses.

For no particular reason, we want to go back to see the *Couvent des Oiseaux*, just to sit down outside for half an hour. That's all. Dalat's Convent of the Birds, like Saint Paul's College in Saigon, was the most enduringly famous institution of French Indochina. There generations of well-bred Vietnamese women sang hymns and learned the fables of La Fontaine in a swirl of cassocks and coifs. There Mme Ngo Dinh Nhu recruited her battalions of anti-communist young women whom she called '*mes petites chéries*'.*

The great ochre façade of the Convent of the Birds still dominates a little pine-clad hill. The former convent has become a teacher's college and the chapel is closed, but there remains an engraved tribute to 'Our Lady of Lang Bian' on

*Tran Le Xuan, the powerful sister-in-law of Ngo Dinh Diem, the South Vietnamese ruler assassinated in 1963. (Tr.)

the pediment of the main building. In the park, as ever, young women are seated in groups of three or four beneath the pines. On the central drive is parked a white Peugeot 203 taxi with polished chrome trim. The passage of time has left no mark on this unchanging scenery.

But it might not take much . . .

LE TEMPS DES FLEURS

A street scene in Nha Trang, central Vietnam. Night is falling on the waterfront and the terrace of the Hotel Haï Yen, where soviet advisors from the neighbouring military base of Cam Ranh used to come to play billiards and look for girls. The beach is an Asiatic Rimini. With Riviera-style projects in the works, Chinese and Korean tourists in the waves, the languor of summer and sleeping pedicab drivers slumped on their vehicles. All along the waterfront, vintage loudspeakers are spouting old proletarian slogans and astounding statistics on 'production records'. Mme D. translates for us: 'The coal production company delivered tons of ore to the people for the construction of the socialist metallurgical industry.' It is the public sound system, the official radio station. Until just a while back it held a monopoly on what is known as news. Today, from sunup to sundown, the more nobody listens, the more insistent it is.

Everywhere beneath the trees are vendors of coconuts, sugar cane juice and grilled cuttlefish; the family-run open-air bistros, which serve cola and *café den* (black coffee), have put in their own sound systems – the private kind. And infinitely more modern. Maximum volume. Compact discs and digital cassettes versus stadium loudspeakers, rhythm and blues versus revolutionary litanies. A stereo cacophony along the beach as we pass from the Everly Brothers (*Greenfields*) to Paul Anka (*Diana*), from *Le Temps des Fleurs* in Vietnamese to the sentimental disco sounds of the pop star Nha Phuong, a native of Huê. Or Than Lan, a former student at the lyceé Marie Curie, who has the voice of a little girl, a sort of Chantal Goya. Here and there we even hear an antique version of *Besame mucho* and an old hit by Hervé Vilar. The overall ambience is at once despairing and mischievous. As if the old Leninist discourse broadcast by the official loudspeakers were being swallowed, subverted and effaced by these decadent popular songs which the People's Committees are forever 'officially' banning. From morning till night, the beach at Nha Trang is dedicated to drowning by decibels the stereotyped drivel.

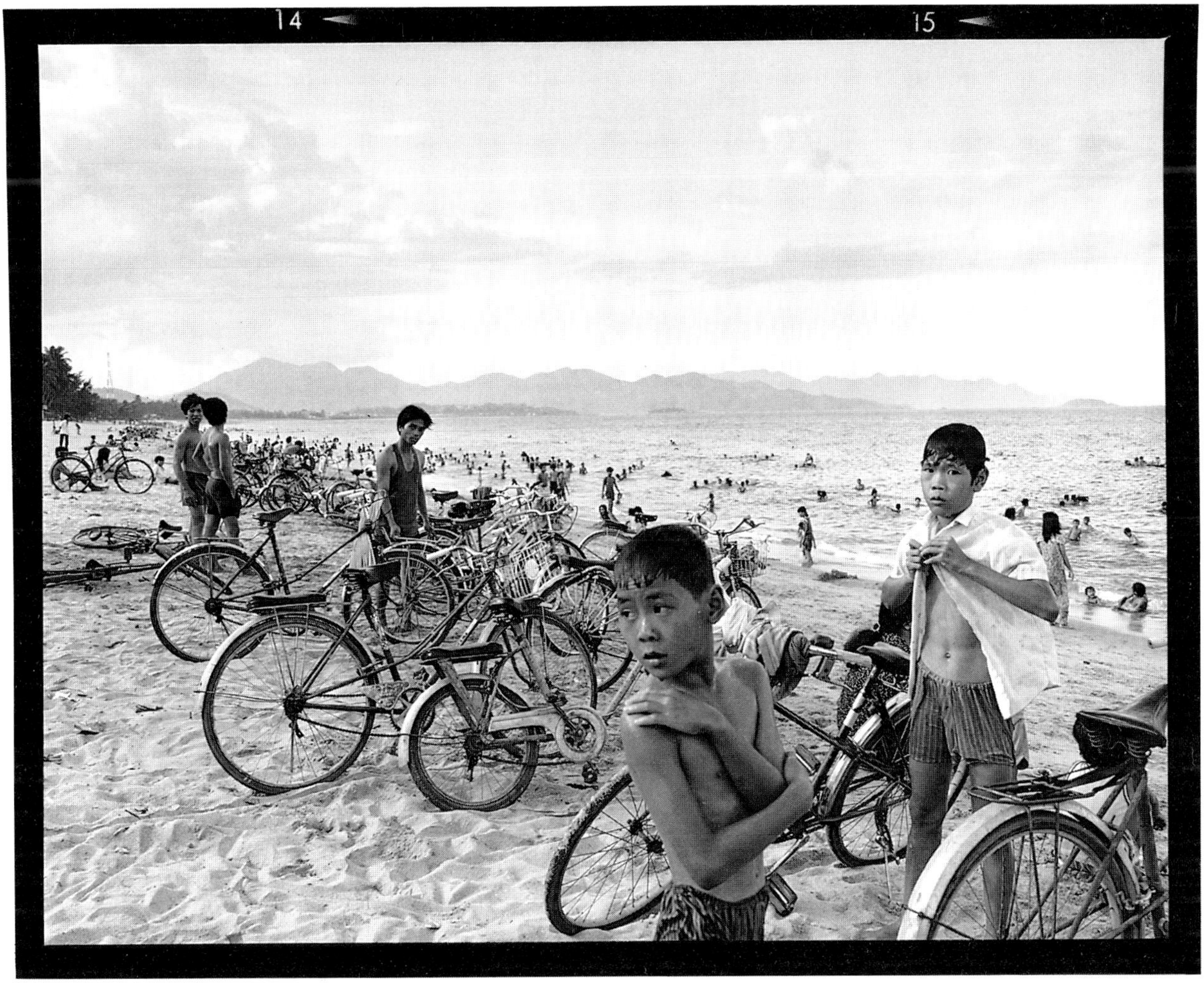

It's summer … the beach, children and bicycles …

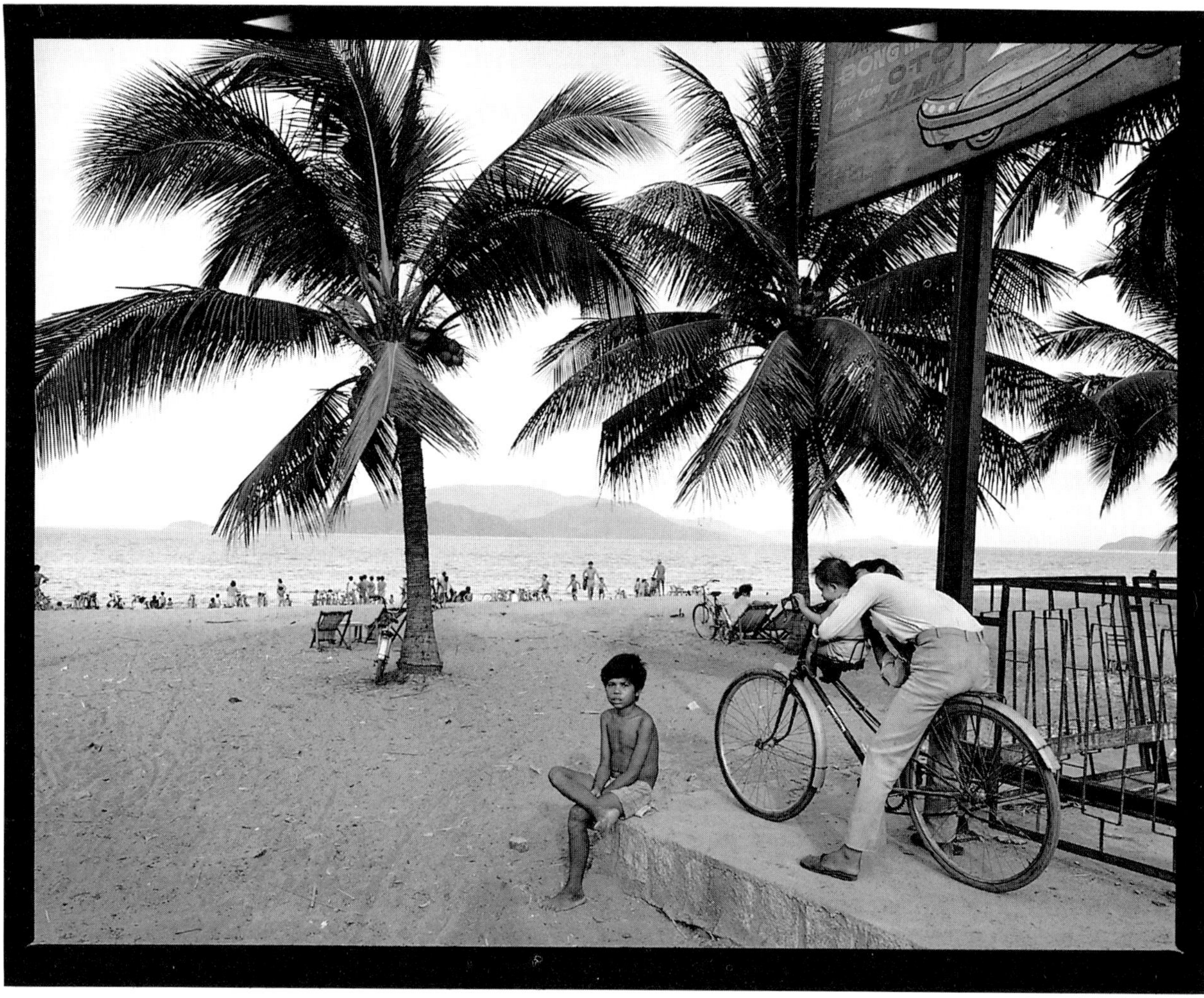

... the sea is splendid ... and the beach.

We have relived endlessly this little scene from Nha Trang in all the towns we passed and along the remotest highways, even in the improbable villages of the mountain province Duong Luong, where we would stop for an occasional coconut juice. The music from the radio-cassette players was often so loud we had trouble talking. Our journey across Vietnam gradually turned into a deafening party beneath the amused gaze of young women. We finally got angry enough to make them turn the volume down halfway.

If private commerce is everywhere besieging collapsing collectivism, music delivers a still more decisive blow. It is inundating the whole of Vietnam, flooding public places, ruining official speeches, occupying mind and space, befuddling police informers and ridiculing the grand opera of propaganda. From village to shop, bus to train, rice paddies to the pavements of Saigon, the omnipresent potpourri of occidental oldies, piercing and hegemonic, is the new language of a nation which has lost the meaning of words.

In Hanoi, on Paul-Bert Street, I discovered an issue of the communist review, *Études Vietnamiennes,* dating from 1973. By chance I opened it at a long, edifying text: 'The Itinerary of an Intellectual Patriot' by one Le Van Hoa. 'The magazines, films and photographs,' he writes, 'the music, dances and songs of the United States, Formosa and South Korea were the usual means for disseminating the corruption of morals. With the flood of GIs, a certain kind of "song-and-dance music" invaded the scene, entered tea houses and dance halls and was played at "sex parties". The struggle against the depravation of culture became an urgent necessity.'

The passage of time has its ironies. Never 'before 1975' did you hear as much 'depraved' music as today, in what is still officially the socialist republic of Vietnam. In the main, music from abroad comes via the two million *Vietkieus* living in Paris, Los Angeles, Houston and Australia. Hence the deliberately 'retro' character of the forbidden refrains, the nostalgic element – all very 'sixties' and 'seventies' – in the music which is listened to – and danced to – all over the country. Sometimes in the original version, or in aggressively romantic bilingual versions (French-Vietnamese or English-Vietnamese). These musical allusions are clearly political.

In Hanoi one evening, Mme D., who had never set foot in the North, and imagined it with some fear, suddenly stopped walking. Among the tunes blasting away on the battery of portable radios along the pavement, she had just recognized a Southern – and anti-communist – hit tune from the 1960s, *The Hill of Purple Flowers,* sung by Duy Khanh, a sort of André Clavaud of his time. Duy Khanh, on the streets of Hanoi! And so loud!

But the effectiveness of this musical subversion is being reduced by video. Thousands of video bars and video theatres have opened over the last two years. All over the place. In the gardens of once private villas. In the converted shops of Da Nang, Haiphong and Cholon. All the Vietnamese youth meet there. And even the video bars no longer have a monopoly on the films and clandestine videotapes. In the state hotels and restaurants where we stay a videocassette player is always turned on, enthroned in some regal spot. They show forbidden films, dubbed by a Vietnamese speaker playing all the roles in monotonous voiceover. You have to tear hotel staff away from their dreamy meditations in front of the screen.

These videos offer more than state contraband. First-run features showing on the Champs-Élysées or Times Square can be seen throughout Vietnam. How? It's very simple. The *Vietkieus* pirate them by camcorder from the back of cinemas and ship the tapes off to Hô Chi Minh City.

As for the music videos, they are full of glitzy singers warbling beneath the Eiffel Tower, on the Pont Neuf or the Golden Gate Bridge. Vietnamese from Paris or San Francisco, garishly made-up girls or rather prissy, impeccably dressed boys, parading round on big motorbikes. In the video bars at Nha Trang and Huê, Dalat and Qui Nhon, the 'new Vietnamese people', hardly out of their teens, sip phony Bière 33 and watch these flickering pictures from another galaxy.

DO YOU SPEAK ENGLISH?

At Nha Trang, I am sitting in the folding chair of a street-seller called Nghia. She is thirteen but looks eleven. Wearing pink pyjamas, with a long wisp of black hair across her forehead, she has eyes like gleaming coal, and chatters away in a lively fashion. 'What is your name?' 'How old are you?' 'What do you want to drink?' Without a mistake. I've hardly sat down before I'm fussed over, coddled and methodically softened up. A grandmother has come up, the eldest brother crouches next to me, the ground beneath my chair is deftly swept, my comfort is assured. Oriental prince or nabob, dignitary or great white god come from afar: the solicitude is exaggerated but never servile. An indefinable sense of irony stops my zealous interlocutors short of ridicule and, of course, obsequiousness. The family treasure set out for me to covet consists of only a set of wooden shelves, three cans of Coca-Cola, two packs of cigarettes, a steaming teapot, ten packages of chewing gum and a few coconuts.

Nghia has already seized my left hand and is pointing to my wedding ring, giggling, 'Madame? Madame?' Vietnamese females, young and old, have a way of getting straight to the point. But it is an innocent game, not tainted by obsessive concern with doing something wrong, as it would be with us.

When they find out that I am French, everyone switches languages without getting flustered. Nghia is the first: '*Tu es touriste*?' '*Tu es déjà venu au Vietnam*?' After a quarter of an hour, we have got into one of those conversational games where each breakdown of vocabulary results in uncontrollable laughter. And besides, a Western customer is a piece of luck to be taken seriously; neighbouring merchants, drawing up their stools, invite themselves into the conversation. For pleasure, or just in case.

The multilingual talents of Nghia and her family are all the more surprising inasmuch as Vietnam is scarcely open to the outside world. Foreigners are not common, and the beach at Nha Trang is a long way off the main 'charter' routes.

Can you imagine, in some corner of the Cantal or Puy-de-Dôme, a market stallholder switching from English to German, or from Spanish to Italian? This curiosity makes me wonder, and I pose the question to no one in particular. Nghia appears confused, hesitates, looks to her grandmother and brother. I persist.

Then, blushing, she quietly hands me a big, worn school notebook. Every page is covered with child's handwriting, carefully formed, covered with red arrows and full of underlined words. There are everyday expressions translated by God knows who and written down in phonetic Vietnamese. '*Le Coca coûte 8000 dongs*', '*Voulez-vous du jus de coco?*', '*Combien d'enfants avez-vous?*'. Nghia recites from the notebook, which consists of at least two hundred pages, from morning to night. At the age of thirteen! This exercise is characteristic of their determined commercial and professional attitude which says much about the urgent necessity of earning a few dongs. For all that, Nghia is embarrassed by her admission, as if she were giving away, not only her own secret, but that of her people.

This eagerness is disconcerting.

But it is the rule, not the exception. Vietnam in this spring of 1992 is like some kind of universal language school, a permanent evening class. Little boys stumbling over English sentences, young people toiling away with *English Streamline*, bookshops prominently displaying Vietnamese–English dictionaries, the old Assimil teach-yourself books, grammar manuals and conversation guides. Determined impatience is discernible in all this. Turning away from weighty Marxist pedagogy, the Vietnamese are energetically flinging themselves into foreign language learning – especially English, sometimes French.

In each city, evening classes are given by universities and, recently, by private institutions. They teach mainly English and computer science. All these institutions have seen their student populations shoot up in no time. In Saigon alone, at least 120,000 people attend classes every evening from 5.30 to 7.30, in some twenty-five night schools. Of their own volition. The numbers are the same in Huê and Can Tho, at Vinh and Haiphong. The opening-up to the outside world, the impending reconciliation of the country with the modern world, is being prepared by the Vietnamese with an unprecedented energy.

This way of literally flinging oneself out to meet the world is not merely security against the future. On this scale it is a vast movement of the soul, a post-communist symptom. It alone guarantees Vietnam a future less bleak than that of the tattered ex-communist regimes of central Europe. Human energy already humming in Vietnam will produce miracles when its force is brought to bear upon the real world. Reputed for their talents, endowed with riches by geography, 66 million Vietnamese are not concealing the fact that they want to become a new 'dragon' of Asia. And why not?

Though auspicious for the future, the hearty and hardworking frenzy of the Vietnamese is dismaying in its immediate effects. An age-old reflex and deep-rooted disposition, this astonishing reverence for all that comes from 'outside' verges upon voluntary humiliation just when it finally triumphs. It is the fetishism of deprived peoples, loser nations, teenage Muscovites, style snobs in Budapest or nomenklaturists in Algiers. A paltry religion whose single credo is that the foreign stamp means superiority: a Western label turns a piece of junk into the most envied of gifts. In Prague they wait in line for hours for the remarkable privilege of owning a pair of Adidas trainers or, in Moscow, of sinking their teeth into a McDonald's hamburger. The deceptive power of imported merchandise is transforming the Third World and will have greatly contributed to the rout of communism. It clearly prevails throughout Vietnam. But the phenomenon here is all the more appalling in that it expresses apathetic resipiscence. Few countries in the world pushed the rejection of foreign corruption so far – and for so long – as wartime North Vietnam. Few refused acculturation so stubbornly, or so strongly affirmed themselves as a bulwark against the American juggernaut.

A resistance that neither B-52s nor Cobras could break is now defeated with chewing gum, Marlboros and Levis without a shot being fired. All over the country, kids strut around in Rambo caps. A pair of genuine Ray Bans is a coveted treasure. In Hanoi they sell fake 'Peugeot' stickers for Chinese bicycles. An American-made felt-tip pen turns you into a big shot. There's no defence against such 'riches'. None of the efforts to rename the old colonial hotels succeeded. The Rex was supposed to become the Ben Thann, the Majestic was to be called the Cuu Long and the Palace the Huu Nghi. A waste of time. A Vietnamese name would seem retrograde.

If the visitor wants to provoke astonishment – quickly turning into mirth – let him ask a street-seller for a pack of Vietnamese cigarettes. Given the proliferation of local brands, and the obsessive care each takes to imitate American packaging, it would seem that Vietnamese manufacturers have tried everything to overcome this contempt for their own product. Without success. A middle-class Vietnamese needs real courage to go out and publicly buy a pack of Vinh Hoï, Du Lich, Mélia, or Thang Long for 1,000 dongs rather than pay 12,000 dongs for Lucky Strikes. And the taste certainly isn't the issue.

To what secret ploy of history, to what interior devastation do we owe this blind devotion, which is ultimately a repudiation of self?

We come to view with distaste these prostrations before objects which are 'magic' because they come from the outside world, and experience an obscure feeling of disaster, regression, of destiny led astray. The triumph of the market economy and of liberalism? An epiphany of democracy? The spirit of liberty? What nonsense! Beneath the 'good news' of post-communism, how can anyone not see the bad? Behind the 'end of history', how can anyone ignore its ugly new beginning? This plundering, all-consuming imperialism of things and gadgets which make the world submit to its law; this revenge of videos, quartz watches and Ninja turtles which brings Vietnam to its knees – are they anything else but an ultimate denial? This bulimic feast, the 'snobbery' of the poor laying down arms may seem bitter in Moscow, grotesque in Bamako, preposterous in Marrakech. It is simply poignant in Nha Trang or Qui Nhon.

Poignant but filled with turmoil. Beyond the never-satisfied fever, the great refusals will soon return. Turbulent forecasts, promised insurrections. No people can contain themselves eternally in reverence and envy. The Coca-Cola and Lucky Strike syndrome, the ultimate Western revenge, remains more fragile than merely vulgar.

REVERED BENEFACTOR

Sometimes we don't talk. Moments pass with no conversation whatever, not even a remark. These are pauses in the journey, parentheses of silence. Near Cam Ranh, we have taken a dirt road eaten up by couchgrass. In the distance you can see the 'strategic' bay and naval base where American helicopters used to drone. The harbour was later offered to the Soviet navy, and Pentagon surveillance satellites followed its development by the centimetre. Today shrimp are farmed here for export. The old salterns are working again. Ancient Russian radar dishes stand rusting beneath the palm trees. The wind raises acrid whirlpools from the sandy earth. Near the main entrance to the base, amid village huts, a few lingering Russians are out looking for a cold beer. The ex-Red Army has been packing its bags for months. Without fuss or fanfare. No one puts themselves out much for the routed *Lien xo* (Soviets). Perhaps Vietnam doesn't like losers. Back in April 1956, just when the last French troops were leaving the country, the brother of President Ngô Dinh Diem, an ardent anti-communist, bade them farewell in his diary: 'Thus the French Expeditionary Force cleared out for good. . . . The tears stubbornly refuse to flow.'

What will they write tomorrow about the Soviet 'brothers' going home?

In choosing this road of dirt and grass, we were going away from the base at Cam Ranh, heading toward the Annamite mountain range. It suddenly grew very hot. The countryside baked in the afternoon sun, the horizon was empty. Not a noise or movement of a buffalo or child, not a bird singing. Our walk was brief. Not far from the old Mandarin highway, a signpost, stuck in the ground at the bottom of an earthen stairway going up an embankment, marked the grave of Alexandre John Emile Yersin. We climbed up.

A short obelisk of stone and ochre-coloured cement, a four-sided stairway and several sticks of freshly burnt incense in a tin can. From this votive eminence, you take in a panorama of the bay all the way to the first houses of Nha Trang.

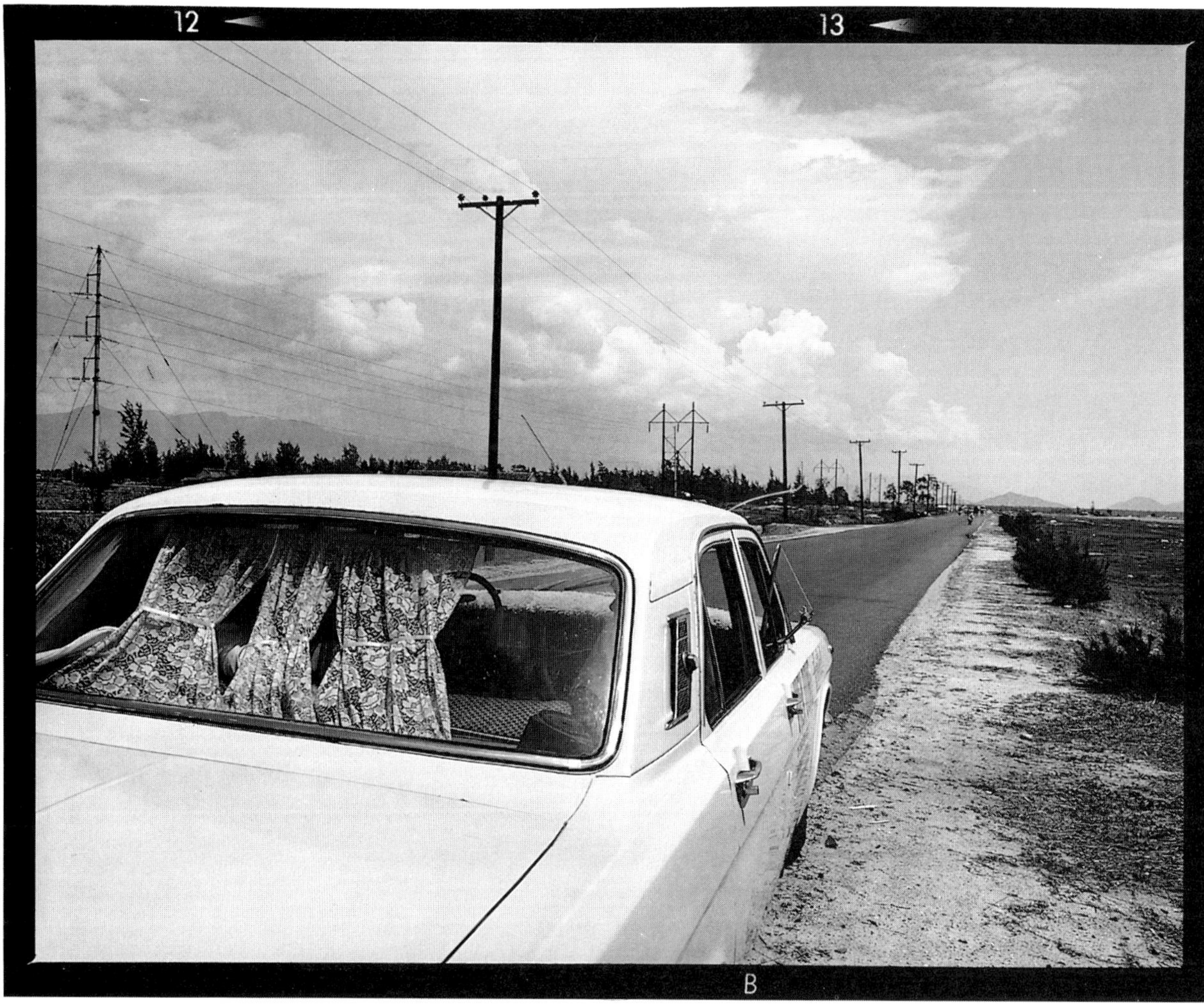

We hire a Soviet car with a chauffeur . . .

The barrenness of the spot, its relative seclusion and certain minor indications – old graffiti on the obelisk and footprints in the gravel which bore witness to regular visits in spite of everything – all gave rise to an emotion for which we were unprepared. Away from the highways and railway stations, on the edge of a plain which was pulverized more than any other by the war's thunderbolts of steel and gunpowder, this solitary tomb, lost in high grass, polished by the rain, has now stood for half a century. One imagines it often surrounded by smoke from explosions, skirted by patrols, flown over by squadrons, perhaps licked by flames. A mausoleum forgotten in the hail of bullets, a sentinel blind but still intact when it all stopped.

Alexandre Yersin, together with the Jesuit missionary Alexandre de Rhodes, is without any doubt the most celebrated French figure in Vietnam. Born on 23 September 1863 in Lavaux, Switzerland, Yersin died in March 1943 at Nha Trang. He discovered the diphtheria toxin, carried out the first survey of the Lang Bian plateau, where the city of Dalat was founded in 1893, isolated the bubonic plague virus in 1894 and – most important – introduced the rubber tree and the chichona tree into Vietnam. A symbolic figure, standing out among the hordes of colonial legend-makers, school builders and epitaph-chiselers.

On his tombstone is engraved a single inscription, in French but in a Vietnamese hand: 'Benefactor and Humanist. Venerated by the Vietnamese people.'

We go back down to the car without talking. I can't get the words of the epitaph out of my head. Especially the word 'benefactor'. A pious homage? Dues paid to the 'civilizing task'? Of course, but that's not *only* how I see them. They are more like a question discovered along the highway. Having come through so many massacres, a 'conquered conqueror' of the past half century, Vietnam is swallowing all its pride and rejoining today's world by going begging to the International Monetary Fund, the World Bank and Washington – and it is bringing us a strange malaise. Are we now about to enter a period of colonial revisionism which still refuses to speak its name? Haven't all the fiascoes, maladministrations and accumulated insolvencies, like so many contrasting negative images in the Southern hemisphere, served (already) to revive Western triumphalism from the dead? Can't the conquering Northern hemisphere overcome its old arrogance?

And so here we are – convinced that we are the exclusive depositories of freedom, goodness and the obscure secrets of abundance. What exactly shall we make of this new 'white man's burden'? Behind all the talk about the rights of man and the 'duty to intervene' is hidden another discourse, which tomorrow will justify a massive armed barricading of the paradise of the rich – indeed, will justify several 'corrections' administered to those teeming, disqualified nations, the 'new barbarians'. (In 1991, the Gulf War was also that – a big stick brandished in the face of the South.)

The tomb of Alexandre Yersin has something to tell us and, with him, so does the whole of Vietnam. For every 'venerated benefactor of the Vietnamese people' how much plunder, how many heads cut off, how many revolts put down by gunpowder? For every 'good work' by the French in Indochina, how many crimes? These are now 'old news' and almost absolved by history. Even their victims, from the depths of their disaster, seem to be on the point of renouncing their past struggles.

Maybe, tomorrow, we will have to ignore fashion and repeat what's been said before. Colonialism was a patchwork of enlightenment and crime, a civilizing discourse corrupted by practice. History advancing through the stench of mass graves, the progress of universal values covering up pillage and slavery. Will all these shadows be dispelled by the light embodied in a single venerated benefactor, Alexandre John Emile Yersin?

I am thinking about the question awaiting us in Paris. 'What's left over there of the French colonial period?'

If only this were all that was left . . .

SPLENDOURS

Sometimes an absurd reserve holds us back. The scenery passing outside our windows like some cinematic back projection is a splendour too long awaited for us to dare talk about it. Even to one another. In any event the fear of cliché renders us speechless, the excessive harmony is paralyzing. As if we feared some kind of verbiage that would be inscribed in the heart of things. Such scruples are understandable but foolish. How could we end up saying nothing about this – the infinity of paddy fields framed by the mountains flecked with clouds? Or about their meticulous division into beehive-like cells which, centimetre by centimetre, control the land and water to the horizon. Or the criss-cross pattern of earthern dykes where women scurry along, shoulders bent under the weight of the poles. Or the gestures and rhythms – two men face one another, swinging irrigation buckets on a rope, in cadence. A team of buffaloes wade cautiously in water halfway up their legs. Other buffaloes, richly costumed in dried mud, monstrous clay statues, follow heavily behind children who tow them by the nostrils or squat on their backs like Hindu elephant drivers. Flotillas of ducks set out on the rivers and ponds in their thousands.

The train sometimes passes so close to houses that we momentarily enter families' private lives: barefoot grandmothers in mud and straw huts, tiny courtyards, oxen sleeping under the broad leaves of the latanier trees. Some women stand up as the train passes, one hand on their hips, tossing back their conical straw hats. The gesture is lovely. This peaceful, archaic universe is repeated for miles; it is without beginning or end, unchanging. Light alone organizes its cycles, which change so much that following the curves of the tracks we cross puddles of sudden shadow, with shimmering intervals and even stroboscopic patterns of sunlight and darkness.

This splendour is not an endlessly repeated lithograph, it *is* Vietnam, a nation three-quarters of whose people are peasants. Here outside the windows of

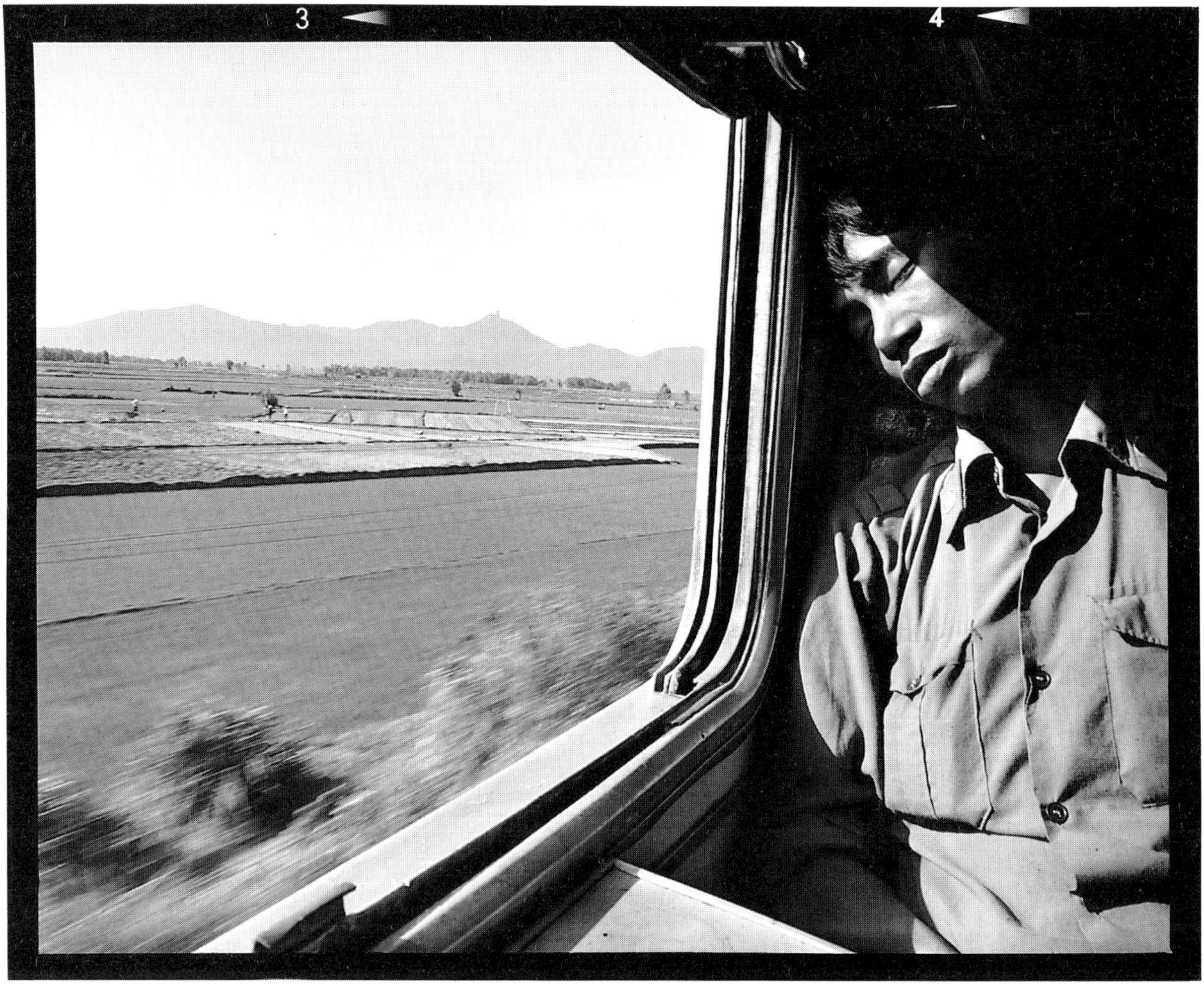

We continue our journey by train …

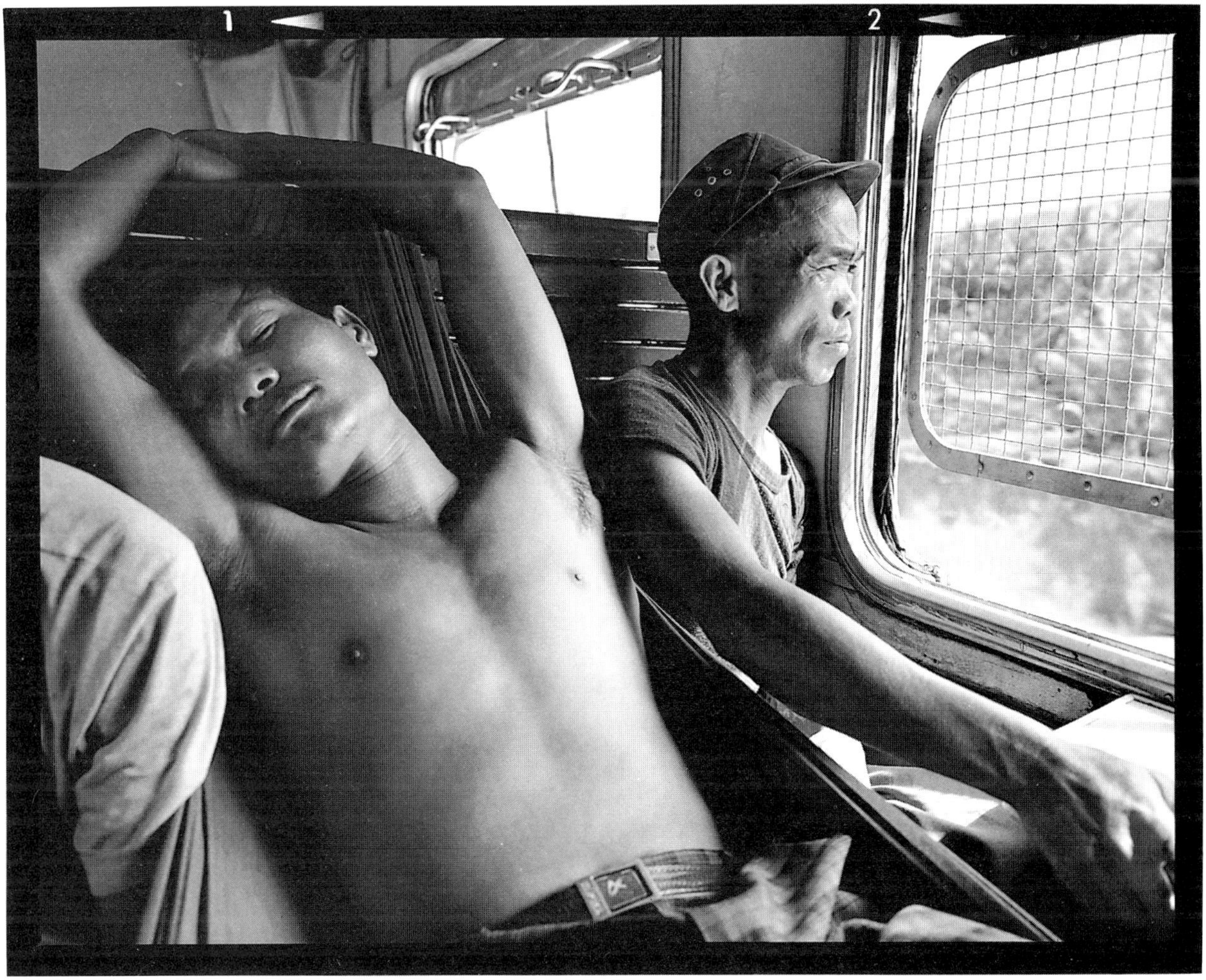

... there are lots of people from the North ...

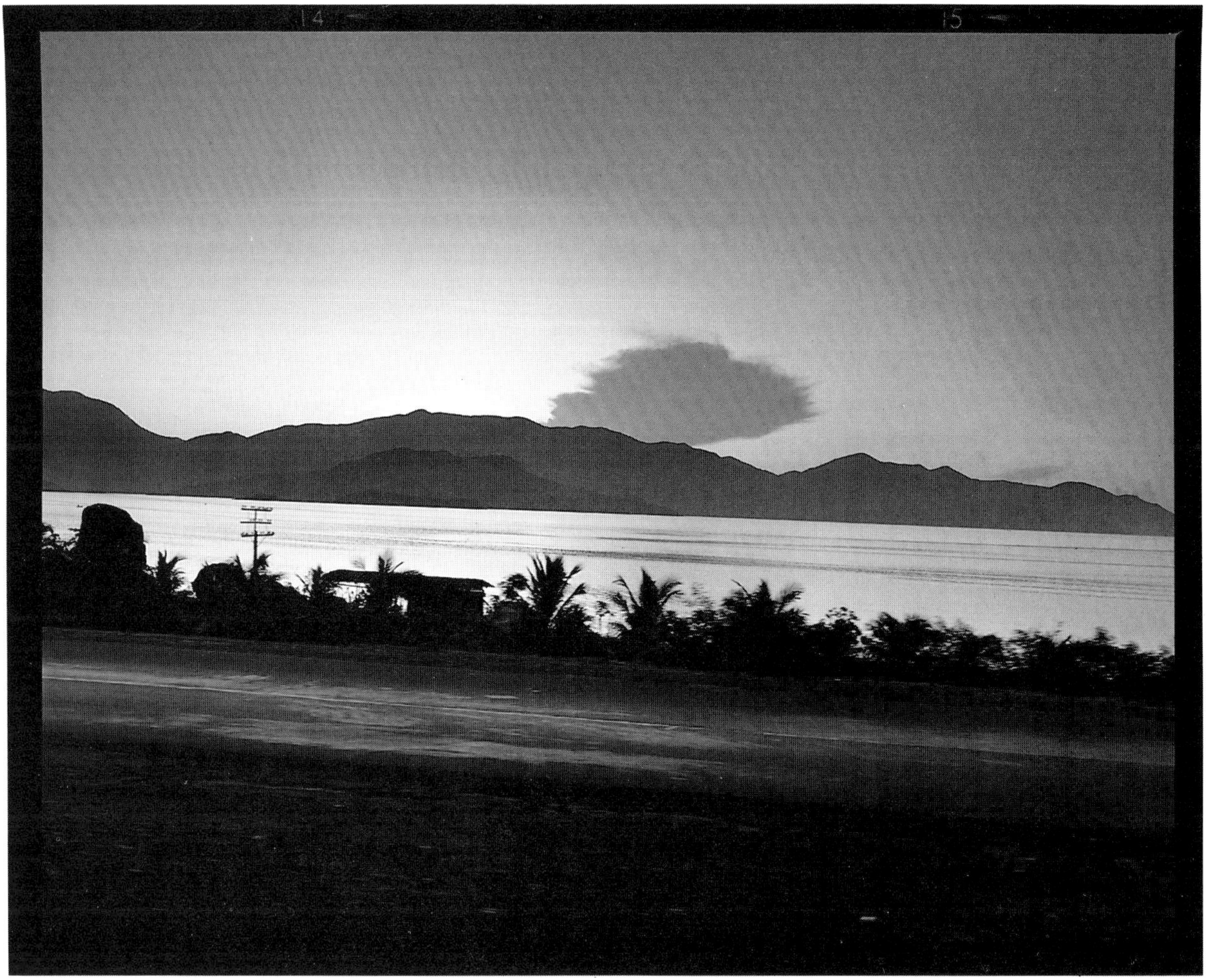

... we frequently follow the coastline.

the *Thong Nhat* is the sturdy Vietnamese identity which endures in spite of war and Stalinism – the keel of the boat, the ballast defying the storm, the reserve held for tomorrow. No doubt the communist 'errors' and nationalizations of the land upset this world to the point of provoking rice shortages and even near-famine at the end of the 1970s. But it has come back. Since the end of collectivization in 1986 and the return to private agriculture, the Vietnamese paddy fields (of the South in any case) have recovered their former opulence. In 1992, peasants of the Mekong Delta and the Annam region recorded their best crop in years. The market price for rice has fallen but a smile lights up every face. Vietnam has again become the world's third largest rice exporter. This disaster of a country, ruined by war and the failure of Stalinism, is once again sitting on a gold mine.

Now that it is a question of going back to square one after being misled by the communist failure, Vietnam finds itself more favoured than Hungary and Russia or the former colonies of Black and Muslim Africa, wasteland countries whose rural areas have always suffered the same devastation.

STORM AT DA NANG

Bac My Ann is at the end of the world, a remote beach where a few children play. The sandy road comes to a halt in the dunes. The sand is yellow and clean. Big filao trees at the edge of the waves form a corridor of cool shade. Two straw hut refreshment stands face each other, with their canvas chairs and three or four low tables. In the distance, above the misty haze which blurs the horizon, emerge the tree-covered summits on the islet of Cu Lao Cham, a sentinel of rock and forest watching over the bay. Long ago, swallows' nests and shells were gathered there. On this side of the beach, several hundred yards behind us, a dozen single-storey barracks provide rooms and collective kitchens for deserving workers. They are all closed.

The woman who runs one of the straw huts serves us a cup of espresso which Italians would envy. She smiles at us very gently, and in a low voice scolds her child, who has taken my hand.

Overhanging the wide curve of the bay to the north is the steep escarpment, *Col des Nuages.* Da Nang, known as Tourane under the French, the main gateway to central Vietnam, is eight kilometres to the south. As for this empty and dazzling beach at Bac My Ann, nothing indicates that it belongs to history. And has done so for a good long time.

This immense bay, stretching to the horizon, is Vietnam's most vulnerable point. In the seventeenth century, French ships dropped anchor here, bringing the first Jesuit fathers who founded at Faifo (today Hô An) a mission which began the partial Christianization of the country. In 1856, *Le Catinat,* ambushed in this same bay, bombarded the port of Tourane, a prelude to French colonization that was 'justified and rendered necessary', according to the terms of the Cochin China Commission, by the persecution of the missionaries.

It was here, too, on 8 March 1965, that the first battalions of American Marines landed, beginning the massive US infantry engagement in Vietnam.

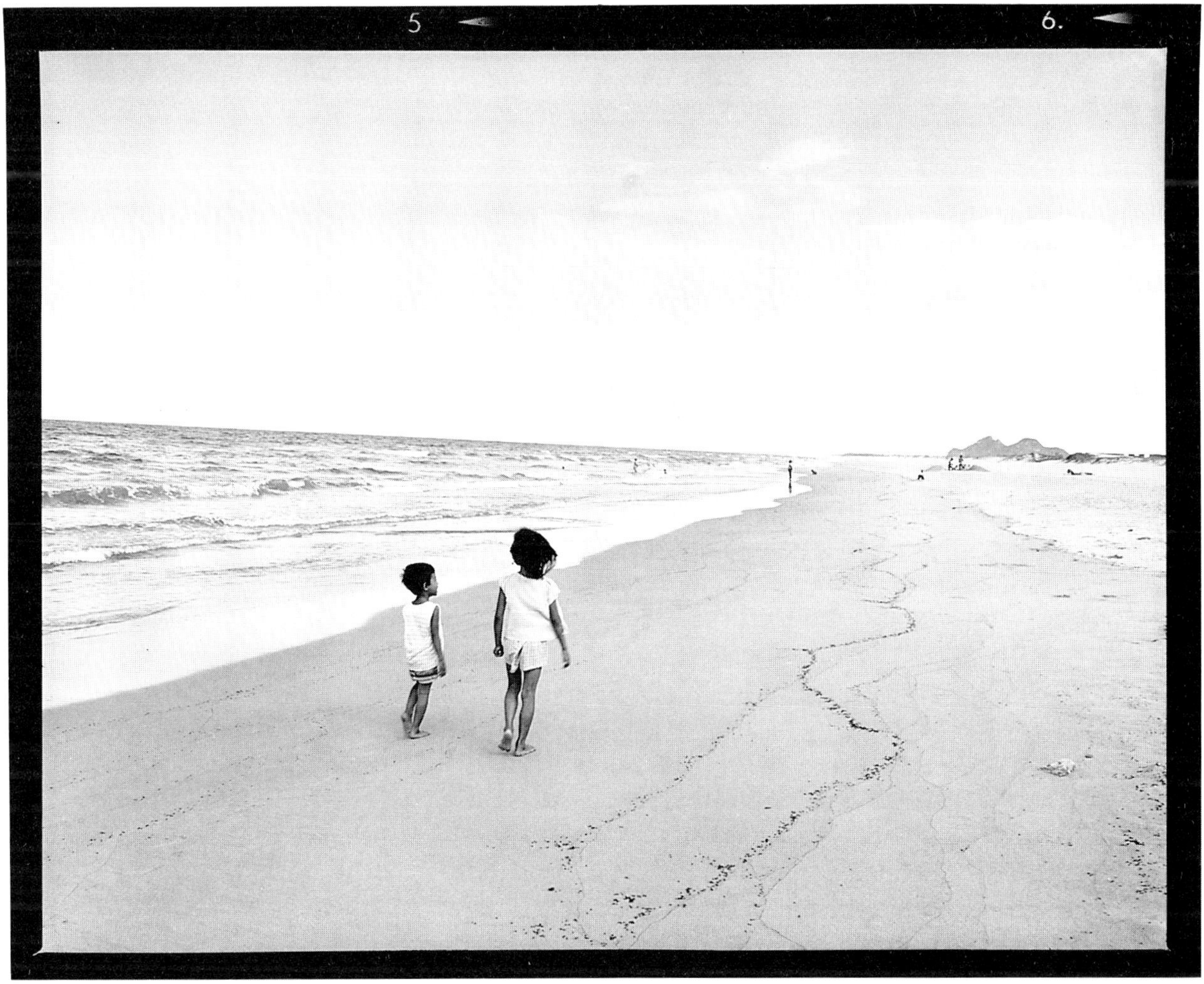

It is here that the Americans landed in 1965.

About the same time, President Lyndon Johnson had launched Operation Rolling Thunder in the North, and B-52s bombed the outskirts of Hanoi. Everybody remembers the panoramic maps shown on television all over the world. Opposite Da Nang the heavily armed ships of the Seventh Fleet, their guns aimed at the coast, blocked the horizon toward the islet of Cu Lao Cham. The sky was filled with helicopters, Phantom F-4 fighters and A-4 Skyhawks. The men, jumping off the landing craft, in their heavy helmets, packs on their backs, clutching the butts of their M-16s, dashed onto the beach in the direction of the line of trees. Behind them, the amphibious trucks were ploughing through the wet sand.

The welcome committee awaiting the Marines was not comprised of Viet-Cong lying in ambush with Soviet-made 130 artillery pieces, but of young women in white tunics, who placed garlands of flowers around their necks. The men stopped, struck dumb, suspicious, dripping salt water. The beach was calm, kids on bicycles passed by along the highway. An unbelievable moment, an unearthly incongruity which created an illusion that would last only a few days. Ten years of savage war was about to commence. Starting in July of the same year, 1965, a little further to the south, on the beach of Quang Tin, two battalions of Marines joined in fierce combat against the 1st Viet Cong Regiment and lost fifty-one men in a few hours.

Today the beach at Bac My Ann near Da Nang – 'Red Beach' the Americans called it – is given over to lovers who walk beneath the filaos, talking quietly, and to cuttlefish and white tuna fishermen who each evening launch long, tapered boats into the waves. To the north, several well-constructed buildings have been salvaged by the Vietnamese army. You can see the needle of a radio antenna sticking out above the dunes, the top of a watchtower and the debonair figure of a *bo doï*, a Kalachnikov on his shoulder.

Leaving the beach, without thinking, we start up along the route followed by the 3,500 disembarking Americans in 1965, who were soon joined by others, bringing to this region a formidable agglomeration of airfields and military bases, with *chevaux de frise* and barbed wire, bunkers, munitions depots, underground command centres and control towers, general stores and squalid whorehouses. Twenty-seven years later, vestiges of this frenzied encampment remain, a backdrop of rust and scrap iron. More than any other city, Da Nang was subjected to this monumental military evisceration, to this earthshaking, mechanical thunder from garrison and convoy, to bar-hopping GIs on leave, and hordes of special correspondents in search of choppers to the front. The city has retained a peculiar look of exhaustion, of defilement, the tired expression of somebody who has seen it all. On the highway we pass old landing strips whose Quonset huts are still standing. There are buildings in ruins, disembowelled bunkers guarded by soldiers, carcasses of GMC trucks lying on their side. Entering Da Nang, there is a hideous statue of the 'Socialist mother of the nation' with blackened lips, opening her muscular arms to the memory of seventeen Viet Cong soldiers killed in battle.

Nothing very pleasant here. Is it fatigue? Weariness from a trip started early in the morning? A viscous gloom weighs on us. Raymond is positive – there are no smiling faces in his viewfinder this time. Ordinarily, the moment he sets himself solidly in front of people, aiming the lens of his large-format camera, the shock lasts only a second. Immediately, faces light up with a glimmer of a smile, there is the hint of a gesture, a vague sway betrays complicity. No matter how slight, it is there, justifying the photo. Or forgiving it. Not here. I sense Raymond is more cautious, embarrassed by the subjects who shy away. Being constantly alert is making us sensitive to the slightest vibrations from the streets.

We walk down Le Duan Avenue which leads to the Han River, still spanned by the old De-Lattre-de-Tassigny bridge, and another just beside it, constructed by the Americans. Da Nang is a grey city. Rusty barbed wire still clings to all the balconies, the buildings are chipped, peeling and precarious. The majority of them in the town centre are low-cost housing dating from the 1960s, which have become foul ghettos with walled-up windows, interior courtyards strewn with rubbish and wrecked motorbikes. As we approach, some police are trying to restore a little order in the crowd. Absurd commotion, excited commands. Some homeless families have elected to live on the pavements of adjacent streets, hanging pieces of faded canvas from one tree trunk to another. They follow us slowly with their eyes.

On Bach Danh Street, which runs along the Han River, formerly a colonial seafront with foliage, stone piers and old villas with crenellated wooden

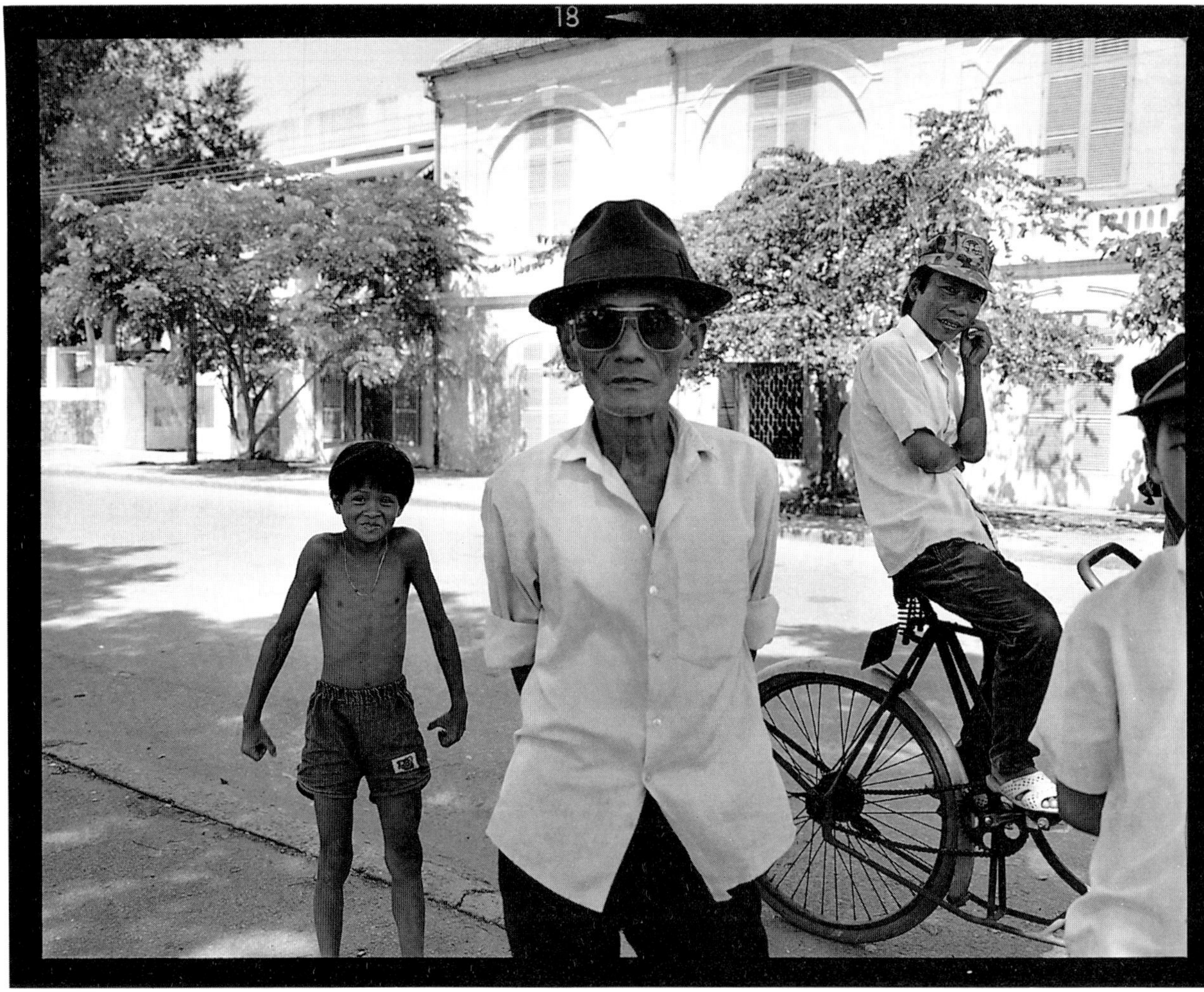

It is better to speak French.

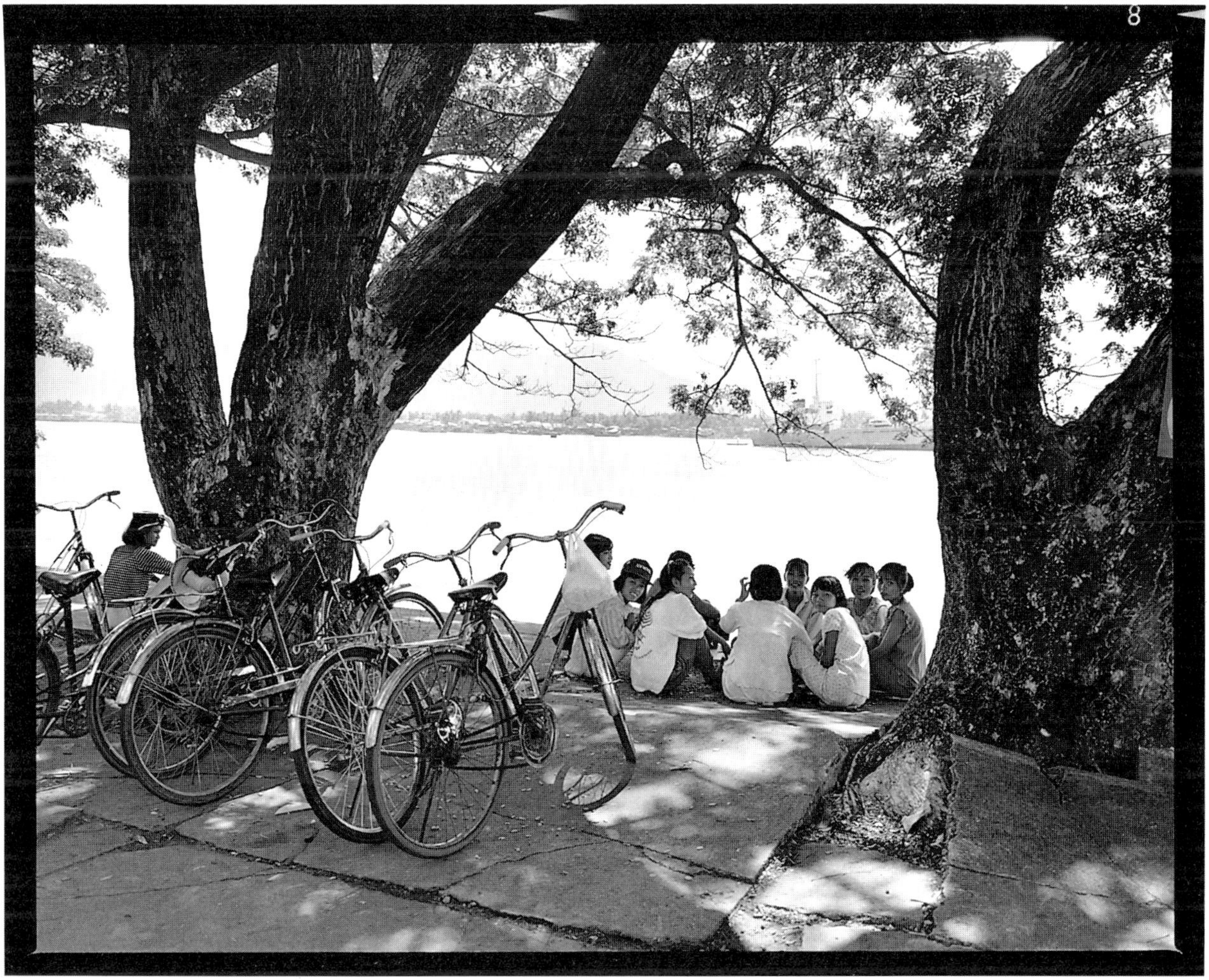

You have to keep your distance with these young girls.

balconies, the melancholy is even more raw. The villas are decrepit – and those which are not, which are freshly repainted and guarded by an armed *bo doi*, betray the privileges of a communist *nomenklatura*, which makes them still more sinister. Some teenagers drunk on beer and boredom follow us on bicycles. Raymond's camera intrigues them. They push each other aside, doing daredevil wheelies. Suddenly Vietnam in our eyes has become another country entirely. Almost hostile. It would seem that at each step something decays, falls apart. The Han River piers are littered with the shells of periwinkles cooked in red sauce, eaten on the spot, and strewn everywhere, still sticky with oil and spices.

Instinctively we shut ourselves off. Old beggars now accompanying us receive no indulgence. Why should people imagine that travellers are endlessly patient and magnanimous? Some of these retirees are pushing old bicycles, all speaking in strange, hollow French, as though with an outdated vocabulary deformed by listening to one another, truncated here and there by lapses of memory. One was a telegrapher in the French army 'at the time of Pétain', he says; then he was a collaborator with the American Signal Corps. In 1975, he had some 'big problems'. Two of his eight children are in Australia. At the beginning they sent a little money, but no longer. He survives, he adds, by serving as a guide or intermediary to the rare tourists passing through. Do we want to rent a car? He knows a chauffeur and it can be arranged. With a piece of cardboard he has fashioned a visiting card with printed letters traced in ball-point, and hands it to me with the caution of a conspirator.

The other old man, perhaps in order to please us, suddenly recites a eulogy, in a monotone, to French colonization, which one imagines he learned by heart from an old history book. Word for word: 'We, the intellectuals, we remember the civilizing work of France. She built highways and, on the large rivers, solid and useful bridges. Doctor Yersin, illustrious savant and tireless researcher, did much for the Vietnamese people.' His oration is so faultless that it betrays a childhood memory resurrected intact, a lesson recited at the blackboard and inscribed forever, like multiplication tables or lists of *préfectures*. From which illustrated history of *l'Empire Français* is this edifying refrain an extract? What is intended by it? What if this nostalgia, recited in sing-song, was simply in earnest?

We consciously shy away from this encounter. We don't want to think about all this. It is too hot. We are tired. The town centre restaurant where we lunched on grilled shrimp and chicken with rice reflected the city itself. Vast, dirty, filled with shifty-looking waiters and female cooks shuffling their feet. Mme D. seems surprised to find us aggravated and uninterested in other people. Every trip is punctuated by such 'air pockets' and observation breakdowns.

Not far from the centre of town, to the north of the mouth of the river, we come upon another beach, notorious in the memories of Yankee veterans. The Americans called it China Beach. They came here on their leaves to go swimming and watch the girls. A celebrated nightclub by the shore has now been turned into a vacation centre. For the rest, nothing has changed. Neither the street congested with bicycles and Hondas, nor the brick houses dotted with bougainvilleas. Only the light suddenly tears us away from ourselves. A storm has just died, the sky is still black above the sea but, like a spotlight in a theatre, a diagonal ray of sunlight illuminates only the beach, leaving the rest of the landscape in the blue-grey gloom of the monsoon. Some kids are running along the sand, elegant women are closing their umbrellas, shaking out their wet hair. *Photo!*

Behind us, twenty years on, Da Nang retains the same colour of toughened steel.

CONCERTO DE L'ADIEU

It was a game at first, a mischievous prank which did no more than make us smile. Raymond and I had in our luggage the *Concerto de l'adieu* by Georges Delerue, composed for Pierre Schoendoerffer's film, *Diên Biên Phu.* The film was just coming out when we were leaving for Vietnam. In the cinema at Odéon, where I went alone, I wept so suddenly and unexpectedly that I waited a moment after the film was over before going out onto the Boulevard Saint-Germain. It was idiotic; my eyes were red. The sudden emotion had brought a lump to my throat, and I was a bit ashamed. I didn't mention it to the others. I made light of it by saying that the film was 'not bad', although a little 'schematic in its construction'. But I ran out to buy the original soundtrack.

That was two days before boarding the plane. I scarcely listened to the cassette but slipped it into my bag.

It all started a little before Dalat. We had stopped in a village and ordered some iced tea on the terrace of a bamboo refreshment stand. We were seated on homemade chairs no higher than doll's seats. Streams of bicycles and carts passed on the highway, throwing off clouds of red dust. People were stopping to stare. How long had it been since they had seen travellers from the west? As usual, a big radio-cassette player was blasting away, driving us crazy. The youngsters at the refreshment stand thought to gratify us by putting on American pop songs and hard rock. The bass resonated in our chests like blows of a fist. It was deafening and disagreeable.

Then I thought of the Delerue cassette in my luggage. I went to find it and without asking handed it to the youngsters at the stand. They immediately put a stop to their detestable *musica* to play mine. Then, and *only then,* did we understand that the scene was extraordinary. We were two Frenchmen in the heart of Vietnam, in the middle of a village in Lang Bian Province, listening to the soundtrack of *Diên Biên Phu* at full blast, with its haunting leitmotif of violin solos accompanying the French Expeditionary Force into hell.

Of course, the young people asked me what this bizarre music was, so radically different from their boombox noise. I suggested to Mme D. that she explain to them exactly what it was about. I attentively awaited their reaction – a serious look, a confirmatory nod, clearly respectful attention. But nothing really conclusive in the end. What did their fixed smile mean, exactly? Were they gratified that in their presence we were listening to a musical symbol of a Vietnamese victory? Or did they find it unpleasant in the company of foreigners to have to listen to a reminder of an 'heroic' event, exploited to the utmost by communist propaganda. I hadn't the slightest idea. In Vietnam, some smiles are more opaque than silence.

Since this 'premiere' near Dalat, Raymond and I continue to listen to *Concerto de l'adieu*. At each stop, feeling that we are pursuing a quest. We put on the cassette in the most unlikely locations: the terrace of the Hotel Thong Nhat at Phan Rang, a cheap eatery beside the highway on the way to Qui Nhon, the restaurant in the Vinh Dong Hotel at Nha Trang, the open air café in Da Nang. People stop talking to listen, sometimes to smile at us. By now it is a ritual. When I forget, Raymond, half-serious, orders: 'Bring out the cassette!' Of course we joke, 'The whole of Vietnam must have heard it by now.' But this 'game' has a serious side.

I was ten years old when the garrison dug in at Diên Biên Phu fell. At boarding school in Villard-de-Lans, the classes all gathered in the dining hall for a minute's silence. 'This is a day of mourning for France,' said the principal. We didn't really understand why, but as the son and brother of soldiers, I instinctively cried. And for a long while. The expression 'mourning for France' seemed irreversible. As the years passed, I buried the memory deep inside. But later, unlike those around me, I never supported the carefree anti-militarism of the 1960s and 1970s – the disdain of political activists and sarcasm of intellectuals to whom I was nevertheless close. Something inside me preferred those who paid cash for their convictions. I felt within an instinctive indulgence toward the soldiers, even those fighting for a lost cause, while still detesting fools and the stupidity of garrison life. But I didn't care for ironic reflections about the mystery of war, period. This was inconsistent with the rest of my life. But too bad. Come what may, I had to live with this 'contradiction'. Perhaps I became a journalist to resolve it in my own fashion, by being on both sides at once – a writer but close to events, conversant with intellectual discourse but never far from tears.

When I got involved in the war for real in the 1970s in Saigon, I often came up against this ambiguity.

Since our arrival in Vietnam, I understand better why I was so overcome by seeing *Diên Biên Phu.* It was not merely on account of the pathos of defeat, the heartbreak of surrender and the horror of the camps. Filmed in Vietnam itself, with the participation of the communist army and some former 'Viets', this film wanted to be the first step toward leaving history behind, a hand of friendship tendered by one side to the other. Its very existence proved this was a road which could be followed. At least, that is how I understood it. At the same time it seemed to me – we cry for less – that my two halves could finally be united.

Since Dalat, we have continued to monitor the reaction of the Vietnamese. But this kind of waiting and watching is not very reasonable. In our haste we forgot something essential. It came to me when I noticed a look of boredom on the faces of two little waitresses in the Hotel Dien Luc at Da Nang. What matters is the unfathomable depth of the past. In short, we had given in to the traveller's perpetual delusion, which runs something like this: going about our business in the world, we make as if 'local' time is small change with no value, which stops when we depart and starts up again the moment we return. We react as if History stopped the clock in the country we left and was waiting for us to come back before starting up again. The world in some way will wait for us to decide it really exists, the way America was waiting to be discovered by Columbus. An old western sin, a false compound of adventure and arrogance.

The proof: it took some effort and mental calculation before I realized that for young Vietnamese the battle of Dieñ Bieñ Phu lies further in the past than, at their age, the battle of Verdun did for us. Nothing but a date in books, an episode grown cold in history recited in school. Were we moved, at the age of twenty, when somebody talked about *poilus, Les Éparges* or *Chemins des Dames*?*

In truth, the Vietnamese we came across had little to say about our *Concerto de l'adieu* or about Diên Biên Phu. Let's say they didn't give a damn. And it's just as well.

**A poilu* was the popular term for a French soldier in the First World War; the small community of *Les Éparges* was the scene of fierce fighting in June, 1915; *Chemin des Dames* was the site of several battles, including a tragic French offensive. (Tr.)

RETURN TO KHE SANH

In the brick-coloured earth of the battlefield at Khe Sanh, twenty kilometres from the Laotian border, grow sensitive plants, *mimosa pudica*, with little fan-shaped leaves. At the lightest touch, they curl up like sea anemones. This sensitive plant, which the Vietnamese call the 'bashful flower', lines a shallow basin one kilometre long and two wide, wreathed in fog. This forgotten area, 1,500 kilometres from Saigon, was the site of the 1967–68 battle known as the 'American Diên Biên Phu'. Today, if you walk over the former Marine bunkers, still strewn with bullets from M-16s and AK-47s, or stroll in absolute silence along what was once the asphalt landing-strip at Tacon, the plants shrink back at your approach, in an extraordinary movement which follows you step by step, like a shudder. There will never be any victory parades here.

In Hanoi they used to call Khe Sanh a 'frying pan'. It was there that General Vô Nguyên Giap, who prepared the Têt Offensive (1968, year of the monkey), drew in and 'boiled down' – in a calculated diversion – the 6,000 GIs of the Marines' 5th division. A hell's kitchen . . . the men listened to Otis Redding's *Dock of the Bay* and Jimi Hendrix's *Foxy Lady*, dug into their shelters. This encampment, attentively watched by the whole world, daily took up to seven thousand mortar shells, rockets or *katiouchas*. The ground is still saturated with them, as at Verdun. There are gaping holes all over the earthen fortifications: in 1992, the 'metal hunters' are still at work. Twelve-year-old kids, boys and girls, hack away with blistered hands under the hot sun and sell their harvest for 100 dongs per kilo to the metal dealers of Dông Hâ. Twenty-four years after the most furious – and futile – battle of the American Vietnamese war, a battle which cost General William Westmoreland his post, made Lyndon B. Johnson give up the White House, and permitted Michael Herr, correspondent for *Esquire*, to write the most incandescent pages in the history of journalism. *Death is a bitch* –

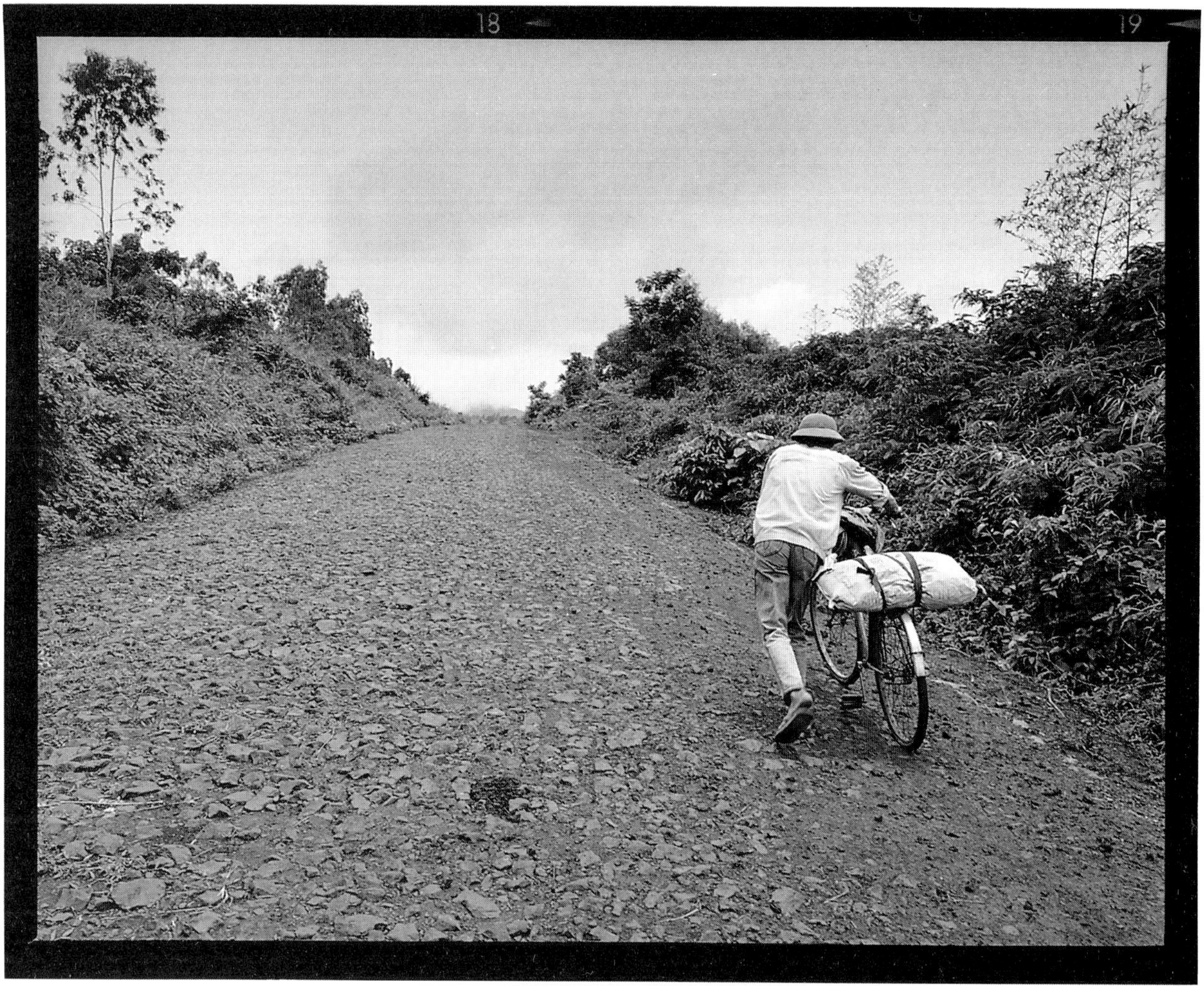

Visiting Khe Sanh … and the Hô Chi Minh Trail …

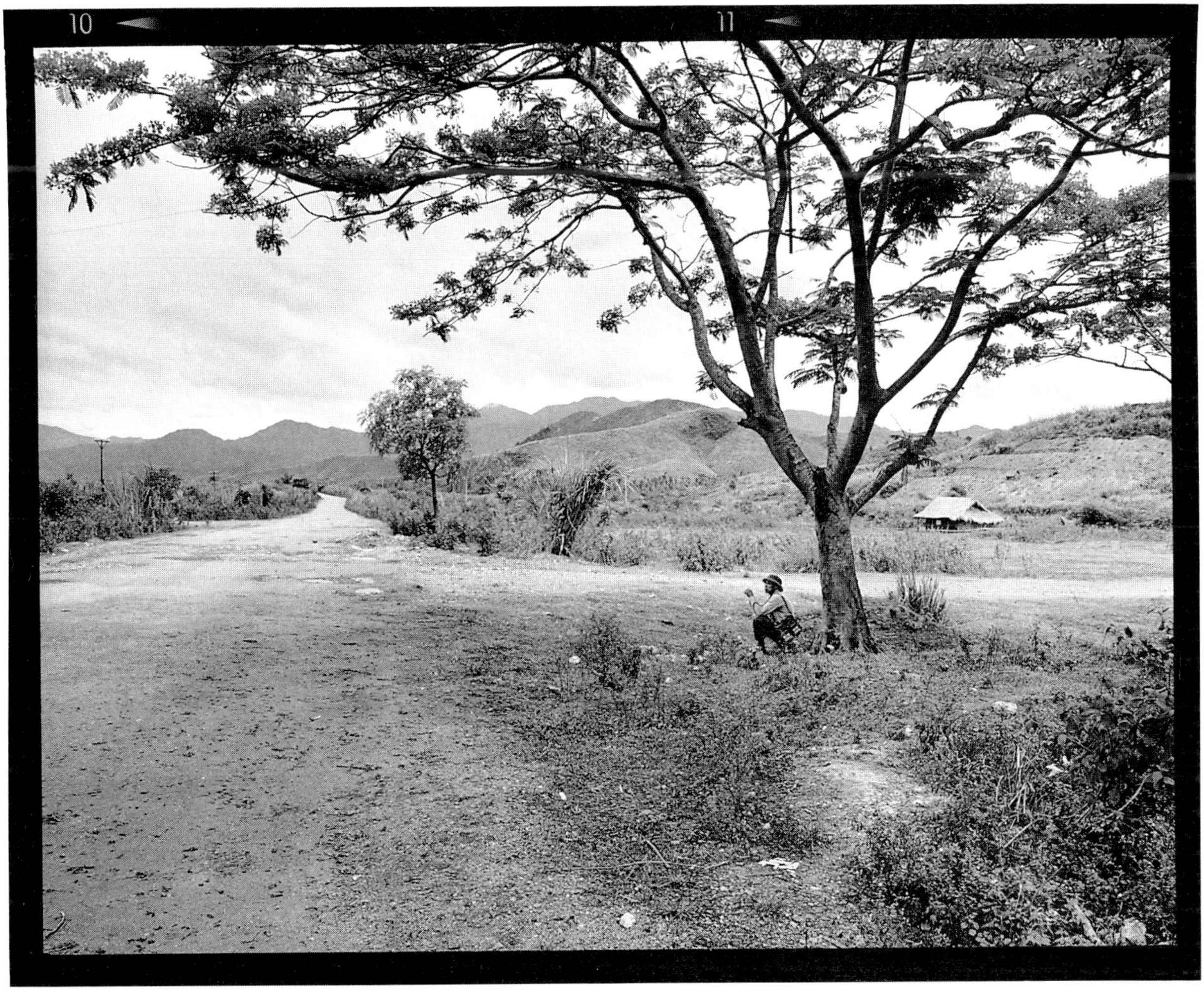

... we went up to Khe Sanh on Route Nationale 9 ...

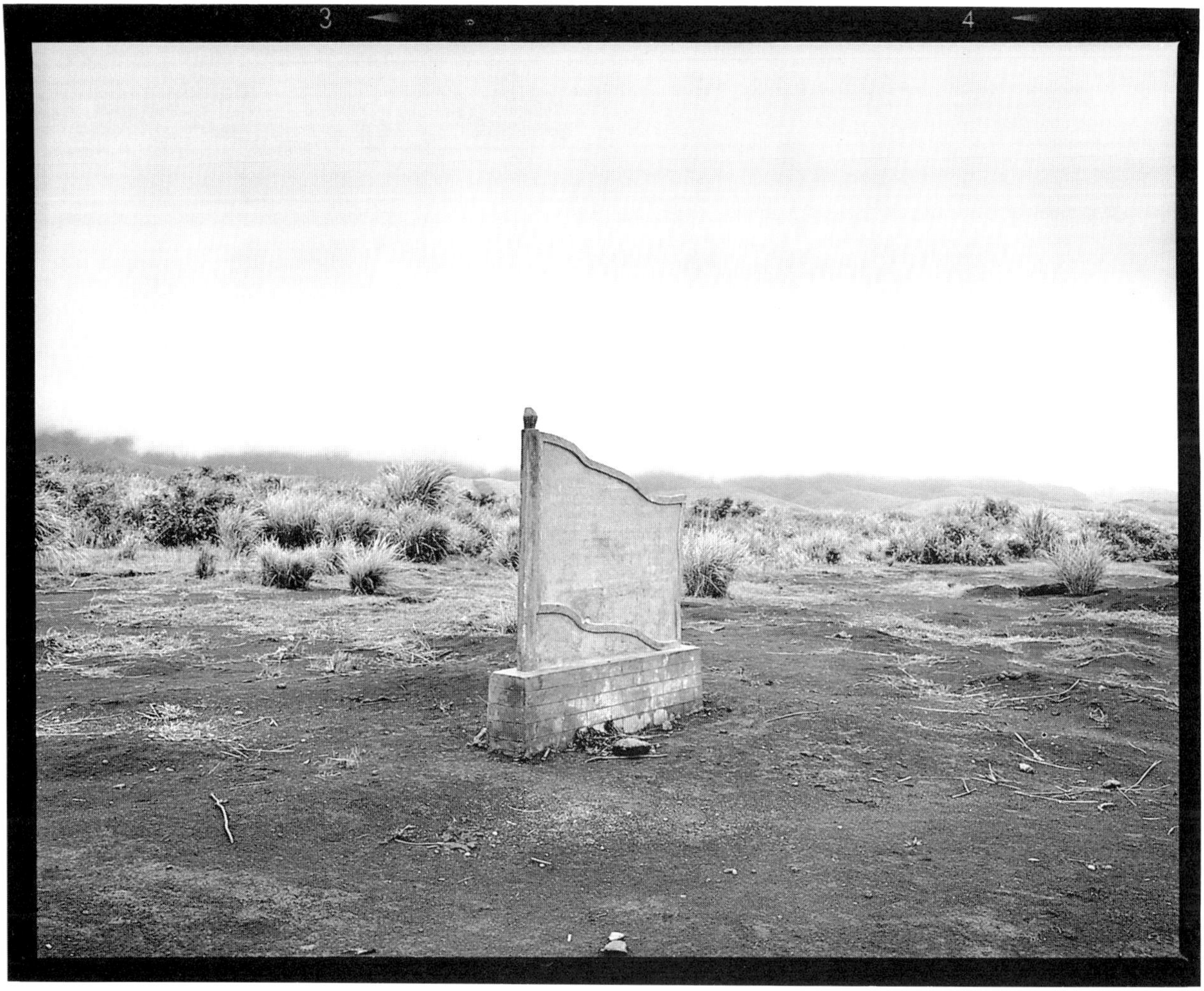

... a small monument ... for a big battle ...

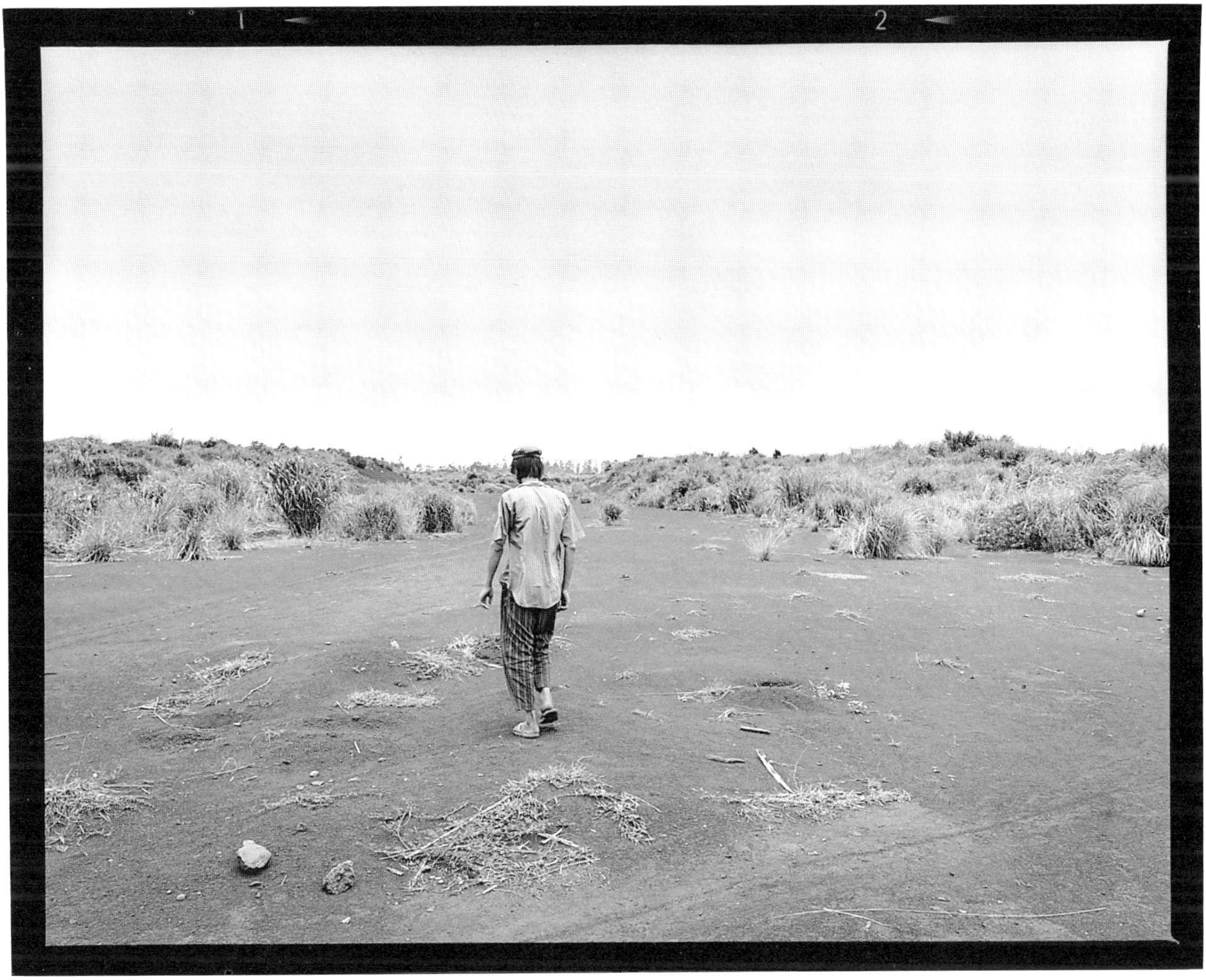

... such sadness ...

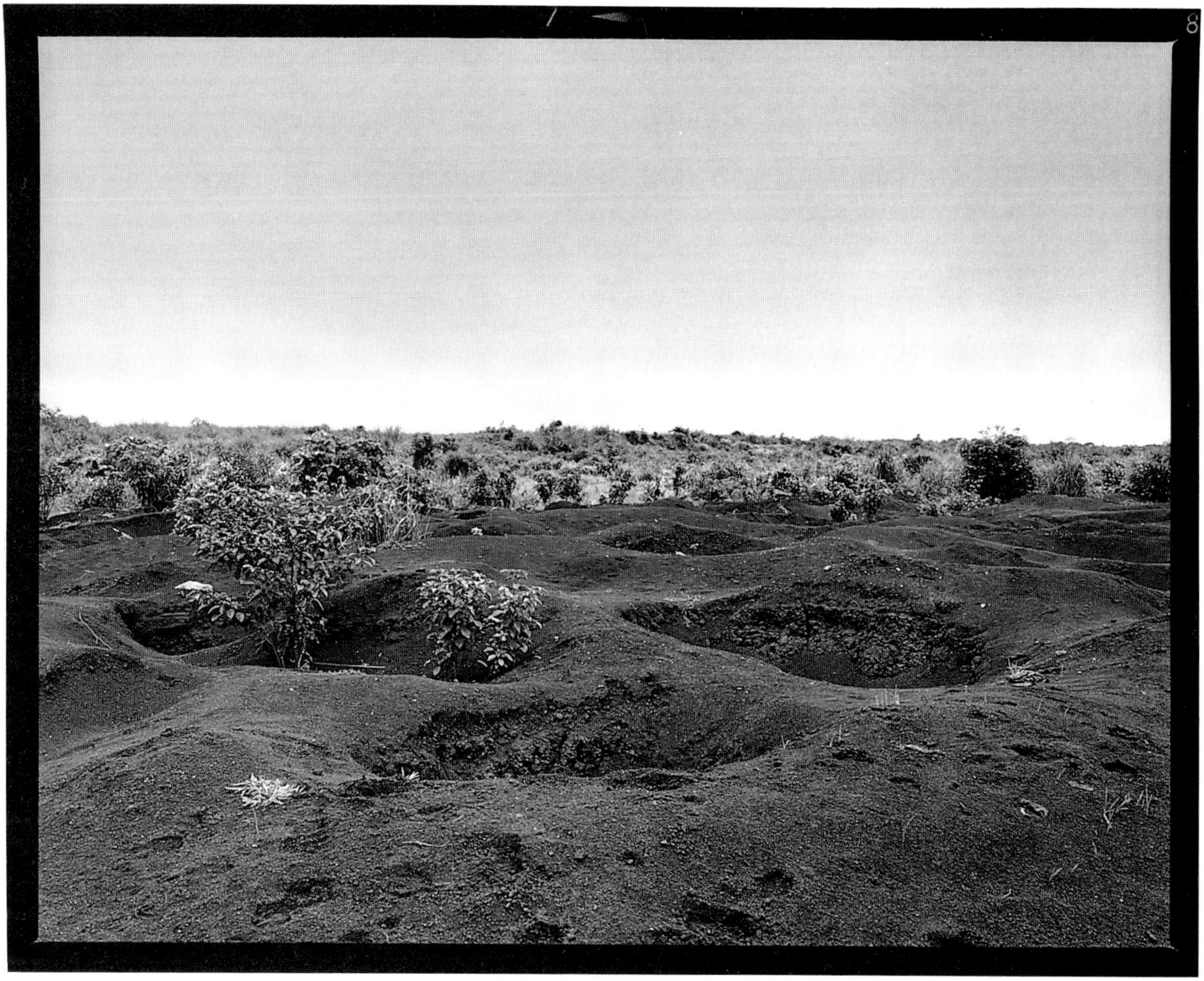

... the place still breathes death.

> Khe Sanh . . . I see a road. It is full of ruts made by trucks and jeep tires, but in the passing rains they never harden, and along the road there is a two-dollar piece of issue, a poncho which had just been used to cover a dead Marine, a blood-puddled, mud-wet poncho going stiff in the wind.*

Twenty-four years later . . . around the beginning of May 1992, a certain John Charpentier (or Charpenter), a Marine Corps veteran, was brought to Khe Sanh (as were we) by M. Nguyên T.D., the official guide of Quang Tri Province. As soon as he arrived he went to an earthen hillock near the old landing-strip. From there he looked toward hills 845, 832, 861 and 881, topped with clouds, then southwest where the old base of operations at Langvei was located, and finally east, toward the firebases of Rockpile and Camp Carroll. He scrutinized the horizon as though verifying his own position. Then, abruptly, the seasoned Marine lowered his head and burst into tears.

Later, he muttered to his guide that often, back home in Virginia, he had put the barrel of a Colt 11-43 pistol in his mouth. The filthy, fucked-up mess that was Vietnam. Returning to Dông Hâ by Route 9 – one of the most bombarded roads in the world – Lieutenant Charpentier (or Charpenter) wanted to stop that afternoon at the memorial of Con Thien ('Hill of Angels'). There on a prominence planted with pines and heveas, little cement tombstones are grouped by province as far as the eye can see. Apart from the graves of twelve heroes and some sixty-six unknown soldiers of the PLA (People's Liberation Army) at the centre of the memorial. Lieutenant Charpentier crouched down before one of the 24,000 *bo doi* graves of the 304th, 320th and 324th divisions of the North Vietnamese Army. Without a word, one by one, he lighted the incense sticks which he had brought with him and stuck them in the ground. For these former *Nyaq,* those silhouettes glimpsed occasionally in the smoke of the bombardments, for his old enemies.

Charpentier was not the first, nor will he be the last. For several months,

---

*Michael Herr, *Dispatches* (New York, Alfred A. Knopf, 1977).

thanks to the partial lifting of the American embargo, former GIs are making pilgrimages to Khe Sanh. There they encounter former communist soldiers that the veterans' associations bring in by bus. They talk to one another and laugh and cry together. Time has passed at Khe Sanh. The depth of the mystery of war ought never to be underestimated.

Today veterans of both sides are brought closer, paradoxically, by the same misfortune. As in America, the hundreds of thousands of *bo doi* have as the price of victory only the ancestral ingratitude of civilian society which, now that peace has returned, is turning away from its former combatants. The US and Vietnamese veterans form the same legion, a disenchanted brotherhood of battered faces, forty-year-old gas attack victims, legless cripples, and semi-beggars. You come across them in wheelchairs in the streets of Hô Chi Minh City, Da Nang, and Hanoi. They weep over their meagre pensions, wave their crutches about and ramble on with the same memories, swearing through clenched teeth that, just as surely as they won the war, the 'politicians' have squandered the peace. Spilled blood is worth little on the Vietnamese 'market'. Some veterans have become pickpockets or small-time dealers, others have turned to smuggling. All express the age-old stupefaction of warriors swindled by History. So many killed to come to this. If any might reach them, it is indeed the former GIs, whose words and tears are like their own. A chilling irony of the war.

Nguyên T.D., the guide, told us all this and a lot of other things. He even recited a piecemeal account of the official-heroic, communist and revolutionary version of the battle of Khe Sanh. In which they lay it on shamelessly thick – 17,000 Americans and 'puppets' brought to their knees, etc. Mme. D. inevitably mutters that Nguyên T.D. was 'giving the communist version'. It seemed to us that his way of putting it was circumspect, indirect, indeed decidedly facetious. I say, *it seemed to us*. Who will ever know the truth about Khe Sanh and the 'adhesion of the masses' to communism?

We ate some sticky rice and boiled chicken in the only eatery in Khe Sanh City, which long ago was razed by B-52s coming from Guam or from Udon, in Thailand. Today, 30,000 inhabitants have come back to this little town, with its coffee and pepper plants, and its big breadfruit trees whose obscene fruits hang down against the trunks. Nguyên T.D. appeared annoyed by our neighbours. A nearby table of 'cadres' was having a party. Dead drunk, in their dull green uniforms, some customs officers from the Laotian frontier were knocking back whole cases of Huda or Zhu Jiang beer, for which they paid cash with money from their trafficking. Their wandering hands fondled the waitresses. Who could possibly resist a tight and merry communist cadre?

The proprietress was dozing on her elbow behind the cash register, ball-point in hand. Dogs prowled under the tables. The heavy silence of the battlefield was still droning in our ears. In a word, the place still stank of carnage and tragedy. As does the former DMZ (demilitarized zone) and the whole province of Quang Tri, one of the most battered, scarred and devastated in all Vietnam. A province of 'heroes' and orphans strewn with monuments to the dead and populated with former refugees. Liberated three years before Saigon, in 1972, it is behind the rest of the country in its slow digestion of all the scrap iron and terror of the war.

For some, the first days of peace here were a windfall. In the hangars of the old base of Ai Tu, in the concrete shelters of Dông Hâ and Cam Lo, those who moved fastest found brand new trucks, stereo sets, electric generators and US-made hardware. They did business. Like columns of ants, the people carried off refrigerators, TV sets, air conditioners and cases of rations. Everybody still remembers. A whole war, a piece of America – move it out quick and recycle it!

Then came the time, which continues still, of 'industrial salvage'. They put the big American GMC trucks back on the highway. Twenty years later these are still rolling all across the country, alongside Russian Kamas and East German IFAs. In the hills and forests of the Ashau Valley, they dismantled hundreds of helicopter and plane carcases and trafficked in the rare metals they contained. The mountains of scrap iron, sheet metal and tank turrets make scrap merchants happy in Hong Kong, Taiwan and Seoul. From tin cans, empty cartridges and canteens found on the sites of US bases, they manufactured coins and beer cans. Finally, they dug away haphazardly in the fields while the peasants, returning to their homes, were trying to work their rice paddies. More than two thousand people have been blown up by shells or land mines in Quang Tri Province alone.

Burrowing underground, the work is an act of exorcism – the ultimate garage sale extracted kilo by kilo from the earth, little by little extirpating from memory the war itself. What else did America do but dump on Vietnam a kind of sub-country of cement and asphalt, a grid of military bases and airfields drifting hopelessly over the real country, never truly touching nor reaching the depth of its being? A formidable machinery, of colossal dimensions, which yet remained as *foreign* to Vietnamese society as the colonial highways themselves, whose fundamental vanity was described long ago by the great Paul Mus.

In my notes from 1972 I found a quote from Mus, copied long ago from his book *Les Vietnamiens et leur révolution.* The text dates from the beginning of the 1950s but can be illuminatingly applied to the 'American mistake':

> Just as the official highway of old ran from the imperial palace to the provincial palace, and to all the institutions of the religious and administrative network, establishing itself above the earth and the people, so our highways in their turn slice into the rest of the country, cross the rivers, cut through the hills and expropriate the paddy fields. They lead us as if from island to island in our own world. The European districts, houses which are socially off-limits, in practice, to the people of the country, were erected and set alongside the asphalt, like the flying castles of the gods in legends. One instinctively understood that European motorcars could only speed non-stop through the country, between these fragments of another planet, superimposed on the traditional countryside. For that countryside had nothing to do with these other beings, nothing whatsoever.*

Thus was the American military infrastructure, at once gigantic and ridiculous, brought to bear on Vietnam. And so since 1975 it has been a question of extracting all this immense ontological scrap from the earth. Has it been done?

---

*Paul Mus and John McAlister Jr, *Les Vietnamiens et leur révolution* (Paris, Seuil, 1972), text established by Serge Thion. This passage does not appear in the earlier version of this book, which appeared in English as *The Vietnamese and Their Revolution* (New York, Harper & Row, 1970). (Tr.)

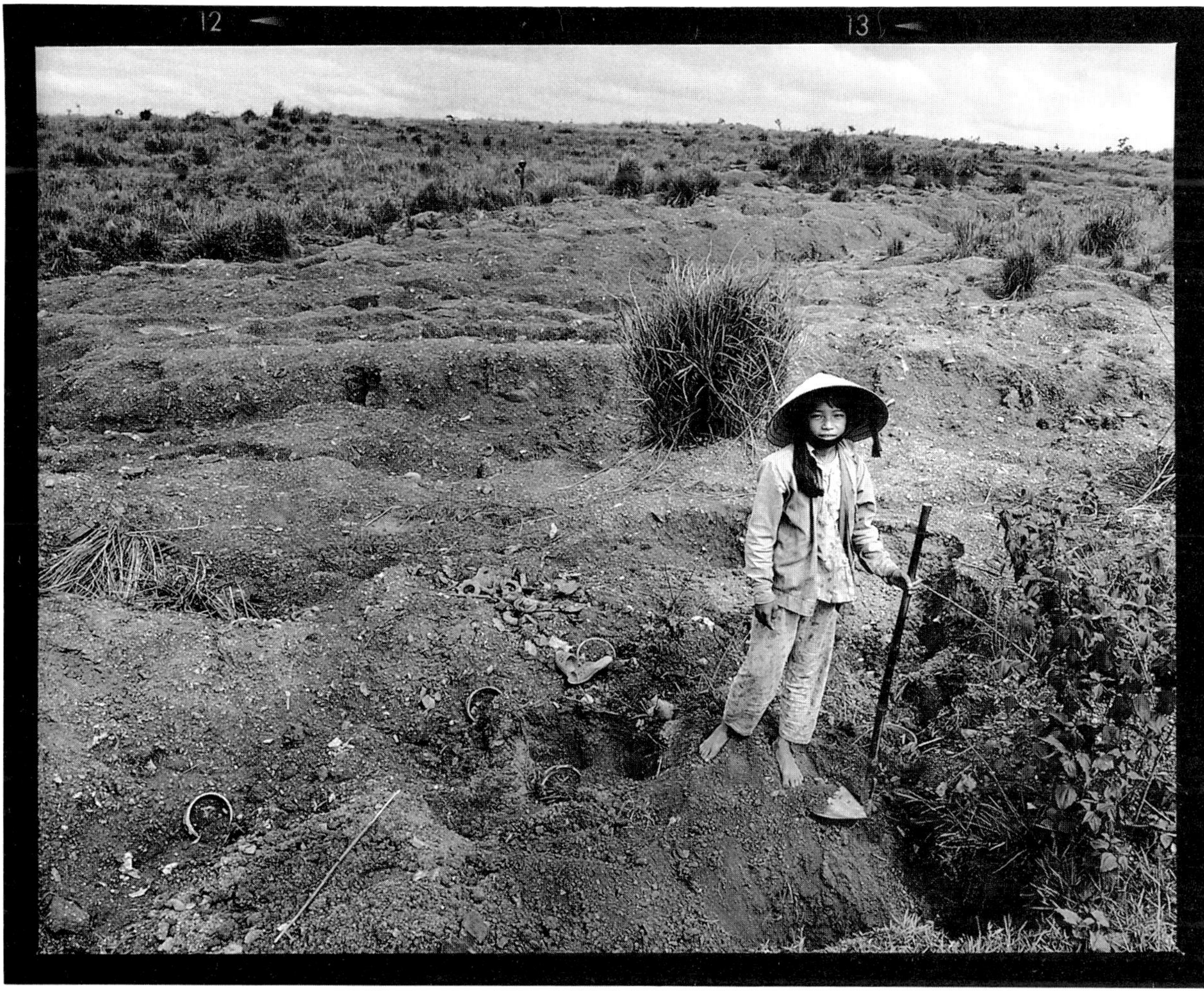

A young woman searches for metal on the battlefield.

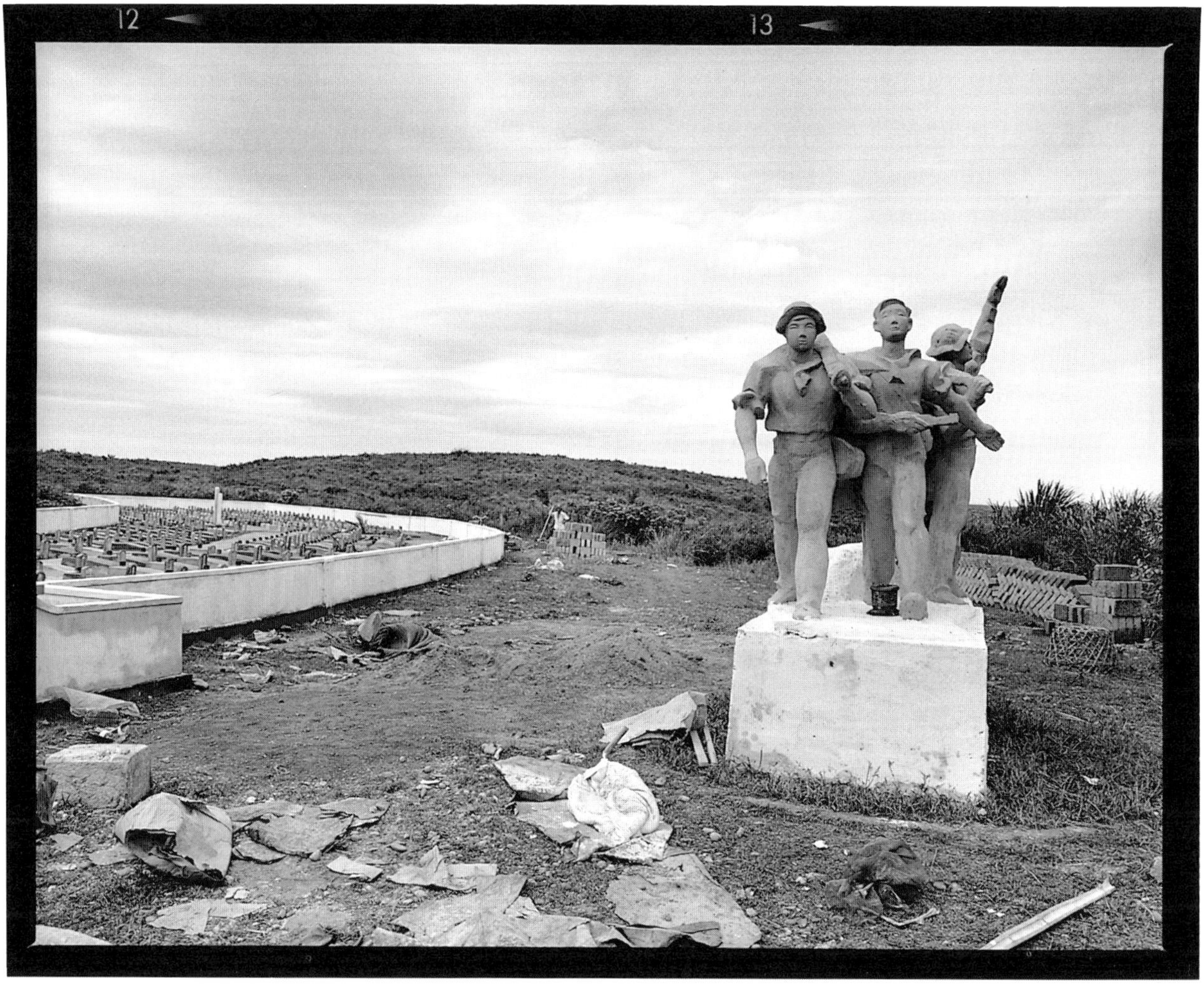

The military cemetery is brand new.

Not yet. At Con Thien ('Hill of Angels') and in the My Chanh River, which marked the front in the spring of 1972, the sludge searchers are still at work, as they are at Khe Sanh. In Huê itself, each morning, from the terrace of the Huang Giang Hotel, we watched kids in canoes, wearing swimming masks, endlessly plunging into the Perfume River. The fragments of shells and bombs which they brought to the surface were never very big. A small profit but a haunting reminder. In front of the wall of the Citadel in Huê, a little girl was selling tourists old bullets from Kalachnikovs and M-16s, mounted on pendants.

However, elsewhere in Vietnam memories of the war seem fairly hazy and the Vietnamese barely talk about it any more. The forests have grown up again, eucalyptus plantations are once more covering the areas on which rained 71,250,000 litres of defoliant (according to American statistics), and twenty million more inhabitants have come along to compensate for the million dead. Of the hundreds of fortified, concrete-reinforced, barbed-wire-spiked American bases, there remain only bizarre wastelands, as at Biên Hoa or Cam Ranh, and bunkers – some of which, like the one at Con Thien, are French. As to the military museums, those at Hanoi and Saigon display the armoured vehicles and US planes taken from the enemy but which, polished by rain and sun, resemble wreckage from another century. More than half the Vietnamese living today were not born twenty years ago. Amnesia so soon?

Not at Dông Hâ in Quang Tri Province – especially not at Dông Hâ – where we return at the end of the day. In the tiny 'tourist office' occupied by Nguyên T.D. a map of the province is thumbtacked to the wall. On it we read in English: 'Principal Centres of Interest in Quang Tri'. Some names of villages, some little coloured symbols. Looking closer, *all are battle sites.* If it can't forget the war, martyr province Quang Tri is going to try and sell it to tourists. The prices are set. Fifteen dollars for the guide, one dollar per person per 'site'. Ready-made speeches to drum up interest in these 'exciting' places.

And there's more! M. Nguyên T.D. is probably not yet familiar with the project being nursed along by the cadres of the People's Committee of Quang Tri who, as representatives of a martyr province, have connections and support in Hanoi. (The Quang Tri 'mafia', it is sometimes called.) A *Vietkieu* partner in the joint venture told me about it with the verve of an impresario. It involves setting up a tour operator at Khe Sanh, as soon as the US embargo is lifted, for former GIs with a yearning to go back. Estimated market: two to three million Yankee veterans. Working title: 'Vietnam Safari'. For $1,700, air transportation included, veterans will be brought from the Midwest by Route 9, which, leaving from Thailand, passes through Laos and Savannakhet. On the programme: Langvei, Khe Sanh, Con Thien and the Hô Chi Minh Trail. For want of hotels it is expected the boys will be lodged in prefabricated structures to be purchased in the Philippines. Such uncomfortable bivouacs may help to bring back memories. . . . In San Diego, some enthusiastic Marines told the *Vietkieu* that they were subscribing in advance.

In swearing their support, they even added, 'If you need 'em, you can borrow our choppers.'

Death is a bitch!

MONTEZUMA'S REVENGE

Nguyên T.D. was counting on his fingers: the Khe Sanh Battlefield, the Con Thien Memorial, the Hô Chi Minh Trail. That made three sites we had visited, four if you included the town of Khe Sanh proper, which was open to debate. He was disappointed. The fee – established by the Committee of Tourism of Quang Tri Province, payable in hard cash – was as follows: fifteen dollars for the guide, fifteen more for the 'authorization', plus one dollar per person per 'site'. Four of us thus made twelve dollars 'bonus'. Not much. Tourists are infrequent in Dông Hâ. Nguyên T.D.'s disappointed expression was painful to see. Were we going to stop there? He could suggest a 'very interesting' addition to hike up his bill: a Montagnard village located in middle of the forest, close to a stretch of the Hô Chi Minh Trail and the bridge at Dakron, constructed in 1975–76 by the Cubans.

We hadn't the heart to refuse. Off we go!

In the car, suddenly Nguyên T.D. can no longer contain his happiness. He is voluble. He croons *Cerisiers roses et pommiers blancs* and smugly quotes Ronsard: *Mignonne allons voir si la rose.* And Verlaine: *Il pleure dans mon cœur comme il pleut sur la ville.* He permits himself a few indelicate quips about what Vietnamese women are like 'in the sack' and concludes, with a glint in his eye, 'Man proposes, woman disposes'. It is thus, amid his ditties and smutty remarks, that we pick up empty and bumpy Martyr Route 9 again, dismal beneath a slate grey sky, then the Hô Chi Minh Trail, renamed 'Trail 559'. It was in May 1959 that Hô Chi Minh decided upon its construction, five years after the Geneva Accords and the partition of Vietnam, to enable the Communist North to lend assistance to the Viet Cong guerillas in the South, threatened with annihilation by the Diêm regime.

Approaching the Dakron bridge, constructed to seal the 'revolutionary friendship with Cuba', a plankboard shop faces a Vietnamese army sentry box. Nguyên T.D. strongly suggests buying 'a few gifts for the Montagnards'. Ten packs of Dalat cigarettes at 600 dongs each, a few packages of chewing gum and four bags of hard candy. Nguyên speaks with new authority. Little by little, his behaviour has changed. With the shopkeeper he is peremptory and rather patronizing; he watches us pocketing the goodies and is full of advice: 'Make sure you give away the cigarettes one by one, at most two by two. For these "minority" peoples, that's already a lot.'

Having found people poorer than himself, Nguyên T.D. has grown ten feet tall.

Conspicuously, Raymond has closed his lens, returned his camera to its case and placed it in the trunk of the car. We are on sitdown strike from the outset. We are no longer playing. The untroubled, obscene way in which this 'official guide' of socialist Vietnam enjoins us to visit the country as though it were a life-size zoo, distributing peanuts to local tribespeople, is in itself revolting. But for such a farce to take place here! We hesitate a moment between curiosity and the desire to turn back. We are curious.

Twenty kilometres further on, having arrived at our destination, Nguyên T.D. scurries along a path below the highway, in the midst of tropical vegetation which suddenly seems out of a kind of Disneyland, full of rubber trees and whistling monkeys. Walking behind him, I am, in spite of everything, assailed by memories. (No nostalgia – we said we didn't come to this country to trot out our old assignments. And yet . . .). In 1971 and 1972 I had done an investigation of the Montagnard minorities being torn apart by the fighting, a subject which hardly interested the major news organizations. The Montagnards, at the time, were the stuff of magazine features, a light subject to take on for want of something better when you had missed the boat. At Camp Holloway, the American base at Pleiku, the press officer looking to make amends for not having found you an available helicopter to the front, invariably proposed a visit to the 'Montagnard village'. As a consequence, in the space of ten or fifteen years their particular tragedy was little covered, seldom told.

It was a French priest with the Foreign Missions in Paris, Jean-Baptiste Etcharren, who had convinced me to become seriously interested in the

Montagnards. Clearly Nguyên T.D. doesn't know that here, in this same region of Khe Sanh, I came to watch the mortal suffering of these 'primitives'.

Extract from an article written in May 1972. At the time, in the midst of the communist offensive, certain tribes – the Brus – were being evacuated towards the South, thanks to an aerial bridge provided by C-130 cargo transports.

> These 2,400 passengers are perhaps the last survivors of an ethnic group which, in 1960, still had 30,000 to 40,000 members. Straddling the Laos-Vietnam border, the Brus were then living in their villages on stilts in the hills of Khe Sanh, in Tchepone, along the Hô Chi Minh Trail. They were one of the largest Montagnard tribes which – together with the Rhades, the Jarais, the Bahnars and the Mnong – form the minority group which the French call the *Mois* (which means 'savages'). Today they are no more than homeless, uprooted and displaced families brought south in the big planes of CIA-funded Air America. This is the last stage of a long ordeal inexorably heading towards the extinction of what was once an ethnolinguistic society with its own culture and territory. The war affected the Brus more severely than any group in Vietnam. Their hills were the first strategic zones, ravaged a thousand times by bombardments. Their men became mercenaries in the Special American Forces and coolies for North Vietnam. With their land despoiled, the Brus became victims of a cultural ostracism which was – to say the least – constant. Under Diêm the forced 'Vietnamization' of the Montagnards attained such a degree of blind brutality that certain tribes formed a united resistance-front – the Bajaraka. Its leaders were thrown in prison.

Here we are, twenty years later, at the same spot, give or take a few kilometres. We walk in single file towards the still 'unmissable' Montagnard village. Our guide is in a jaunty mood. Not us. Today the Montagnard minorities – to use the official terminology – include about 1.5 million people. Since 1975 their situation has hardly improved. 'Quite often,' discreetly writes Nguyên Tan Dac, a North Vietnamese ethnologist from Hanoi, 'the dominant ideology has come into conflict with beliefs and local traditions.' A careful, almost risible, way of recalling the disaster of forced assimilation, which was the rule under the communists just as it had been under previous regimes. The only provinces remaining out of bounds to foreign travellers in 1992 are in the highlands – Pleiku, Kontum, Dak

Tô – where the majority of the Montagnards live. Whatever its desire to further the 'opening-up' and tourism, Hanoi wants no witnesses in these 'problem' regions.

Here is the 'village' of Bru Van Kieu: four or five houses on stilts in a clearing, a handful of women in rags, children in their arms, a few snot-nosed kids running around squealing among the hens. On the steps of one house, an 'elder' is sitting, his ruined mouth frozen in a smile. Nguyên T.D. circulates in this milieu like a provincial cleric at a church club. He browbeats the 'good guys', frowns while talking to the children, introduces the old man to us as the chief of the village. Docilely, mechanically, the Montagnards line up for the handouts: cigarettes for the adults, sweets for the children. Mouths full of rotten teeth smile up at us.

It's a disgusting scene.

We cut it short. Nguyên T.D. who sees us swiftly getting rid of our presents, is desperate. We icily decline his proposals to do 'interviews'. In any event the houses are too new, the unfortunate people stupefied by fear and alcoholism; the place is a *trompe l'œil*, the 'site' artificial. We bid *adieu* to the Brus enlisted in the service of 'Vietnam Safari', farewell to these poor among the poor, pulverized by History, the redskin gooks of Heroic Vietnam! The return trip is morose. Nguyên T.D., whom we have lectured, searches desperately for subjects of diversion, makes himself small, rebukes the chauffeur, ventures to recite a fable by La Fontaine, pretends to sleep. The road is long.

We are in no mood to listen to the fables of La Fontaine. In a year or two, whole busloads of American senior citizens will be stopping here, bags of candy in hand, to view the 'primitive tribes of Vietnam in their native setting'. I imagine they will put in a handrail along the forest path and a sponsored rubbish bin for the sweet wrappers. In five years, moreover, the Montagnards will themselves have set the price to let themselves be photographed. They will stink of beer and rice spirit.

Montezuma's Revenge, everybody knows, is the persistent intestinal illness that spoils the good humour of tourists in the tropics. Could there be a Montezuma's Revenge of the soul? There could. We caught it.

DÔNG HÂ: TO THE EAST OF THE MOUNTAINS

At first I thought I was dreaming. Tonight, someone knocked lightly and insistently at my bedroom door. Not fully awake, I ran to open it. The hotel maid was standing in the doorway, looking a little weary. A Vietnamese woman about forty years old, her fingers red from doing laundry. She rubbed her palms together and gazed at me without speaking. It was nearly midnight, I didn't understand what was going on. We were the only guests in the Hotel Dong Truong Son, whose name means, 'To the east of the mountains'. Was somebody sick?

The woman kept looking at me. Finally, she repeated a single word in a hollow voice: 'Massage? Massage?' At the same time, she awkwardly made faces which she supposed were lascivious or tempting. For a moment I stood there incredulous. She must have thought that I was weighing up her proposition because she stepped up her mimicry: 'Massage good. Massage . . '. In fact, I was not surprised by this development. Since leaving Saigon, we have been solicited every day. If all Vietnam is throwing itself before foreigners, the women – whether regular prostitutes or not – are obviously the most enterprising. And only a hypocrite could claim that he has never – ever! – been susceptible. But this incident had not occurred just anywhere and anyhow.

The hotel itself, this concrete edifice planted in a wasteland, an old hospital transformed into a communist 'palace', exuded regimented dreariness, with its sleeping desk clerks and its abandoned pools full of stagnant water. The city of Dông Hâ, epicentre of the war's wounds, a precarious settlement rising up from massacres and exoduses, is itself a sort of exaggerated symbol of the disaster. The thirty-year tornado which passed over it – Paul Mus's 'molten history' – has left

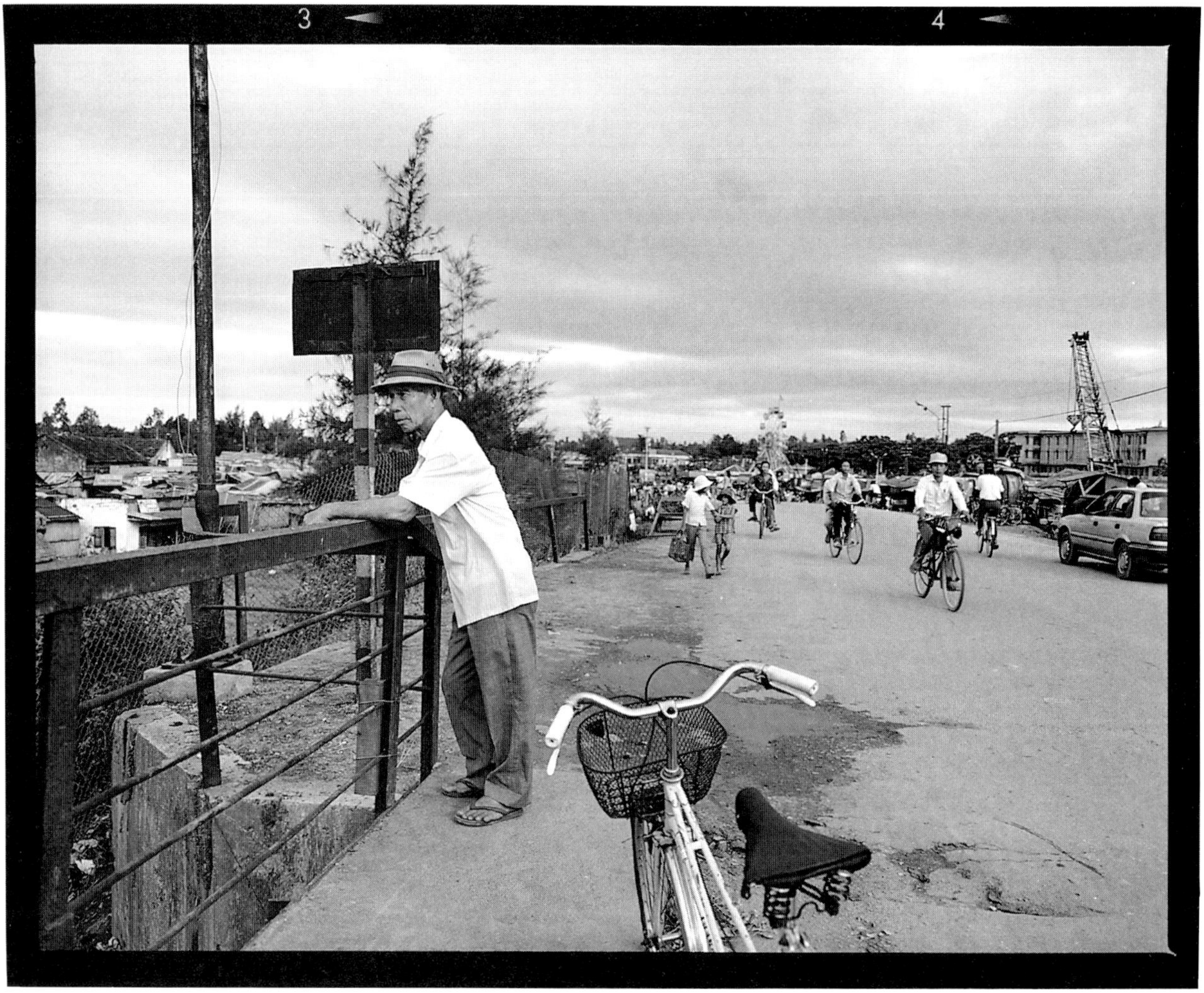

Dông Hâ, everything is destroyed ...

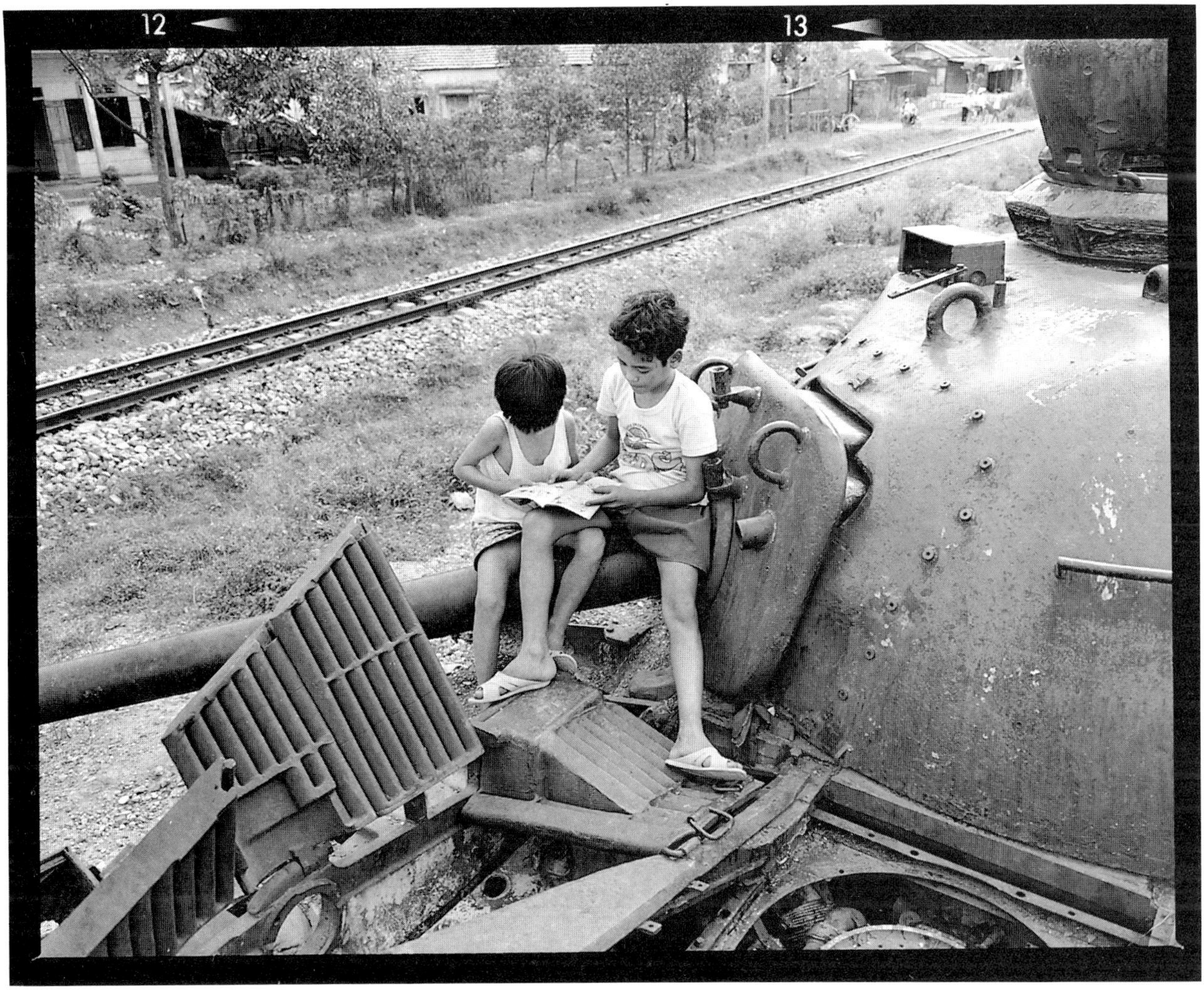

... a few American tanks remain ...

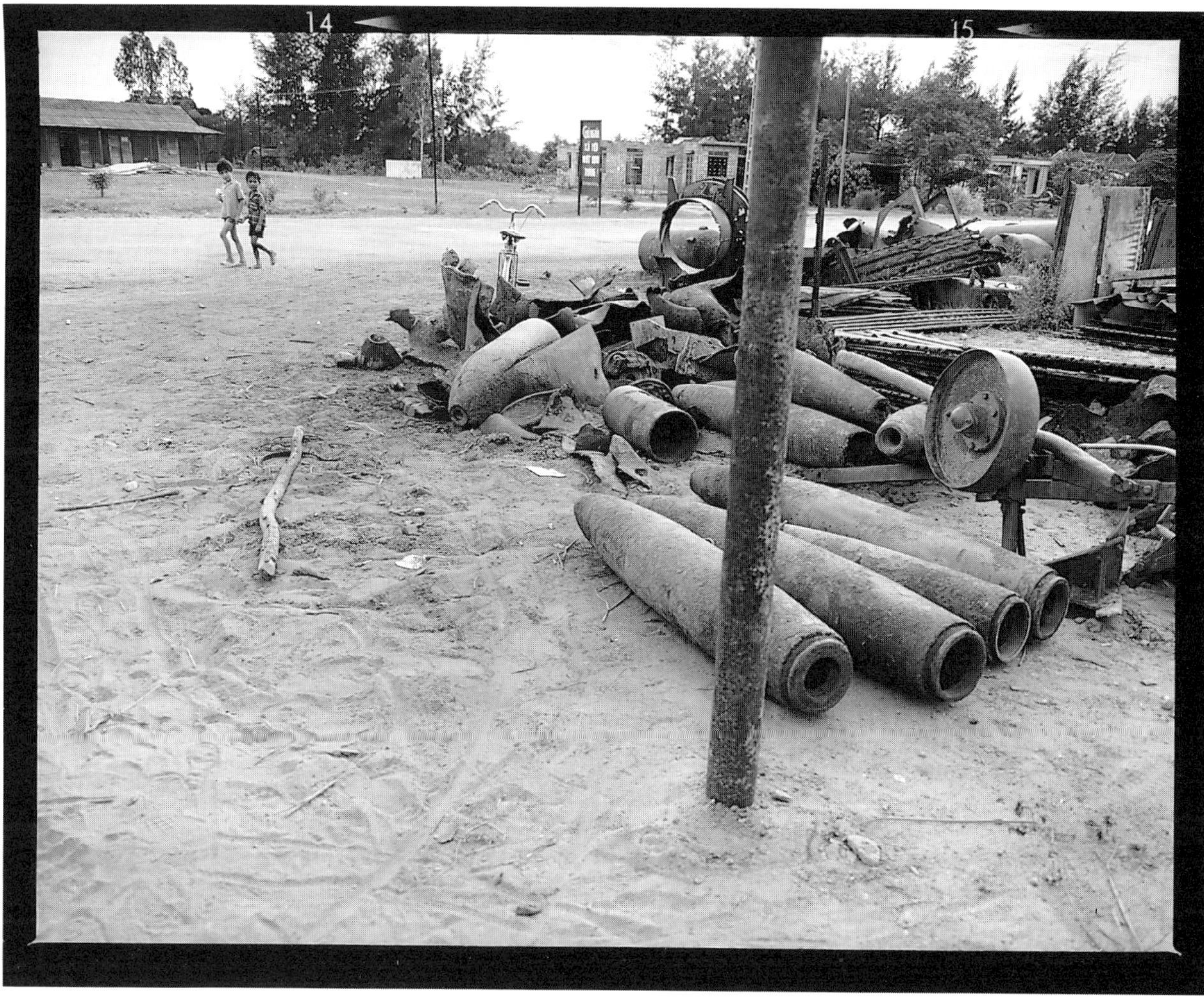

… and shells for scrap metal.

behind an idea of devastation which time does not erase. The poverty of this woman with her sunken cheeks, spindly in her work pyjamas, all made the scene horrible. Rudely awakened, I was confused. Perhaps I should have smiled?

The woman persisted, gradually insinuated her way into the room. I gave her a ten dollar bill while shaking my head. I smiled to make her go. She clearly no longer understood anything, and we stood facing each other in the yellow light of the Hotel Dông Truong Son, at Dông Hâ, in the exact centre of Vietnam. The waiting became absurd. Outside, a violent monsoon rainstorm had just begun. Torrents of water were bouncing off the flagstones. The woman held the ten dollar bill in her hand. Her face expressed not gratification at largesse so easily obtained but rather sadness, in spite of everything, at being scorned.

I gently pushed her outside, repeating, 'Thank you . . . thank you . . .' It was nothing to be proud of. For either of us.

It is past midnight. A deep silence descends once more on the hotel, a silence scarcely broken by the last gurglings of the passing rain. I go back to bed in the clammy room where the air-conditioning hasn't worked for years. Sleep has left me. I toss and turn in one of the twin beds; the sheets are damp with sweat. The awkward bargaining with the floor maid has brought back a feeling of discomfort that I have been trying to repress all the time we've been staying here. The return to Dông Hâ is not what I was expecting. Ever since we arrived in this ersatz city, assembled bit by bit at the crossroads of two important strategic highways (from Hanoi and from Savannakhet, in Laos, via Khe Sanh), I've been besieged by memories. More tenaciously, more hauntingly than anywhere else. Nothing keeps them away any more. As if something in the setting was unstable, as if the same anxious urgency hung in the air today as it did twenty years ago.

I get up once again to open the window looking out on the entrance to the hotel, which is surrounded by concrete walls. A whiff of damp smells – of the sea, of wet earth – invades my room. The moon appears intermittently behind running clouds. A faint glow in the distance – rare, flickering fireflies of electric light – outlines the contours of the city. It is springtime. That makes it exactly twenty-one years since I last saw this same city, bathed in darkness.

It was May 1971. Dông Hâ was yet again under attack by communist maquisards. Staying with the parish priest, Father Jean-Baptiste Etcharren of the Foreign Missions of Paris, I climbed onto the roof of the presbytery with a young Vietnamese priest. We were counting the flares falling all around us, floating down on their parachutes. The rattle of automatic weapons changed direction confusingly, toward the right or left following the battle. From time to time, the dull thud of a mortar shell shook the windows of the house. Then, for a minute or two, absolute silence would return. A routine engagement, the indecipherable ripples of war which the inhabitants discussed in the same way you might talk about a thunderstorm. 'Tonight, the attack will be longer than usual,' murmured the young Vietnamese priest, crouching beside me in the dark. 'It is the anniversary of the great victory of Diên Biên Phu.' (This young, francophone priest, this Catholic anti-communist from the South, said 'victory' without a moment's hesitation.) He had added, 'Nights where there is no attack, people call "peace". It's the only kind they know.'

The following morning, we went out in the streets with Father Etcharren. The shops were open, the city was back to normal. Some children were running and laughing along the main street, some peasants chattering beneath their conical straw hats as if nothing had happened. In the centre of Dông Hâ, some laid-back ARVN servicemen were occupying the old French-built lookout tower. Everything seemed relaxed and peaceful. Save one detail: at the foot of this freestone tower, lined up along the street's dusty asphalt like trophies of the hunt, were the corpses of three communist soldiers. The bodies were flattened and broken, their muddy hair like tufts of thick hemp. Some people went up to them with a false indifference, sometimes turning one of the faces with a foot. The dead were kids from the surrounding area who had joined the Viet Cong, willingly or under duress. Their bodies were on display to inform their families. And to intimidate them.

That day Etcharren took me in his Dalat (a Citroën manufactured in Vietnam) to visit several villages in the region. The people talked to him with confidence. He sometimes encountered Viet Cong representatives, who spoke with him in an indirect way about the relationship between politics and religion but in the end left him in peace. Here, the war no longer in any way resembled the one we were 'covering' on the military bases and with the American helicopters and infantry platoons. It was not the same enormous and thunderous tragedy. You could have said that here it broke apart into a multitude of tiny stories, a cacophony of family dramas which it would be futile to try to sort out. Such and such a family had two children in the underground and another in the ARVN; another had seen their only son recruited by force in the middle of the night into the ranks of the Viet Cong. I recall the observation made by an old man in one of the villages around Dông Hâ, which, brought back to Paris or even Saigon, would have seemed incredible: 'The war has gone on too long. Now may the best side win.'

All these people were unaware that I was a journalist. Etcharren introduced me as a relative from France. Going off with him for a long drive through the country in his Dalat, followed by a stay at Dông Hâ, I was suddenly snatched away from familiar surroundings – from briefings, military operations, dinners with journalists and helicopter trips. I had left behind the military war properly speaking, the clearly demarcated 'sub-county', to enter the real Vietnam. The one which no GI ever encountered. All day long I was thrown headlong into these infinite labyrinths, amongst these hesitant villagers, these divided families. Each evening I returned to the presbytery more troubled than the day before. Nothing was as simple as it was said to be; nothing could be judged at face value; nothing corresponded to the generalizations of strategists and war correspondents, of all of us.

I experienced a sort of professional despair which has never entirely left me. An absolute feeling of powerlessness and futility. What could I write? How could I give an account of all this? What good was journalism? Every element of what I was learning here would have required – ideally – to be reported with the greatest care, introduced at length, corrected and nuanced. These kids enlisted by force, for example, absolutely contradicted the image of the maquisards on the outside. But that fact did not in itself mean that all Viet Cong were fighting under coercion. In the same way, the normal life which returned after each attack corresponded poorly with the vision of apocalypse which, even in Saigon, one had of this province bordering the 17th parallel. But how could you say that without improperly minimizing the savagery of the conflict? A thousand other examples aggravated my confusion.

The Vietnam War, viewed from here, was becoming an impossible story, reality as *trompe l'oeil.* In the little bedroom of the presbytery where I stayed I passed whole evenings lost in doubt. Was I learning my trade? Trying to estimate the maddening limitations of being a witness in general, and of journalism in particular?

June 1992: I watch the sparse lights of Dông Hâ from my room in the hotel Dông Truong Son. The discomfort is still there. So is the question of bearing witness.

AMERICAN ON A BRIDGE

It is a bridge falling to pieces on a river which smells of rotten grass. A barrier stops all vehicles coming from north or south along the old Mandarin highway. It is not a customs station nor even a checkpoint. The man working the troublesome bamboo gate with a string is only half in uniform: a khaki jacket, but patched-up jeans; a *bo doi* helmet but a bright yellow T-shirt and sunglasses. This fake sentry with his mismatched clothes has been standing guard at the approaches to the bridge for three long months. His mission is not political but belongs to the Vietnamese makeshift brand of survival – to prevent two trucks from simultaneously starting across this structure of rusty girders and cracked beams, which could collapse with the least bit of overload. Beside the gate, a little girl is selling chewing gum and cigarettes; she has an appealing way of screwing up her eyes against the bright sun. The helmeted man, the little girl – from a distance, two figures frozen in the light.

Some trucks – old broken-down heaps themselves – drive carefully onto the bridge. The land on both sides of the river is fallow. There are no paddy fields here, nor plantations, nor forests, only a barren and bumpy expanse from which emerges, here and there, the roof of a pavilion. A mile post indicates 'Hanoi 735 km' and, to the south, 'Huê 91 km'.

The place is ugly, with no view apart from the mountain range, far to the west, muffled in clouds. We approach. The man working the gate swears that a lot of painters come to set down their easels by the bridge. Vietnamese, of course, but also some foreigners and, among them, even Americans ('*Ong my, Ong my...*') Are they attracted by the absolute desolation of the place? The banality of the landscape? At the north end of the bridge, a rock stele has been erected, above which a concrete soldier stands guard. The centre of the obelisk is decorated with a profile of Hô Chi Minh and offers the following inscription in Vietnamese, chiseled into the rose granite: 'Vietnam is one. The rivers may

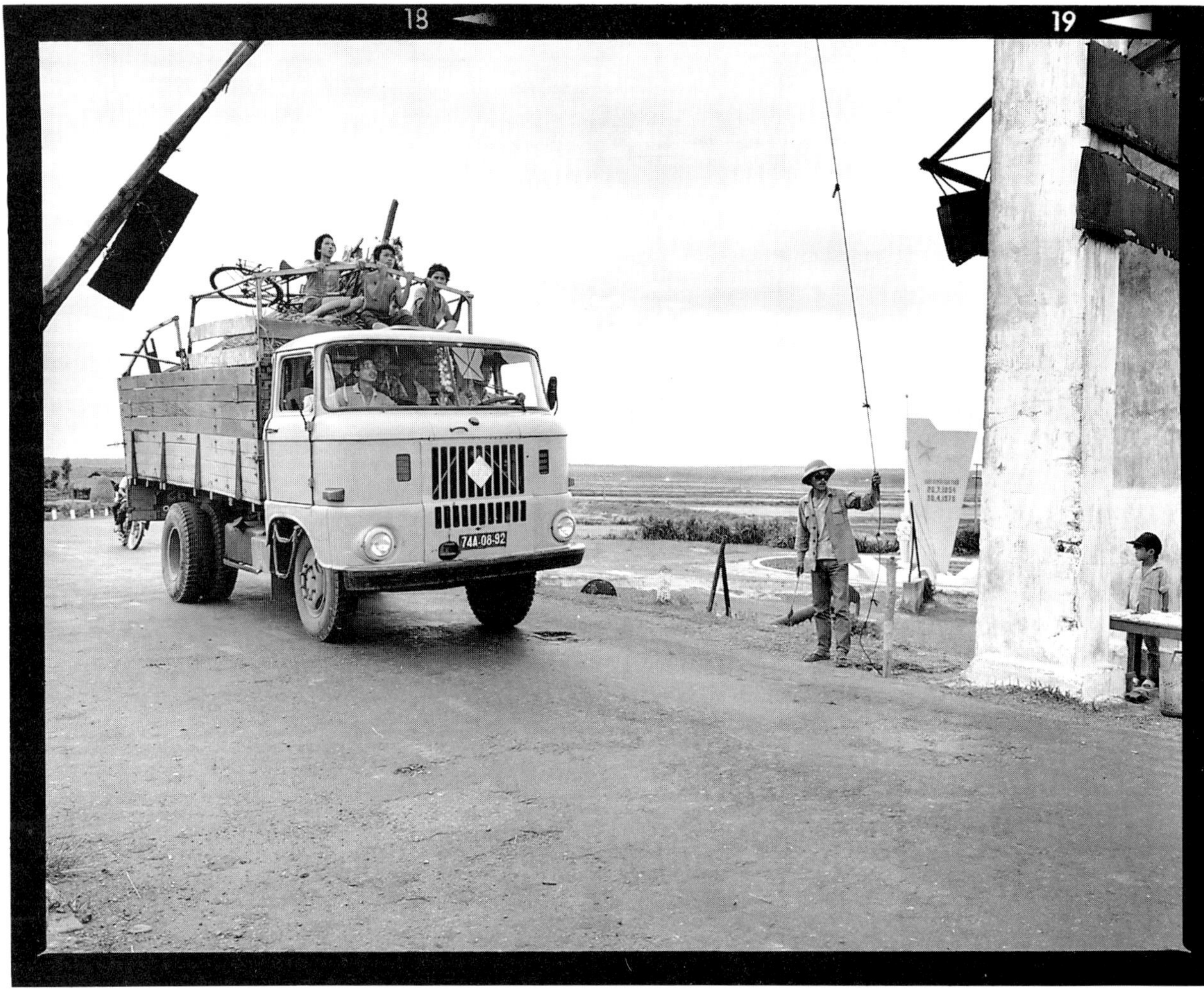

The Ben Haï river …

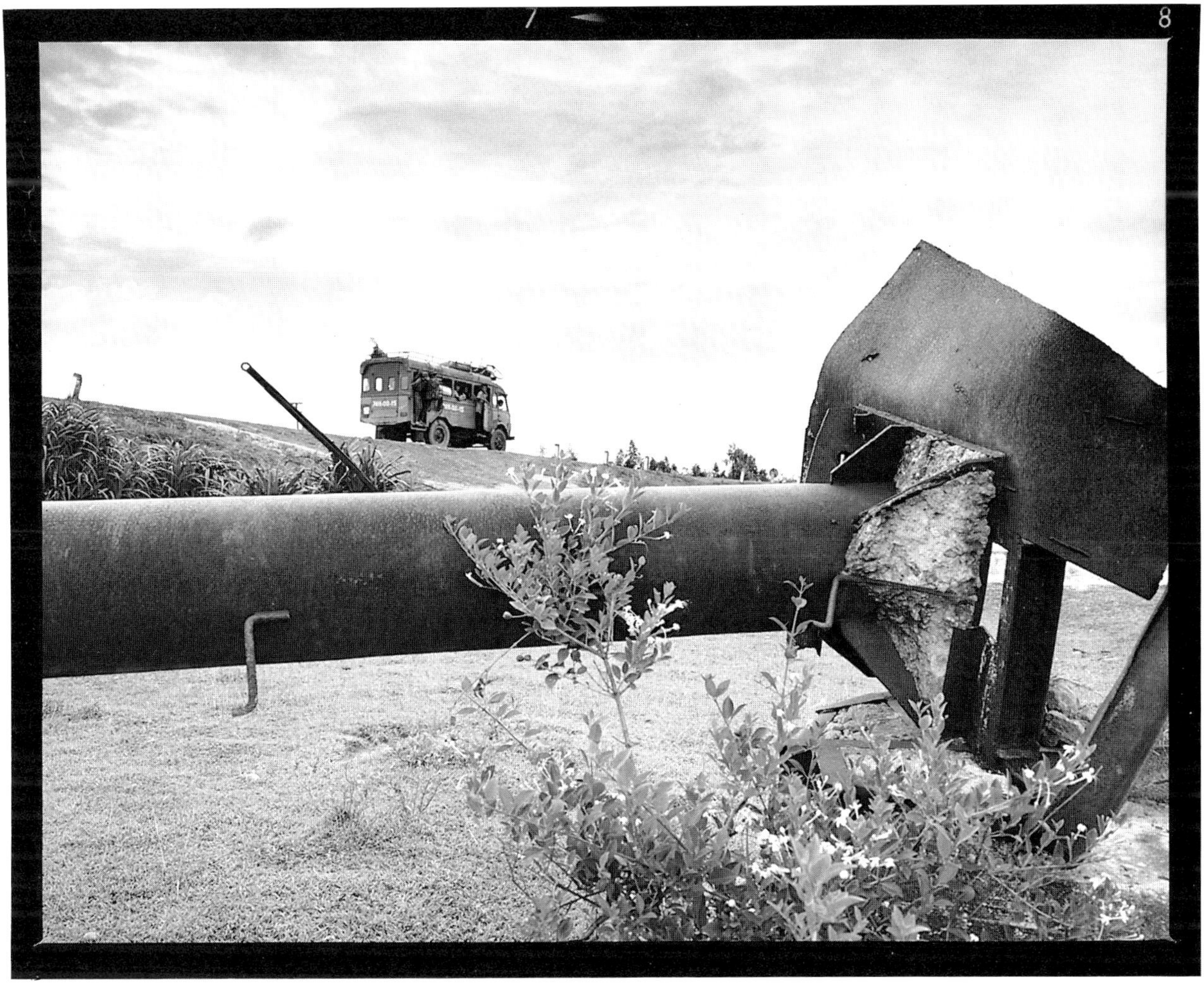

... so many died for this bridge!

run dry, the mountains may fall, nothing will change this truth.'

By themselves, would Uncle Hô's homily and the ungainly monument attract all this curiosity? Nowhere is it written that this bridge was, over the course of twenty-one years, one of the most extraordinary strategic and military epicentres of all time. It stands in a stretch of countryside more severely bombed and shelled than any other in the world. These rolling expanses on each side of the river, and the grassy pampas where a few water buffalo sluggishly roam, received the equivalent of one tonne of bombs *per minute for three years.* The mounds and craters in the earth, which scar the countryside like a tenacious pox, bear witness, twenty years later, to this monstrous bombardment.

This is the place of Vietnam's greatest sorrow, the precise locus of the madness.

The river is called the Ben Haï. Its course coincides with the 17th parallel. It was chosen as the border when, following the Geneva accords in 1954, Vietnam was divided in half: communist North, liberal and 'bourgeois' South. The river's length determined the famous DMZ (demilitarized zone), reinforced in 1967 by a system of defence that America, in its worship of technology, believed impenetrable – the McNamara Line, a tangle of land mines, bunkers, man traps, sophisticated sensors and electronic listening systems. A fearsome and futile set of bars at the junction of the two Vietnams. A military padlock which stopped nothing. All through the war years, thousands of trucks, cars, bicycles and carts crossed the Ben Haï River by night. In April 1972, even several squadrons of T-54 tanks crossed the river, to the west of the bridge, and swooped down towards the south, towards Quang Tri and Huê. Here also began one of the sections of the Hô Chi Minh Trail. A formidable concentration of fire and guile, of molten steel and lunatic escape routes. The code names the communists gave these improbable parts speak for themselves: Fireground, Bomb Pocket, Iron Triangle. Some grim figures: in this region alone, on both sides of the river, there were 135,000 killed and 180,000 mutilated. In the course of the last twenty years, seventeen million explosive devices have been recovered.

We are sitting on the north bank. How could I describe, at this point in our journey, halfway between Saigon and Hanoi, our retrospective stupor? 'It will have taken us twenty years to cross the river,' says Raymond.

* * *

Twenty-one, to be exact. In April 1971, like many journalists, I had come to the south bank of Ben Haï. An ARVN bunker – 'Post 46' – was buried beneath sandbags, covered with anti-aircraft and machine guns. The most advanced outpost of the Republic of Vietnam under American protection. I remember. Using binoculars, you felt a touch of dread in seeing the red flag of North Vietnam flying over the enemy post on the other side of the river. At the time I arrived, an 'incident' (as we called it) had just taken place.

Near Post 46 there extended a dense network of corrugated metal huts, old rags and junk – the shanty town-village of Quang Ngang where 19,000 refugees, chased out of the demilitarized zone, were bivouacked. Some came from the mountains near Khe Sanh, which they called, with tongue-in-cheek nostalgia, 'Heaven'. A strange shanty town, an absurd conglomeration in the very heart of the war. During that week in April 1971, the Viet Cong had just made a punitive incursion. Under the noses of ARVN troops entrenched in their bunker, 200 communist maquisards, armed with AK-47 rifles and B-40 anti-tank rockets, had searched houses and, without any sort of trial, executed three cadres compromised with the Southern regime: a village leader, a civil servant and a civilian guard. Then they had picked out three Honda motorcycles and blown them up with sticks of gelignite as a sign of condemnation of 'bourgeois capitalism'.

I recall those wrecked Hondas in the middle of the village. Burn, capitalism, burn! Destroy these petty-bourgeois baubles! Today, the very same Honda 70s are invading socialist Vietnam. One of them, owned by the man in the yellow T-shirt, stands by the bamboo gate.

Raymond isn't talking any more. The man in the T-shirt, looking weary, raises and lowers his barrier. The little girl selling cigarettes is still smiling in the sun. An old lopsided-looking bus crosses the bridge. The passengers wave to us. In the distance I notice one bicyclist who is in a greater hurry than the rest. He is pedalling furiously, head down over the handlebars. Amidst the general torpor, the frenzied pace of this strange apparition from the edge of the horizon captures our attention. The cyclist approaches. His bicycle is a model unknown in Vietnam, a mountain bike with dérailleur gears. Soon he reaches us and stops.

It's an American.

He smiles at our astonishment. Christopher Schneider is twenty-three. He is a mechanic from Olympia, Washington. What is he doing here? For his vacation he decided to 'do' Saigon–Hanoi by bicycle. In sixty-kilometre stretches, staying with local people on the way. Has he had any problems? He bursts out laughing. 'I've never felt so welcome in all my life. Pampered, even.'

Time has passed along the Ben Haï River.

A hundred metres from the bridge, a wooden sign carries an inscription in yellow on a red background, that rain and sun are wearing away. *Chu nghia xa hoi nhat dinh thang* ('Communism must be victorious'). It can hardly be read any more.

THE CHINESE DRAGON

At Huê, the imperial capital of central Vietnam, things are more permanent. Here time is tallied in centuries; the real power remains in the hands of the bonzes, and the Citadel of the Annam emperors, in spite of chipped ramparts and fragile pagodas, resists the insults of time as it did the furies of war. We rent bicycles and pedal for hours around this sleepy provincial city, its air heavy with the scent of frangipane and jasmine. We mingle with parties of visitors from Hanoi strolling by the ornamental pools carpeted with waterlilies: we climb the steps of the Purple City and wander around the central market and the quays of the Perfume River where sampans are moored, their decks roofed over with half-moons of matting – shelters, not so long ago, for finely-manicured prostitutes.

A dreamy sweetness pervades everything. Swarms of cyclists criss-cross in the shade of the south bank, laughing schoolgirls riding side-saddle. In the bookstalls along the river, English dictionaries and computer manuals have not yet driven out the tiny hand-sewn poetry collections full of '*bien-aimée*' and '*dernier printemps*'. There's no point in summoning up memories to measure what has changed. Nothing has changed. I check in at the Huong Giang Hotel feeling as if I had only left the night before. Beneath my window, the pond decorated by a concrete deck has not moved an inch. In the wide bend of the Perfume River sail the same junks with raised sterns, gliding close to the water. The reinforced-concrete covered market – an attempt at modernity twenty years ago, with its slanting roofs and gothic touches – has not aged badly. It seems to me that even the scents are those preserved in my memory: a melange of sugar and spice, pepper and honey, blossoms and urine.

On the hotel terrace, where swing doors open onto the river, I was almost surprised not to see the olive-drab combat uniform of a crewcut American adviser, or to find scattered over the tiles the travel bags of those bedraggled special correspondents who used to stay here every time the communist advance

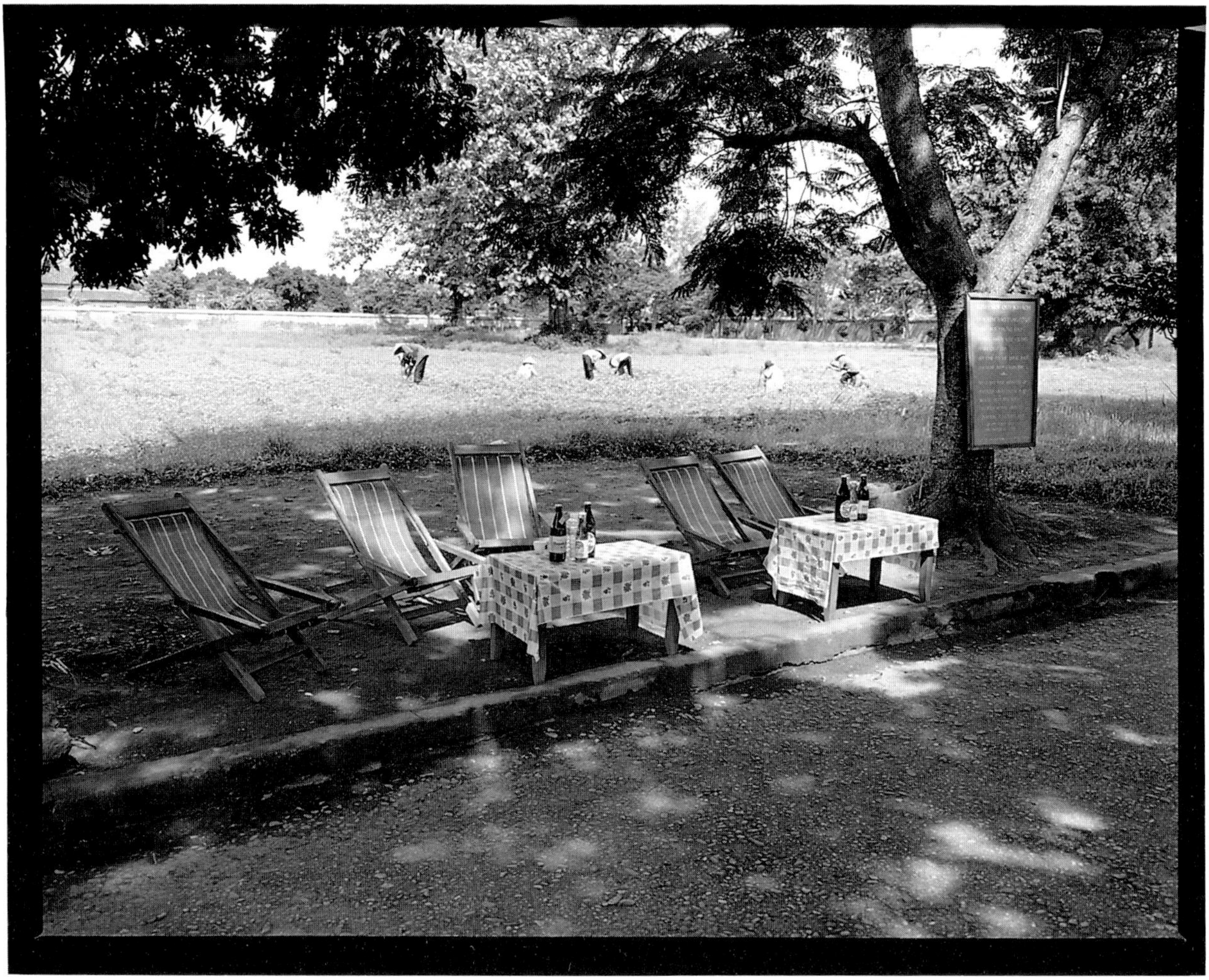

Huê, the imperial capital ...

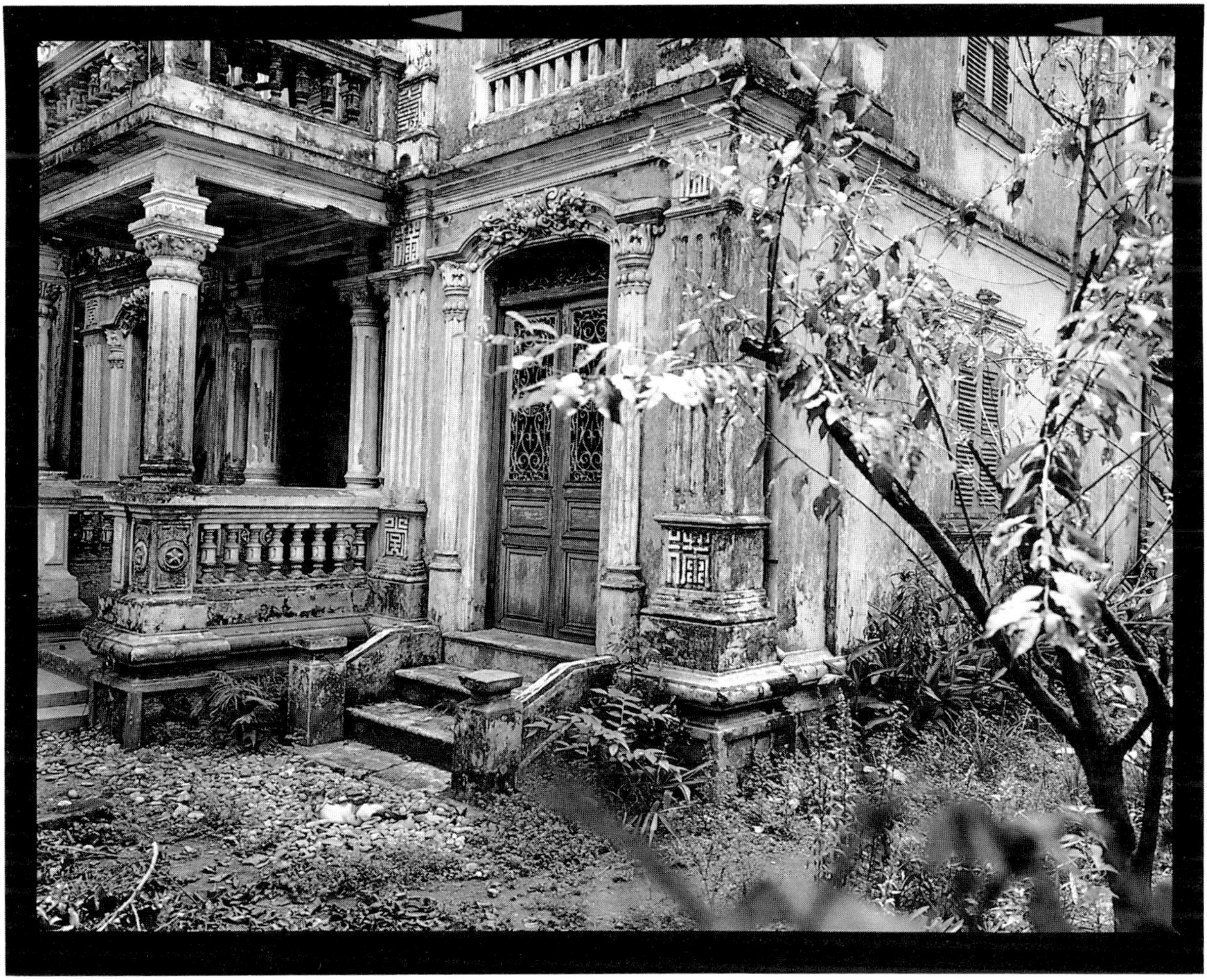

… old houses and big gardens …

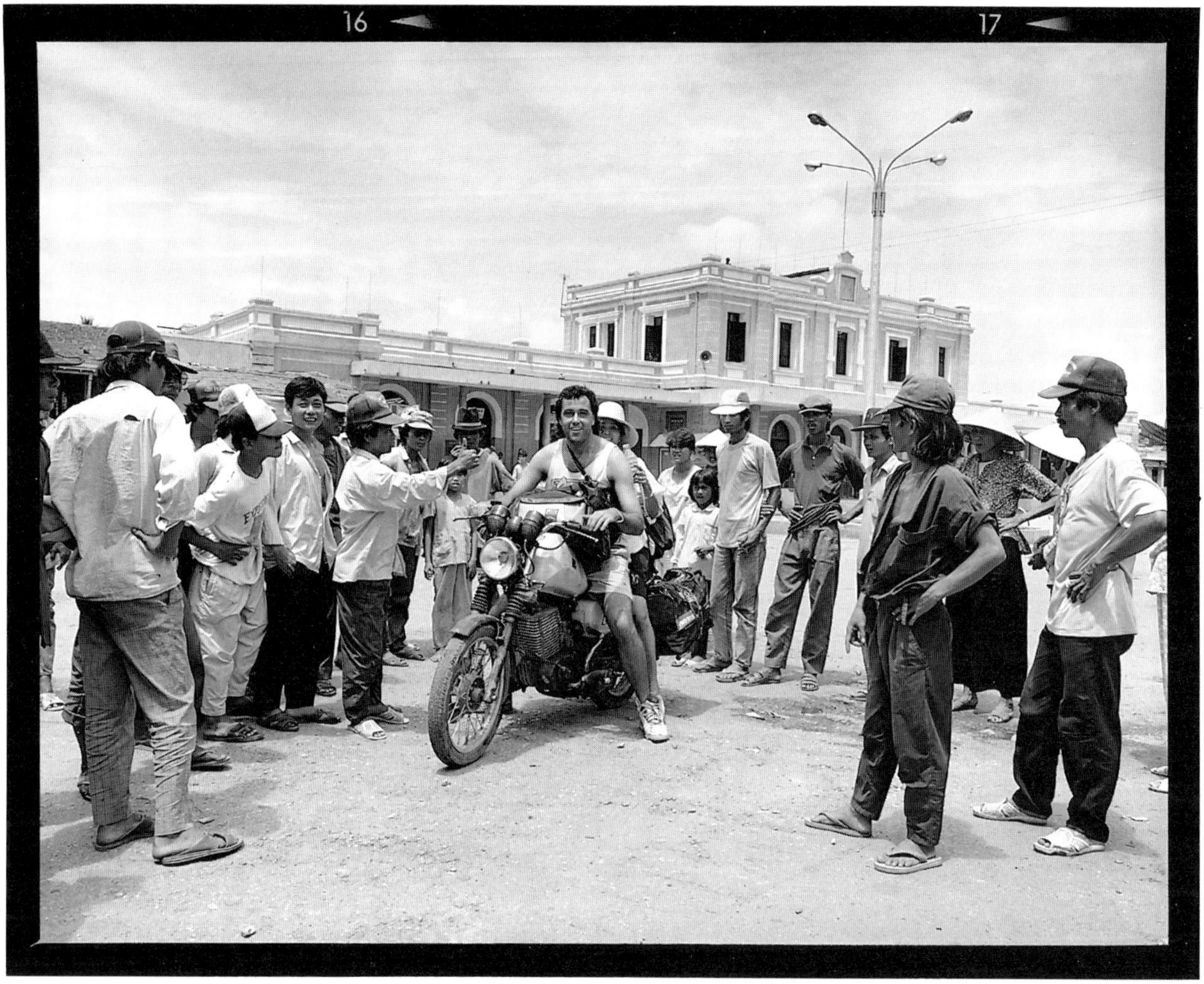

… at the station, we come across two American tourists on a motorbike.

emptied the city of its inhabitants. Behind the bar the waitresses whisper the same asides as they did twenty years ago, and have the same uncontrollable laughter.

We cycle around endlessly, aimlessly, just enjoying ourselves, accompanied everywhere by smiles and whispers. We linger with some students who, stammering a little, ask about the West. We drink tea with Mlle Vy, a shy and entrancing twenty-five-year-old French teacher at the university, whose teaching material comes from a few ancient and much-thumbed Parisian magazines. With Mlle Vy, who hesitates and blushes, puts a hand to her mouth as though repressing some unspoken audacity, another Vietnam reveals itself. Which is Huê precisely, traditionalist and literate, curious about the outside but refusing to compromise itself, attentive to nuances but unmoved by passing turbulence. Mlle Vy, whose family is intellectual and bourgeois, can't get over the fact that she has agreed to take tea with us on the terrace beneath the flame trees. Out in the open! Triple transgression – drinking in public, with men, and foreigners! Before coming, she hesitated for a whole evening. We guess that now, overwhelmed by the situation, she is both anxious to get it over with and intoxicated by this lucky encounter with the outside world. Her confusion, the way she keeps shifting about on her chair, show clearly the effort she is making. She gives her hair a shake, mops her brow, and loses her French. She repeats: 'I'm upsetting you. I'm boring you. I can't answer your questions.' There's a lot more to this than coquettishness. The enthusiasm for 'opening-up' Vietnam must now be irresistible, if it can make Mlle Vy sit out on the terrace of a public cafe in Huê!

This Vietnam, on the Perfume River, is neither busy and cynical Saigon nor lugubrious Da Nang nor the stubborn and eternal rice paddies, nor the more austere North. Today as yesterday, Huê embodies a self-confident nonchalance and peaceful pride rooted in the imperial past which come together in the merest conversation. This seamless harmony surprises us. How did Huê resist? How did it survive? How did it come through thirty years of turmoil? Unlike Dalat, which was a colonial creation, Huê was not spared the war. In 1968, at the time of Têt and the 'general offensive', the city was captured and devastated, the Citadel retaken metre by metre by American Marines and Southern Rangers. Here also took place the bloodiest 'revolutionary cleansing' attributable to the communists – several thousand selective executions which precipitated countless exchanges in the world press. (Was it a CIA lie or an incontestable fact? An old argument. . . .) There were also renewed exoduses, panics and fleeing Southern soldiers who (in 1972) were an unwelcome presence in the city. Finally, as elsewhere, there was the long *imperium* of proletarian materialism with its committees and its commissars, suspicions and remorseless utopias.

Yet, in spite of everything, Huê has not changed. Is it hiding its wounds? Covering up old fears? Could it conjure them away by holding to the 'steady wind' which endures forever and, invariably, returns. In this climate we intuitively comply. We navigate the city with light steps. We give way to surreptitious caution. How can I put it? In Huê, above all, we don't want to disturb anything. Not this time.

A wasted effort. A disturbance happens anyway. Even worse, it is unexpected and symbolic. We are at the Huong Giang Hotel – Mme D., Raymond, and I – when a busload of tourists noisily invades the lobby. The personnel bustle about, luggage piles up in front of the desk, an interpreter takes charge, with a badge on her bosom and a ring of keys in her hand. The visitors are Chinese from Taiwan on a group excursion. Almost imperceptibly, Mme D. scowls, something which at first I attribute to the secular antagonism between Vietnam and China. These Chinese, it is true, are potbellied and surly-looking. They flaunt the disdain of people with money, and in no time at all they have colonized the hotel, shouting at one another, waving their camcorders and 24 × 36 cameras about with unpleasant, swaggering greed.

Even when they have all finally found their rooms, the untimely agitation continues. Once they have unpacked their capacious luggage, the Chinese descend again, bizarrely dressed, wrapped in crêpe togas with papier-mâché headgear. Then come the Vietnamese prostitutes – duly summoned, one imagines – with painted cheeks and even shorter skirts than those found in the *Ông Bars* (mini whorehouses).

These violent preparations have rapidly dispelled the hotel's torpor. A prelude to what? One wonders, but not for long. Outside, around the pier which juts out into the Perfume River, other activities are taking place. A motorized junk has been strung with paper flowers and decked out with electric lights. On the bridge, tables have been set up and food and alcohol laid out. The visitors from Tapiei, we are told, have rented the junk for a 'party' on the river. They will leave tomorrow.

Having seen some of them on the stairway in full costume, Mme D. has already realized what sort of party is involved – a merry and orgiastic little pastiche of the imperial ceremonies at the court of Huê. The Chinese men made up as Annam emperors and dignitaries fondle their favourite girls. Big fat smiles, photo flashes, a battery of camcorders. The celebration starts right away, scarcely two hours after the group's arrival. The efficiency of Taiwanese tour operators is no less impressive than that of their Japanese counterparts who offer 'Europe in four days'.

As a Vietnamese patriot, Mme D. makes no more attempt to conceal her rage. She says she feels humiliated. To see the memory of Huê grossly parodied, its great court travestied in a stupid, drunken spree? Soon, in a blare of music and laughter, the phony imperial junk appears on the Perfume River. The expressions on the faces of the hotel staff, so obliging and attentive only minutes earlier, are unmistakeable: sorrowful, impotent disgust.

We dine that evening on the hotel terrace while below us the phony junk drifts noisily from one side of the river to the other. Late into the night, the party is still going on. At dawn I notice two prostitutes without makeup staggering out of the hotel. Finally, at breakfast, we attend a showing of the nocturnal celebration, videoed at interminable length and screened, after a fashion, for the beaming, comatose Chinese, glued to their chairs by fatigue.

At ten o'clock the rooms are vacated, the luggage counted, the bus loaded. The Chinese dragon, Vietnam's voracious neighbour, leaves the way it came.

Huê regains its sweet tranquillity. But it's an uneasy peace, and a temporary one. The Far East which surrounds Vietnam will never go easy on this bargain basement.

FREEZE FRAME

Raymond never uses his camera like some sort of machine-gun. Bulky and slow-moving, he sets himself up in front of the Vietnamese and focuses his large-format 'box' which looks like the cameras of old-time photographers. This act interrupts movements, freezes smiles and suspends gestures. Too much so sometimes. Then Raymond lowers the lens and lets the camera drop to arm's length, without moving. He smiles at people, as if to reassure them, to obtain silent consent. This face-to-face can go on for several minutes and does not always succeed. Raymond then moves off without having taken a picture. Nothing has come of it; an encounter has not happened.

Deliberately, Raymond keeps his distance. To each his own way of working. His approach rejects aggression, immediate familiarity, intrusiveness. Even if it means missing that *target* implicit in other photographers' talk of going on a *shoot.* Raymond explains himself by waving his right hand, palm open, as though he were wiping the mist off a window pane. He wants to *show* things, to increase the depth of field, avoid tightly-composed framings – 'Fragonards' as he calls them. Timidity or respect? I don't know. But I like this obstinate austerity, which touches people's lives without knocking them off course.

Sometimes we separate. When I sit down on the sidewalk to talk to a Vietnamese I've met, Raymond leaves to walk around the streets at random. From a distance, I see him stopping here and there, hesitating for a long time, scrutinizing the surroundings. I get the feeling that he too is trying to eliminate the clichés – postcard snapshots, conventional angles, the temptation of prettiness – which are to photography what repetition and redundancy are to writing: trivialities.

But chance can play its own tricks. When he presses the shutter-release, Raymond sometimes catches a moment of stupor, of fleeting gravity which comes over people like a shadow. Just after the click, a big smile lights up their faces, as if with relief. Too late, the photo's been taken. I often think of all those smiles

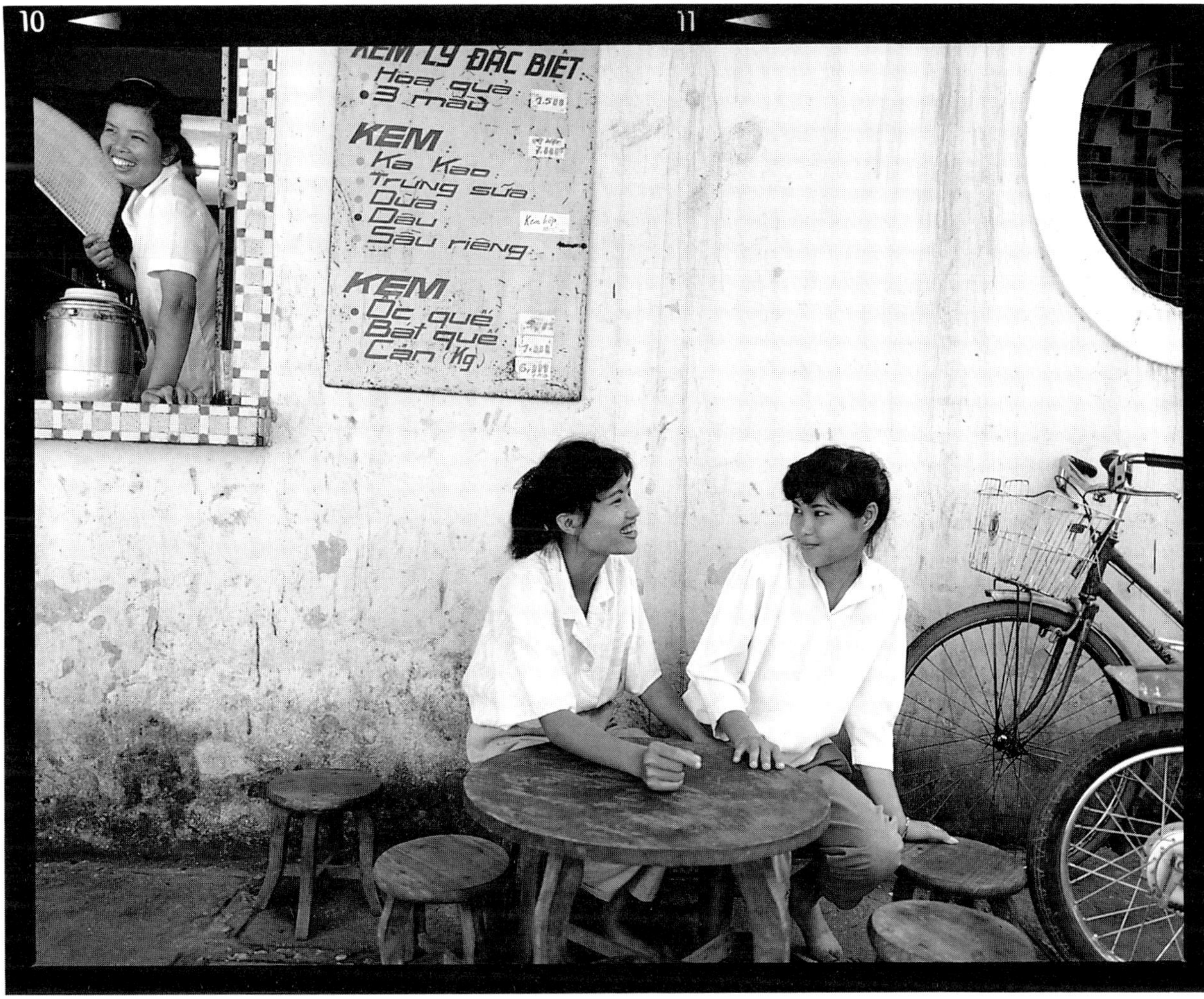

Hanoi: how do you photograph the charm of the Vietnamese women?

following us which the photos won't show. We talk about it. I am afraid Raymond's camera may bring back a Vietnam that appears sadder than it really is. Where is the truth of a journey? How could we not lie a little? What is the right balance between the general poverty, the mean, cheerless surroundings, and the infectious happiness which, despite everything, we encounter everywhere? How can we best reproduce this union of opposites?

It is amusing to leaf through the new brochures and guides to Vietnam. The glossy photos, depicting colourful marketplaces, smiling crowds and rainbows illuminating dark green paddy fields at the foot of towering mountains, are well-meaning lies. They portray an ideal country, dressed up in its Sunday best, which we have never encountered. They are as unreal as those American magazines which throw the châteaux of the Loire and the markets of the Auvergne into the same Technicolor stew. La Belle France as seen by Hollywood. Which does not mean that in the case of Vietnam the extraordinary happiness and harmonious colours are *totally* invented. We find them in the form of traces, associations, exceptions, all along our way. It's just a matter of finding the right proportions. Raymond has the same problem as I do.

When he is standing still, camera in hand, I suppose he is waiting to seize some particular moment in the general movement of people and things. The moment where the different elements are combined in the right proportion. The real moment, in a word, which doesn't actually exist but remains the traveller's magnetic north. We're both chasing the same illusion, doggedly trying to reconstitute a disappearing reality. This question of how to look, how to show, is the real challenge of the journey, the only uncertainty which counts. In the evening, back at the hotel, we take time to talk about it.

Raymond, for example, is firm about one thing: the seductive power of Vietnamese women, that famous magic which once bewitched lieutenants of Cao Bang or special correspondents at the Hotel Continental, is impossible to photograph. In Hanoi parks, we linger in front of the display panels of travelling photographers; plywood boards where they show off their best snapshots. There are stylish women posing on Hondas, young married women in their Sunday tunics, girlfriends smiling together by a lake. There is no trace in these photos of the magnetic beauty of the peasant women, the waitresses, the street-sellers. It is as if the film's emulsion did not record that casual grace and elusive eroticism. The photos only show nice, simple girls, with arms dangling, wearing too much makeup. But in fact they're the very same people . . .

The same phenomenon occurs with the photos of stars which adorn records and cassettes of Vietnamese music. With their self-consciously languid poses, these singers may be beautiful but are never disturbing. Why? Raymond suggests that it is a matter of movement. The Vietnamese women whom we come across seem to scatter gestures around them like sparks: the position of a hand, the tilt of a neck, raising an arm to hold back the end of an *ao dai*, its transparency barely revealing a slender figure. Could a snapshot show all that?

Raymond admits his powerlessness as a photographer. That omnipresent fundamental grace that has surrounded us ever since Saigon – that of women – is not some documentary fact which could easily be reproduced. I doubt that even a film could convey it. It is a mirage, which can only be perceived on the spot. Which is undoubtedly why in France the dreamy bedazzlement of soldiers and colonials returning from 'Indo' was taken as a sign of a slight mental disorder.

Raymond says: 'You have to talk about this in your text.'

It is not so simple. Sometimes words are no more faithful than a photo. It occurs to me that in thirty years of war and journalism one hardly spoke – or only badly – of Vietnamese women. And we accepted as a kind of secret that was too difficult to share the fact that their image was everywhere. In the soldiers' bars and the jungle, in the GIs' melancholic yearnings and the diaries found on the corpses of *bo doi*, in the rice paddies and on the pavements. Contemporary, communist Vietnam is not to be outdone. Women still hold first place everywhere: shopkeepers and street-sellers, roadmenders, railway workers in overalls, tireless kids running their own little businesses: but also hotel managers, businesswomen, intermediaries and interpreters, indomitable grandmothers. . . . All of them seem to spread about them, as though inadvertently, the lively seductiveness which they share with Vietnam itself.

I don't know if this sovereignty is the reverse side of social or political oppression. Some Western feminists have written that it is. Vietnamese women novelists have affirmed the opposite. Could our photos and words be enough to dispel these mysteries?

THE RUBIES OF NGHÊ TINH

At Huê another train takes us north. Night soon falls. There are bodies asleep in the aisles, uniformed female inspectors going to and fro on their rounds, party cadres sleeping in their seats, briefcases on their laps. But at every station the whole train is instantly awake. Children jump down nimbly on to the platform, conclaves are held beside the carriages, obscure negotiations take place concerning the availability of seats. Wads of dongs change hands.

We have passed Quang Tri, the martyr city whose citadel was razed to the ground in eighty-six days of fighting in the spring of 1972; then Dông Hâ and the Ben Haï River. Towards ten o'clock at night we are in the former 'North Vietnam'. Mme D., for whom the prospect of going 'north' was so frightening, sits up in her berth to watch the obscure railroad stations come to life as we arrive. Is she expecting a raid by political commissars or bandits? The only thing which actually assails us is the smell of grilled fish.

Yet as we go further north, the small traders and hustlers become less common. The station platforms are less crowded, and the people move more slowly. An indefinable stiffness is perceptible all around us, contrasting sharply with the cheerful Southern anarchy. This ascent towards Hanoi follows a regular gradation: from pandemonium to relative order, from exuberance to reserve, from indiscipline to voluntary obedience. The old North–South axis of Vietnam. Aboard the train, the railway's Northern personnel gradually relax as they geographically and mentally re-enter their own territory.

We are in a hurry to get to the station at Vinh, in Nghê Tinh Province, birthplace of Hô Chi Minh. Ever since Saigon, rumours have warned us against this province and this city, which was destroyed by American bombing and reconstructed with Soviet aid according to the canons of proletarian architecture – square concrete blocks, geometric open space – '*Moscovinh*', the Vietnamese call it, with a grimace. 'Whatever you do, don't get off at this station! It is full of thieves and murderers.' It is true that the arid, hilly province of Nghê Tinh is the poorest in Vietnam. And so it is here that *doi moi* and the opening-up to capitalism have generated the greatest number of unemployed beggars.

But the rumours don't stop there. In any ruined country, from the depths of the greatest poverty, dazzling hopes spring forth, firing the imagination and setting whole peoples in motion. Gold rushes, the promise of an Eldorado at the end of the road, the incandescent prophets of the Brazilian Northeast, the fantastic secrets which echoed through the Peruvian Andes. Whether dream or reality, these promises are a measure of the despair which gives them birth.

The Vietnamese have been getting agitated about Vinh for the last couple of years, describing the place variously as ugly, ungrateful and frightening. Secrets 'from a good source' circulate in whispers, 'indisputable' details are added, gossip spreads all the way to the back room of the Café Givral in Saigon. It is an exemplary story. Here it is.

In 1989, in the mountains near Vinh, two Vietnamese geologists working for the government were searching for traces of zinc and uranium. Vietnam remains potentially rich in minerals, largely unexploited not least because war ruled out serious prospecting in whole regions of the country for several decades. Whether real or exaggerated, this untapped treasure trove – much coveted by Japanese and western corporations – is one of the great hopes for the 'opening-up' of Vietnam. But that year at Vinh the two government geologists, digging away in the distant hills, found something they weren't looking for – rubies, large ones.

Aware of the enormity of the affair, it is said that they concealed their discovery while waiting to report it to the authorities. But they were seen or heard – no one really knows how – by the local people. The astonishing rumour spread in a few days to Vinh and throughout Nghê Tinh. Hope and unrest took hold of the populace, particularly all the good-for-nothings, beggars, layabouts and other desperate adventurers. A stampede was started which nothing could contain; a mad race unhindered by the authorities' attempts to restore order. Armed with picks and shovels, crowds of men, women and children headed for the hills. As in California or the Klondike in the last century, stories spread and were quickly embellished. So-and-so had found $500,000 worth of gems, somebody else had made a million. . . . Crazy figures, delirious arithmetic in a country where the minimum wage for workers employed by Western companies is under forty dollars a month. Little by little 'ruby fever' took over, emptying factories and schools, turning things upside down.

Thai traders notified of the windfall came running from Bangkok to buy the gems. At rock-bottom prices, one fears. A clandestine commerce was organized, all the more easily because corruption in the party, administration and army has become the rule in Vietnam, to the extent that it has become a hobbyhorse of the official press. There was talk of export networks set up by communist cadres and officials of Air Vietnam.

If I am to believe the account of a young geologist whom I met in Saigon, events took a still more disturbing turn. A murderous anarchy soon reigned in the province, with rackets, gangland-style killings of ruby hunters and middlemen and fatal accidents burying inexperienced prospectors in hastily-dug mines. Everyone armed himself as best he could. Prospectors were protected by bodyguards, then by armed gangs, eventually by private militias. As might be expected, rumours multiplied the 'details' of all this to the point where it soon apparently required about fifty men armed with assault rifles to protect a single prospector. As to the police and the army, some say they gave up trying to intervene, others that their attempts simply failed.

What truth is there in this story transmitted by word of mouth from north to south, from Saigon all the way to remote villages in the highlands? The Vietnamese press sometimes referred to it, but only elliptically or coyly, as the 'situation in Vinh'. In private, people talked of 'exaggeration'. It is hard to know. But the elements of fantasy translate a clear wish, and the chronology coincides too closely with Vietnam's 'opening-up' to be ascribed to chance. Thanks to the rubies of Vinh, the country imagines a fabulous future for itself and draws the envy of audacious and unscrupulous adventurers; it brings centre stage the corruption of the regime and the greed of neighbouring countries; finally, it embroiders a dreaded social disorder, a fascinating, mortal anarchy which looms up – by chance? – in the heroic home province of Hô Chi Minh. When she speaks of rubies, and the 'murderers' haunting the railway station at Vinh, Mme D. is really quite happy to remind us that it is all to do with 'Northerners'.

True or false, the message is clear.

It is past midnight. The train bumps along on the single track with its uneven roadbed. This half of the railway line, situated in what was North Vietnam, has indeed suffered more from the war and bombing than the South. The patch repairs have not been sufficient to erase the difference. Tonight we seldom go faster than forty-five kilometres an hour.

At half past midnight, we enter Vinh.

Mme D. gives up any idea of leaving her berth, and Raymond is asleep. I jump out onto the platform amid the peasants and children reeling from sleep. There is nothing there. Nothing but a gloomy railway station, groups of travellers looking for their compartments, conductors in green uniforms and an unlit concrete facade.

In the moonlight, far away in the distance, you can barely make out the silhouette of the mountains where the fabulous rubies still slumber.

GENTLE HANOI

Early in the morning, we reach Hanoi. The dawn is mild. Bicycles proceed *en masse* along the tree-lined avenues. The ambient noise of this capital resembles no other – a slow hum instead of a din, a soft murmur in place of a racket. With countless 'Northern' passengers, we watch through the windows of the old, exhausted train which has finally made it home.

The Saigonese Mme D. discovers the city with us, her anxiety ill-concealed. For a Southerner, Vietnam's capital unquestionably remains 'the breeding ground of communism', the invaders' lair, the fatherland of the conquering *bac ky* (Northerners) whose yoke people of the South still feel around their necks. Faced with police from Vinh or Haiphong, Northern cadres and military officers, nitpicking civil servants and sadistic jailers, the Saigonese still have an acute sense of being occupied by doctrinaire and uncouth 'BKs' (a pejorative abbreviation and play of words on 'virus'). In the mind of Mme D., Hanoi probably figures as a Spartan city of sullen inhabitants and charmless women. Rather like Beijing or Tirana in the mid-1960s.

So as soon as we get off the train, Mme D. is looking for what her eyes expect to see: squads of cyclists in dark tunics marshalled by traffic police, helmeted *bo doi* in the streets and state stores with forlorn-looking shelves.

Mme D. is dumbfounded.

So are we.

Total astonishment is the best description of our first reaction to the new Hanoi in spring 1992. In less than a year, the capital of Vietnam has embarked upon a transformation all the more surprising because it constitutes a break with thirty-eight years of Stalinism – not seventeen. I think of the remark of a diplomat I met in Huê: 'The differences between the two Vietnams are becoming blurred, you will see. But it is the North that is showing the way.' An austere city? Not in the least. It welcomes us with languorous grace and untainted freshness. For the

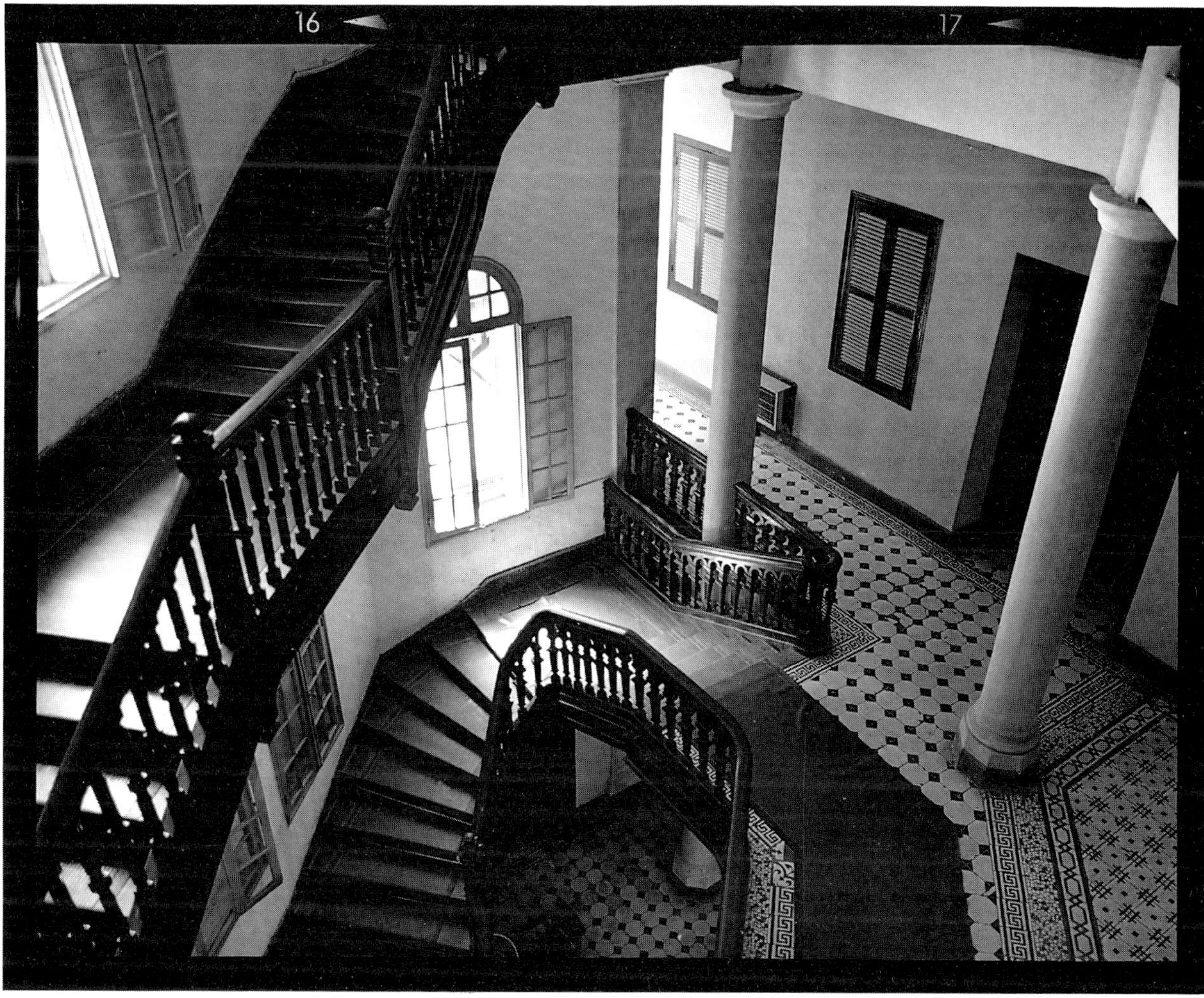

The staircases of the Hotel Hoa Binh.

first time, Hanoi is trying out freedom. And perhaps pleasure. Do we have to count all the Hondas again, all the Simsons and Babettas (East German motorbikes) which fill the streets? Must we photograph the smart, over-made-up women on the pathways of Hoàn Kiêm Park? Should we describe the bustling proliferation of private window displays, terraces where *mah jong* and *tô tom* are played – a proliferation which more and more rivals that of Saigon? Talk about all the sparkling colours which now brighten up every street? The effrontery of litchi nut sellers who comment loudly on the appearance of foreigners? Who will tell you everything they have for sale – but in a low voice this time – along the city-centre pavements which, towards evening, take on a festive air.

Where does the money come from? Not from *Vietkieus*, but from 'comrades' returned from Eastern Europe who, in this precipitous change, have played a role comparable to that of the former boat people in the South. In the ex-USSR and in the countries of the East, a good million North Vietnamese workers who were 'lent' to brother countries were initiated into the art of wrangling, the black market and the underground economy. In Gdynia and Leipzig they learned the limits of proletarian discipline and even anticommunism without tears, before being persecuted by crackpot skinheads from the new Germany. From there, they sent back money orders and goods. This is the meagre accumulated 'capital' which, in the form of motorcycles, shops and merchandise, suddenly appeared on the streets of Hanoi as soon as 'renovation' allowed. Thus did remittances from Eastern Europe favour the first 'opening-up' to capitalism and Hanoi's first step towards . . . Saigon.

But here the alchemy of change operates in a city which remains, thanks to the war and communist isolation, one of the most unsettling in the world. A place which lingers behind the times; a carefree city of the 1930s, a sepia photo which *doï moï* is bringing to life. We take our first steps in a state of shock which is not so easy to analyse. The apparent changes – this efflorescence of commerce and commodities – are altogether just as stupefying as the permanence of the cityscape, which seems to have been frozen for three-quarters of a century. Over the decades, Hanoi has become, without knowing it, a museum of colonial architecture, the French Empire's very own Venice Preserv'd, the sumptuous conservatory of a squandered century.

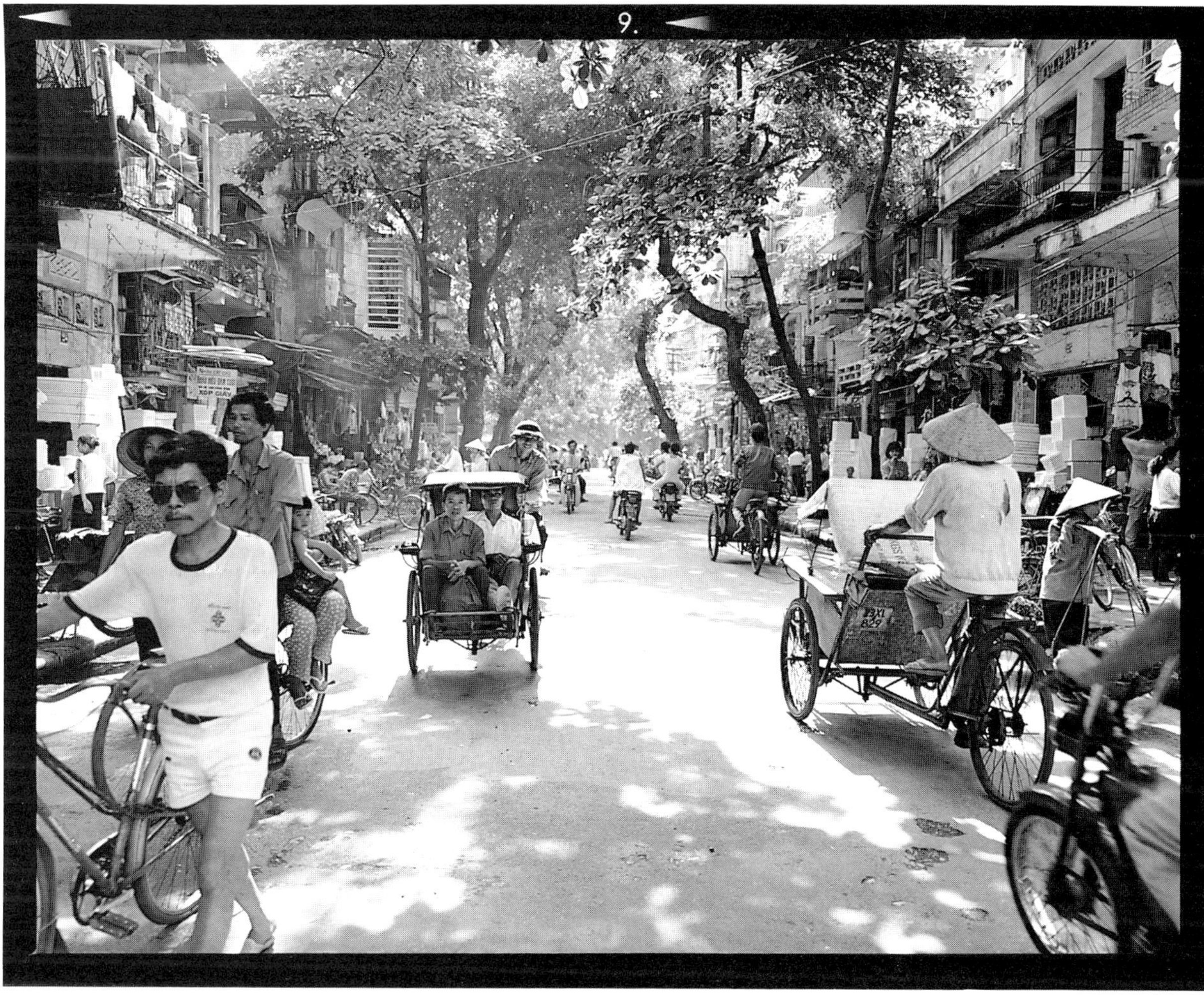

I discover the streets of Hanoi for the first time …

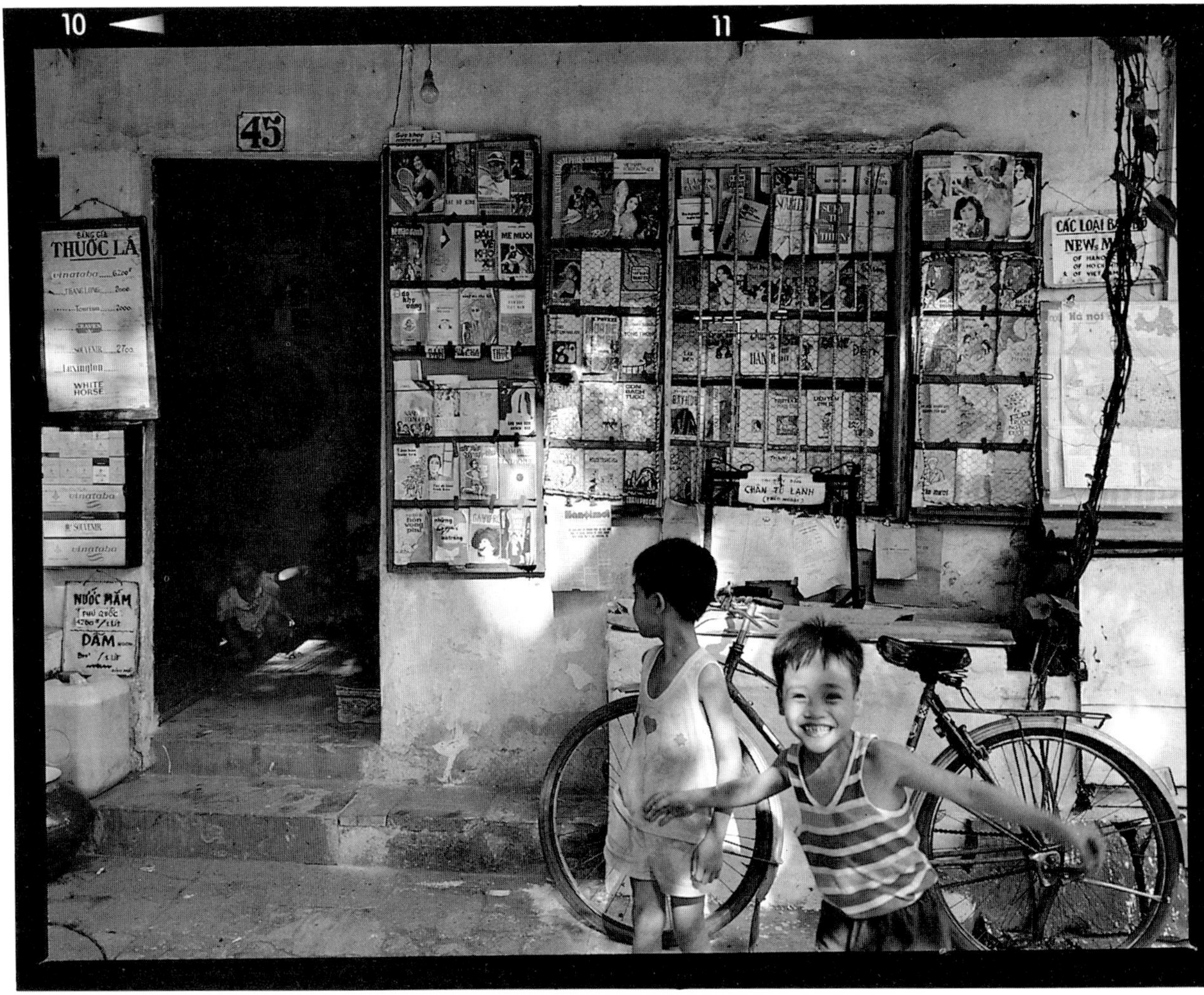

… I could walk in the streets of this town for hours …

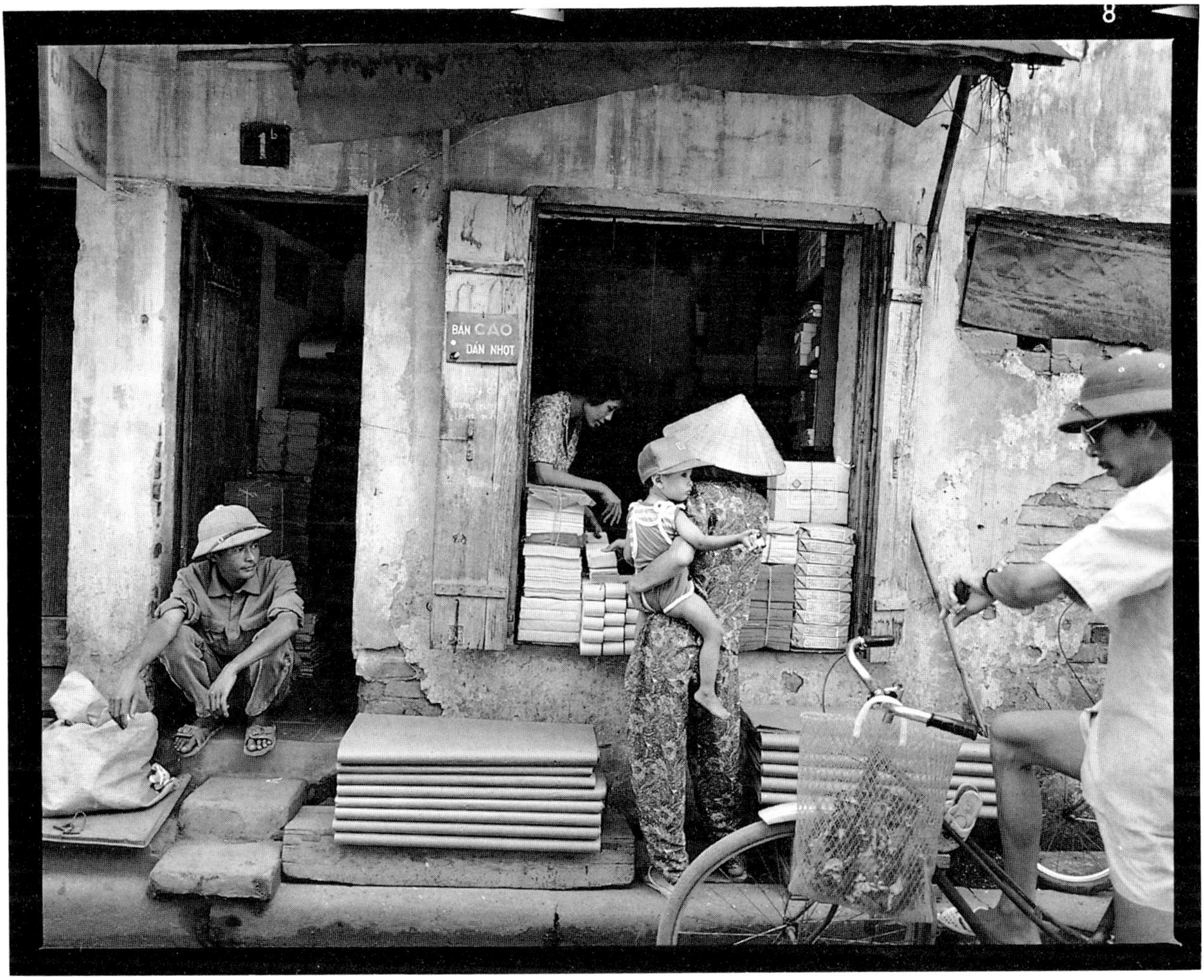

... in the old town ...

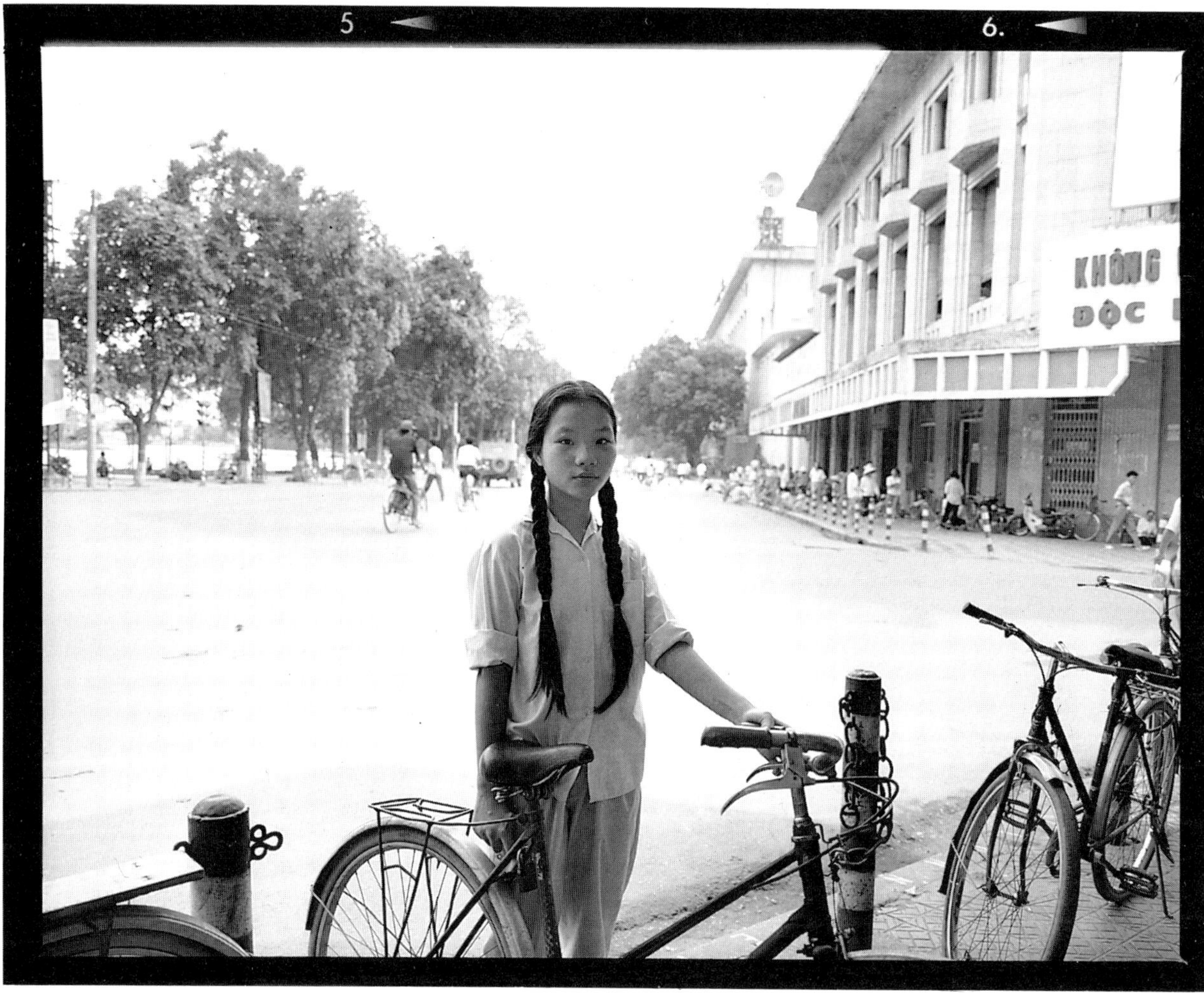

… in the centre, in the French streets …

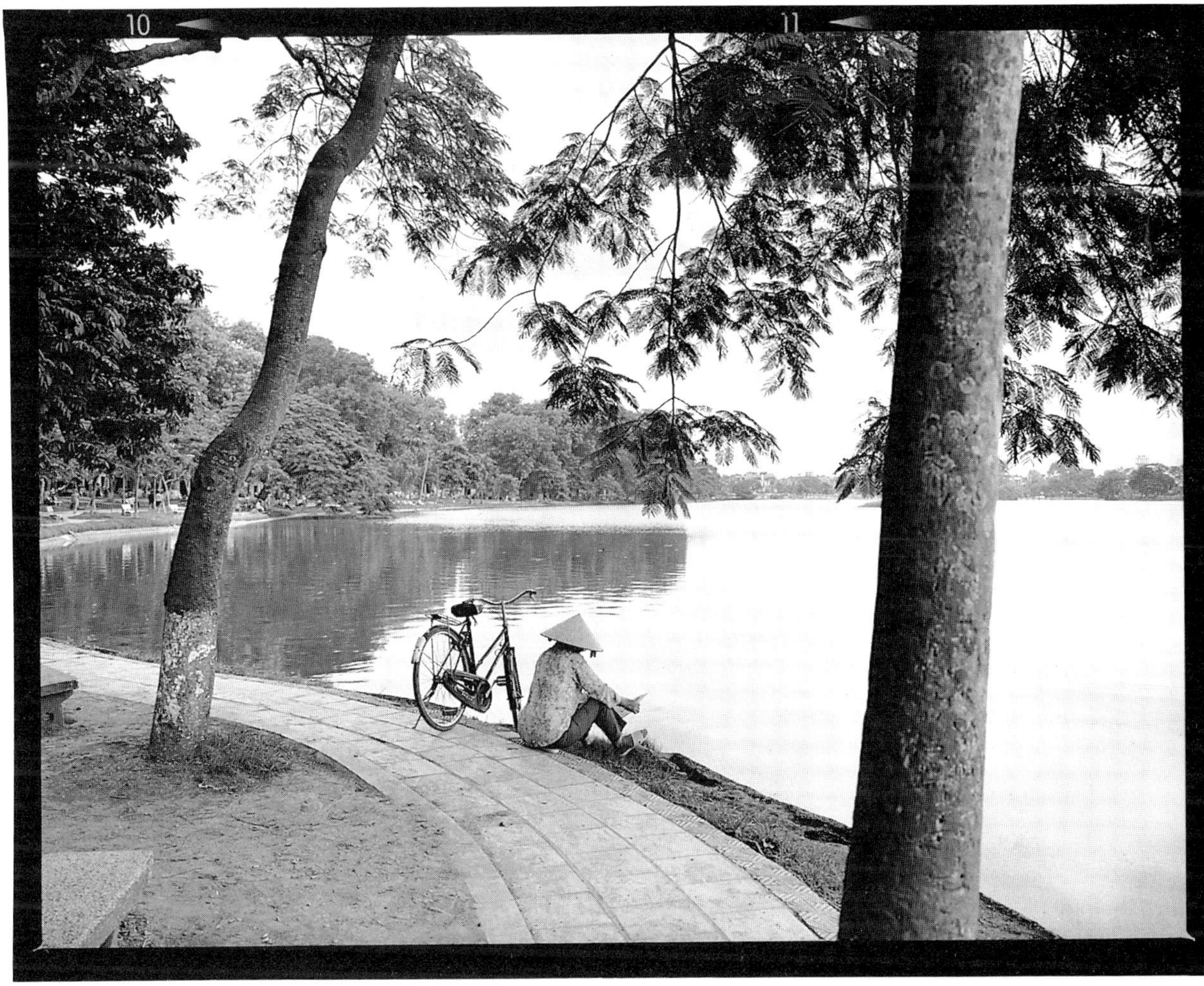

... by the lakes ...

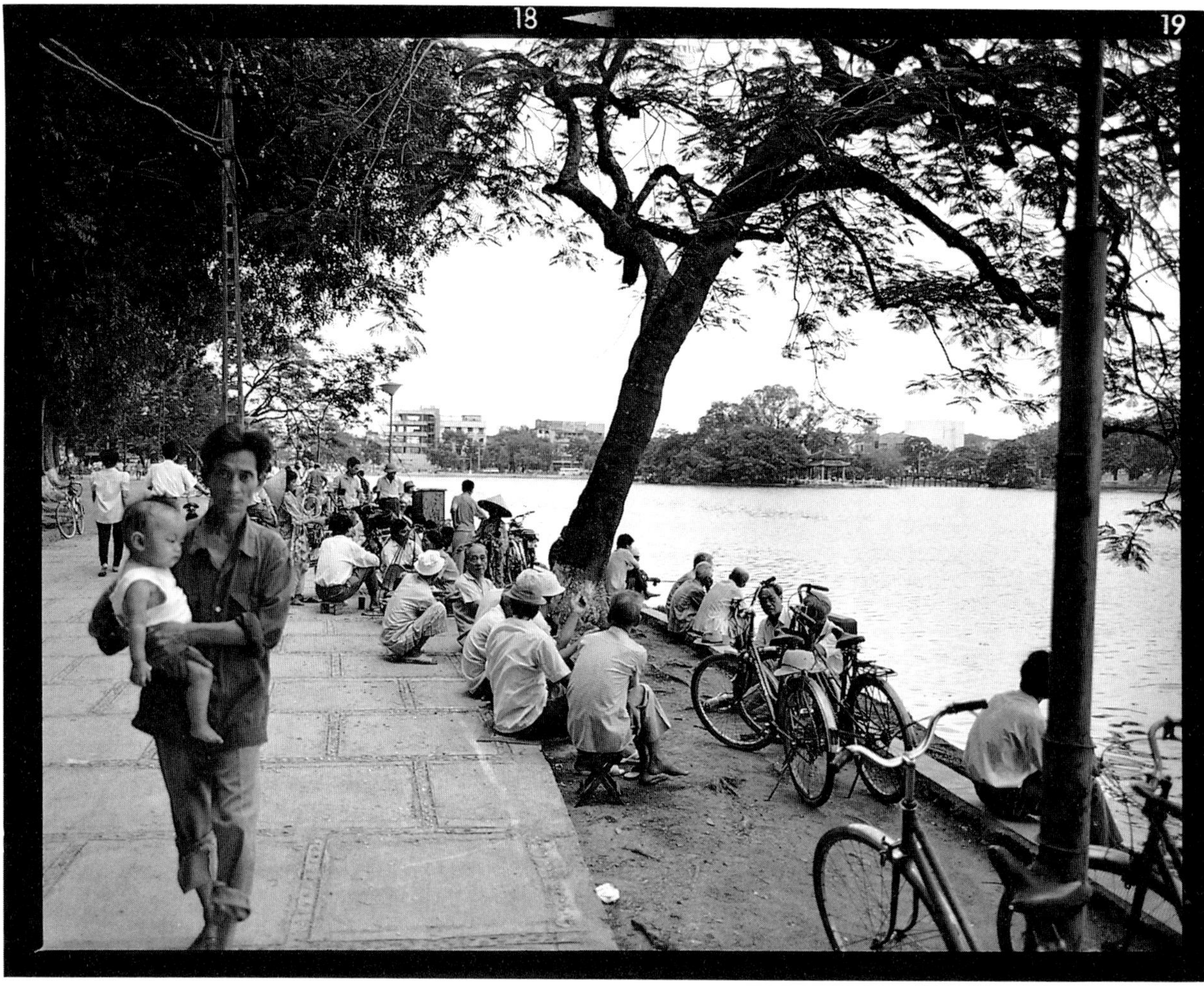

... *in the evening* ... al fresco *with the crowds* ...

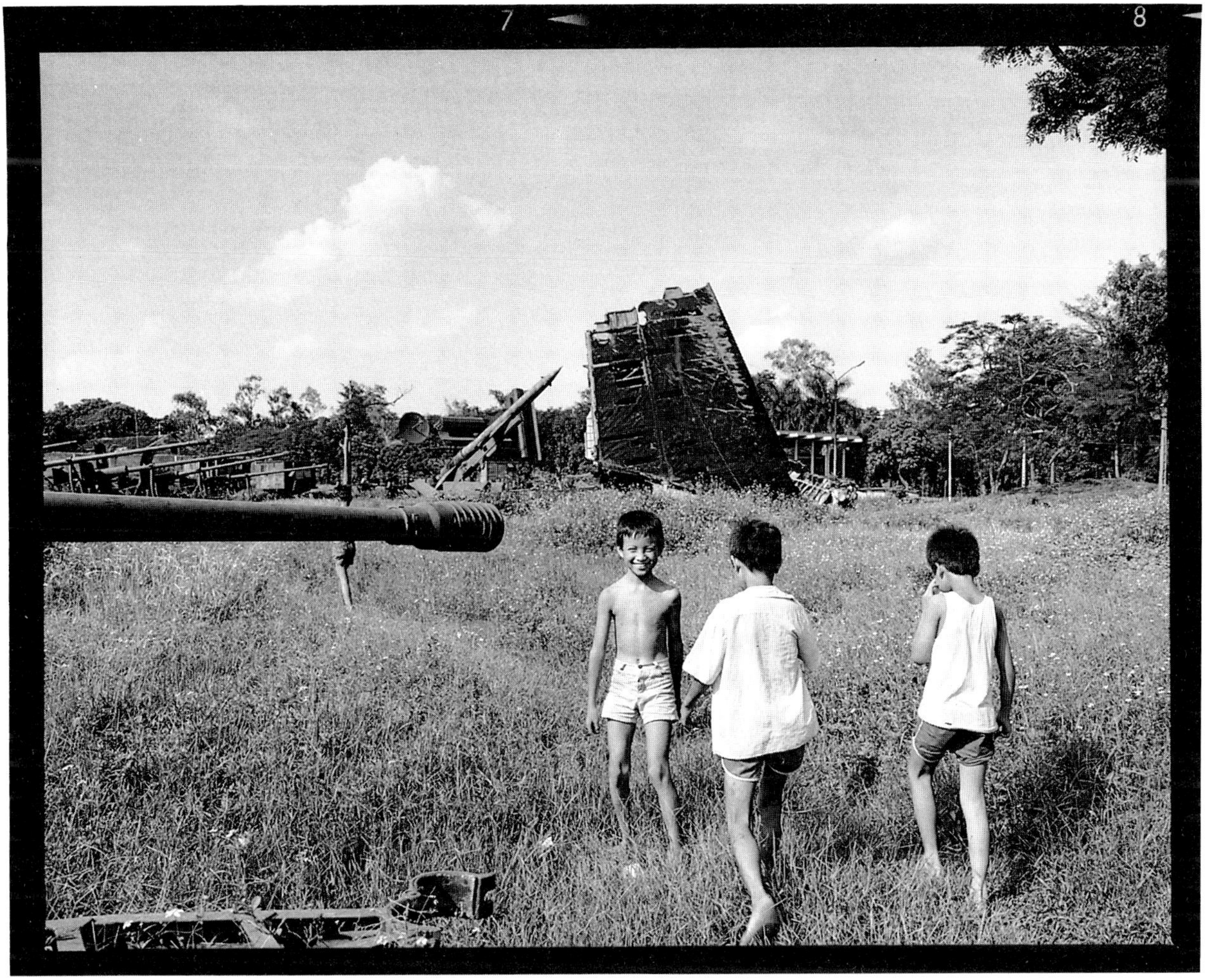

… in Lenin Park, with the children …

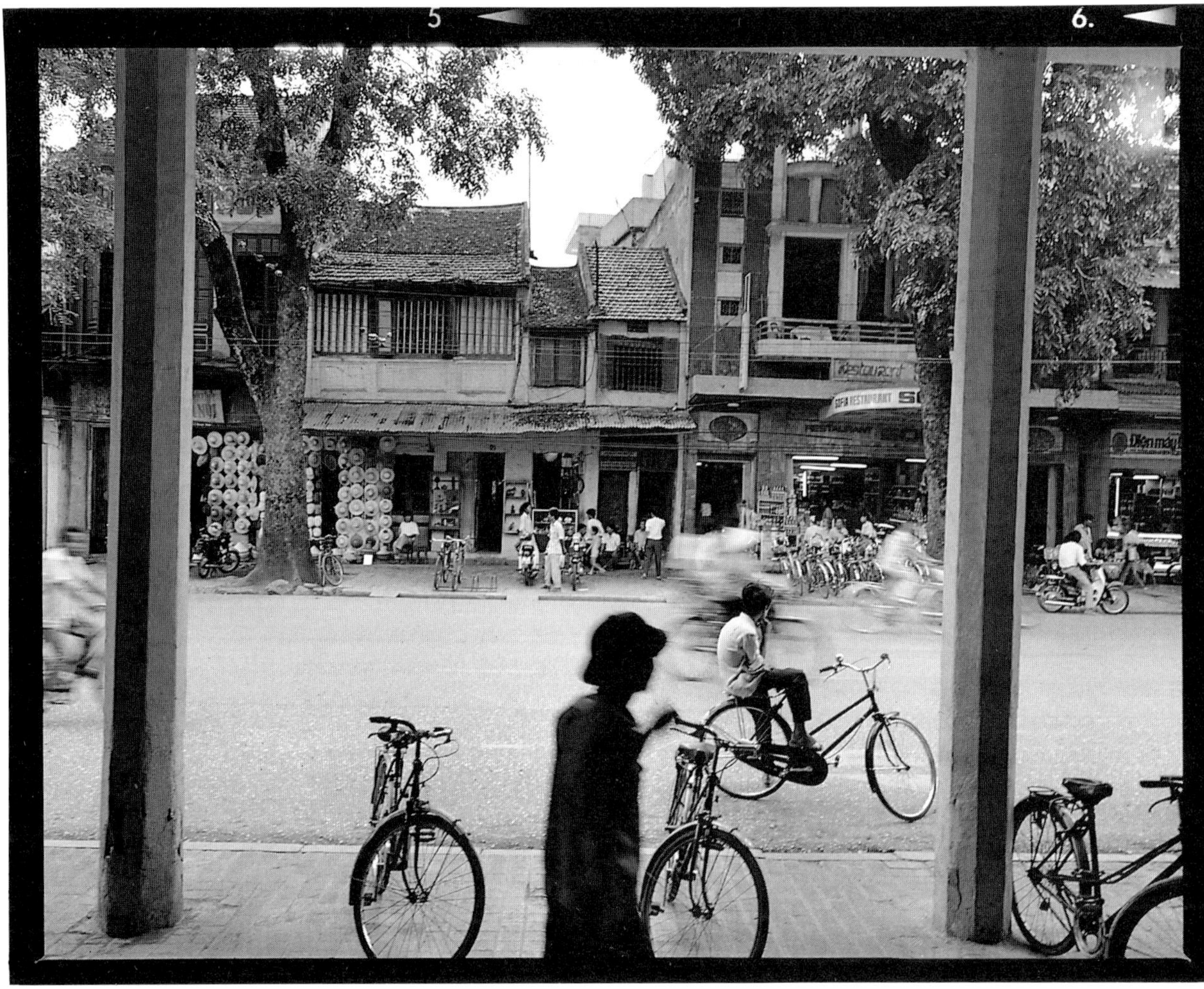

... there are places where time seems to stand still ...

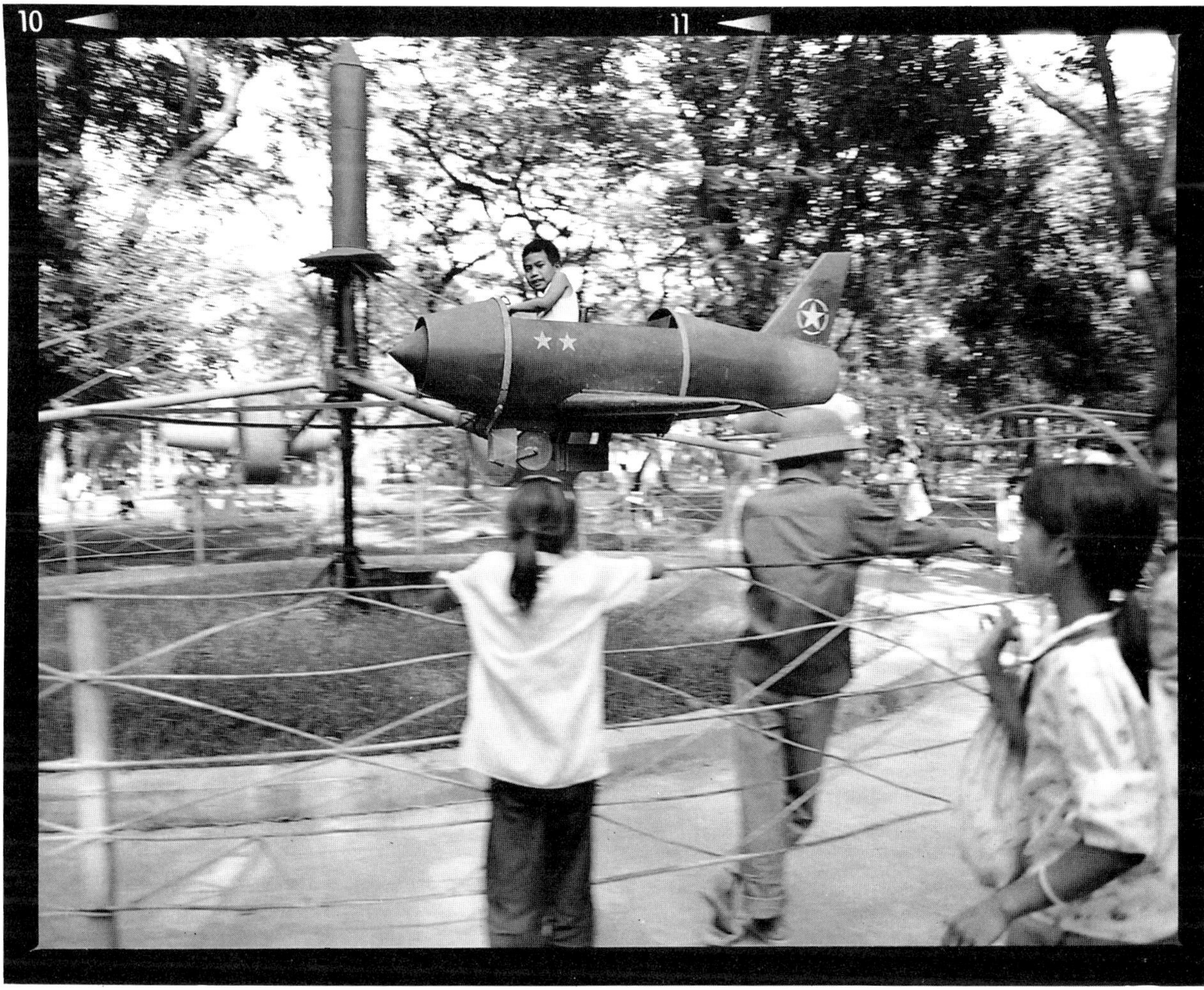

... the war is still present ...

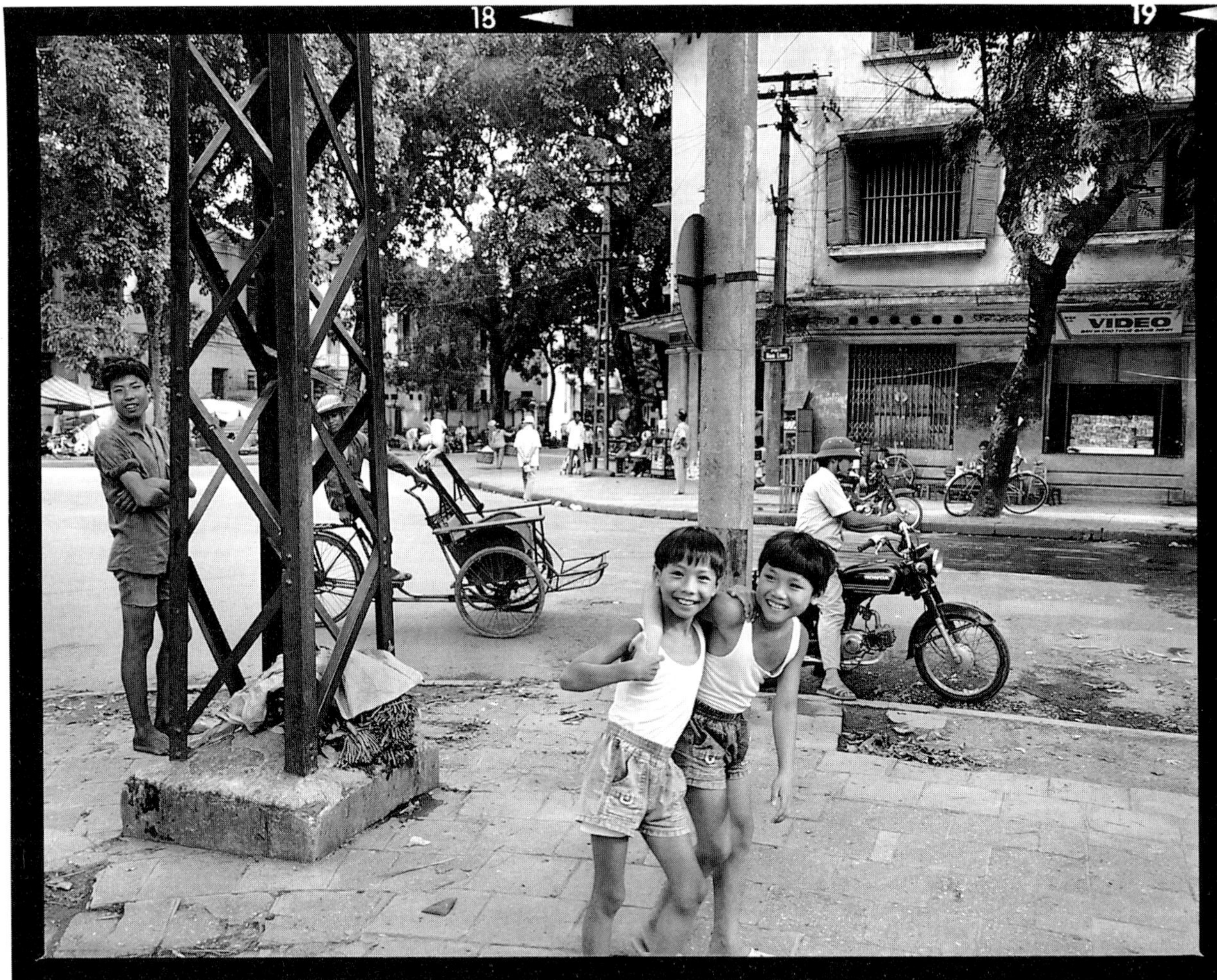

... but the children don't give it a thought.

Ochre façades with cornices and verandas, buildings with monumental stairways, steps decorated with flowers, shady parks where old men dream over books by Victor Hugo or Anatole France, girls who apologize for carrying around, for want of anything better, a copy of *Scarlet* in Vietnamese ('Oh, excuse me, I know it isn't really literature!'), peaceful lakes where lovers pose for photographs, the old rue Paul-Bert and the Provincial Opera House where you expect to find haughty French officers with their elegant wives in tropical dress. We survey all this green and gold glory, with bated breath, like speleologists who have discovered a cave-painting soon to be obliterated by air from outside.

I have hardly ever experienced anything more overwhelming than this arrival in Hanoi seventeen years after the war, three years after the death agony of communism. I feel all kinds of vague nostalgia, and a sense of intruding on the privacy of a sleeping beauty who is just waking up. Waking up, that is, to this new freedom which, still more spectacularly than in Saigon, is sending the inhabitants of Hanoi rushing out to meet the outside world. There is no fear any more, not the slightest reticence in these meetings. No longer is every single academic or professional whom a Westerner invites to a restaurant accompanied by a political cadre who notes down times and conversations. That sort of spying, at least, has been given up. And the ordinary people of Hanoi, almost imperceptibly, have started talking again.

From abroad, one imagines there would be ruins and devastation. Wrongly. The city suffered little from American bombing. Except for the Khan Thien district, where a monument perpetuates the memory of citizens who perished in the rubble. And the Paul Doumer Bridge, whose scars are still visible. Everywhere else is suffused by a delightful, antiquated elegance.

Hanoi is a flower which is opening. Still timorous. Not truly certain that the loosening Stalinist vice will not tighten again tomorrow. A fragile flower which welcomes foreigners without the cunning – and caution – of Saigon. In this ravaged country, Hanoi is a place of harmony, of conservation and innovation. Of course something remains of communist torpor and of the bureaucratic stupidity which has diminished but certainly not disappeared, which still persecutes – mechanically – 'dissident' writers such as Duong Thu Huong, Pham Thi Hoâi or Hguyên Huy Thiêp, subtle harbingers of a springtime still to come. Even so, each passing day lifts the lid a little more.

A less corrupt city than Saigon, Hanoi is also less culturally corrupted, more independent. Perhaps it bears fewer emotional scars. To us, it is like an epiphany, a fleeting moment of grace suspended between two histories, two challenges. Hanoi smiles at us and lowers its guard.

Is this what it has become, once more, this capital of war and revolution, this heroic city that stood firm against the bombs, this victorious, central metropolis? A delicate, soft-cheeked young peasant woman, awkwardly advancing into the improbable jungle of change. The jungle where Saigon, now that the scene has shifted, contests the law.

With a thirty-eight-year lead.

NIGHTCLUBS AND VIPs

The discotheque in the Boss Hotel in Hanoi, on Nguyên Du Street on the shore of Lake Hô Thien Quang, has been open since 15 April 1992. It is a night club on the cutting edge of history. There they dance awkward lambadas while watching video-clips on a large screen. A trendy place, with twenty-five mini-skirted hostesses, it is also an exemplary joint venture. Offered, a touch eagerly, as an irrefutable symbol of 'change', it brings together *Vietkieus* living abroad with apparatchiks from the Ministry of the Interior – that is, with the communist police, who share in the profits.

Admission costs four dollars, each drink a bit less. There are embassy cars parked outside, but also Hondas belonging to locals and a few vehicles with green number plates owned by the city authority. As for the Boss Hotel, once home to the French *sûreté*, it now houses *both* the Vietnam mission of Americans Missing in Action and the Hanoi VIP Club, where those who 'do business' hold their pow-wows. The whole place is a kind of bridgehead established right in the centre of Hanoi. Shall we go in?

We are formally introduced. The twenty-five girls in mini-skirts and high heels still have all the disarming freshness of novices. Just yesterday the majority were university students in pigtails or Young Communist militants. Now they are shyly trying their hand at secret whispers, blushing a bit while they engage the 'customer' in conversation. Even when they try, they don't have the 'pro' look or the disillusioned artfulness of Saigon's bar hostesses. On the dance floor they sway their hips with embarrassment relieved by giggles, are ebullient with a naive pleasure which one imagines will not last past this first spring.

One after another the girls approach us to offer conversation. In French, with schoolgirl intonation and studied charm. It is hard to forget that a year or two ago the same little mouths were reciting Marxist-Leninist dogma. Amid the deafening tumult of the sound system, Mme D. indignantly raises her eyes to the ceiling. She does not find any of this very amusing. She would like us to leave. Why? The deliberate choice – or renunciation – of these twenty-five girls inclines her to gloomy comments on the 'Saigonese' fate soon to overtake Hanoi and of which this Northern nightclub is the first, sniggering herald. Surprised not to have found any of the Spartan austerity which she feared, she is sorry nevertheless that Hanoi is already giving up some sort of more dignified and 'Vietnamese' reserve. The ambiguity of this reaction neatly expresses the attitude of all Vietnam, at once seduced by, and afraid of the 'Thai' future promised by the new capitalist logic.

A Southern patriot and fervent anti-communist, at bottom Mme D. would not be unhappy if Hanoi remained stoically in its 'different' camp which, without appearing to, defined the division of roles between the two rival capitals. She is disappointed and shocked at how quickly it is renouncing this difference, and learning to copy. And clearly revolted by the innocent enthusiasm of these student-hostesses who, for less than a month, have been apprentices of venality.

For the moment, they are swaying about on the dance floor. They are beautiful and can laugh about it.

Across one wall of the nightclub parades the world news according to CNN. A kaleidoscope of sound and fury, accompanied by a 'factual' commentary drowned out by the music – Russian disaster, African famine, Yankee political conventions, Californian riots. All pieced together in a loop in colours straight out of Disneyland.

Undoubtedly the music and beer have gone to my head. I feel a bit dizzy. Here I am in the heart of Hanoi, watching all-American global news against a background of disco and amateur hostesses, under the distressed gaze of a Saigonese woman lamenting the dissipation of virtue. Seventeen years after the 'fall' of Saigon! Sure, history is crazy. But all the same . . .

We move on into the bar of the Boss Hotel, which is next door. The waitress is more impassive, the drinks still charged in dollars. Here the silence of business is barely disturbed by whispered formal negotiations. Sitting at our table is a playboy just turned forty. Let us call him Mr Tuan. He is a hero emblematic of today's Vietnam. His passport is Swiss, his Saigonese mother lives in Los Angeles, his father is a Californian. But his uncle is a lieutenant colonel in the ex-North

Vietnamese army. Tuan is a *Vietkieu* with white teeth and good connections, trained in the best American business schools. Accompanying him is a Chinese woman from Cholon, all legs and bust, wriggling her hips, or docilely putting her chin on his knees while she listens to him talk. 'My number-three wife', he explains.

Tuan does business. He is at his best with certain high-level communist cadres. He runs from one joint venture to another, navigating between Los Angeles, Paris and Hanoi, perfectly at ease in 'renovated' Vietnam. Tuan is the archetype of the enterprising 'yuppies' who have sprung up all over the country. A pragmatic generation in a hurry, which, as in Moscow or Warsaw, is replacing the old party men and hero-soldiers on half-pay. The Boss Hotel is one of their HQs. Incidentally, it's here you might bump into the son-in-law of the secretary-general of the Communist Party, Mr Do Moï, in person, huddled in discussion with some slick executive.

Tuan's final comment on his activities in Hanoi. 'Payoffs, sure. But no more than 5 per cent. And payable afterwards. For me, that's a matter of principle.'

LITTLE GIRL ON THE FERRY

We keep our distance. We have no choice. Travel doesn't only broaden the mind. It is said to sharpen the gaze and strengthen the soul. Perhaps so much so that in the long run it bolts something down inside you. You can't survey all these disasters without some internal protection; you can't chase after the world's upheavals and anguish without secretly steeling yourself, with a minimal degree of toughness. Otherwise, how long could you keep going? All real trips – and some more than others – are made holding your breath.

So Raymond and I cross Vietnam laughing a little too much. We turn certain discoveries into jokes, we make ironic comments on the troubled nostalgia which, from time to time, assails us. We dissipate the more specific – or personal – bouts of melancholy by making fun of the Southern 'fears' of Mme D. In the evening, at the hotel, we often ward off serious thoughts with outbursts of laughter. When, without thinking, Raymond yet again brings up his friend Gilles Caron, lost in Cambodia in 1970, I instinctively change the topic of conversation. When I recall certain names, he turns it into a joke, just as I need him to. In short, we keep an eye on each other, making sure we don't let our guard down too much. Mentally holding our breath.

As a consequence we carry with us something like a surfeit of words, a heavy load of bottled-up emotions. It is good that we do. And indeed it's the least we could do. How could we dwell on our own feelings in the middle of this rout? Compared with the anguished wanderings of 65 million men and women, what does it matter that we are filled with vague disquiet at the ultimate wreckage of the 'Vietnam story' and the way it marks the end of an era (and reminds us, every step of the way, how old we are)?

The fact that we are twenty years older is not Vietnam's problem! Our bitterness in the face of the obvious, unbearable, incredible *retrospective* uselessness of the slaughter in Vietnam is of no great use to the survivors. By keeping an eye on these untimely sentiments, we are not only looking to protect ourselves. It is a matter of what is rightly called decency.

But of course the result is a build-up of unspoken thoughts and repressed feelings. We seem weighed down with them sometimes. And then follow the sudden fits of anger, the hesitations and indecisiveness which are so disconcerting for Mme. D. Raymond will lose his temper over bad light or bad timetables, then stop himself and lapse into silence. I will make a fuss about all the stops and starts, or the mileage, before realising how silly I am being. Inexplicable outbursts and tantrums. We feel strangely accountable for every hour, personally responsible for the tiniest detail of the itinerary. As if this trip would not allow us to enjoy for a single moment the splendid innocence of the traveller. All the same, we constantly talk about 'coming' back, even though we haven't left yet. It's absurd, but it's not coincidental.

I have a reason for reporting these ups and downs. I think they have plenty to tell us about the ambiguity of a return trip that we wished weren't so serious. But which was serious, in spite of ourselves. As proof, there were real tears, at least once. Suddenly bursting out of this silence.

On the Pha Binh ferry, between Haiphong and the Bay of Along, I am pestered by a dozen or so little girls selling things, tugging at my sleeve. The situation is familiar to us. We normally refuse all goods offered with enough firmness and smiles to avoid getting snared without being harsh. Usually, we aim to wear them down patiently, although in this game the little girls are formidable opponents. So this time, as usual, I shake my head and gently brush aside the knick-knacks being offered. It is not enough. The kids are barely ten years old. They grab my arm in turn, uttering a few words in French, competing with their supplications and wheedling.

All around me the ferry passengers are amused at my difficulties. For the twenty minutes of this crossing I am at the mercy of these obstinate children, with no way of escape. '*S'il vous plaît . . . s'il vous plaît . . .*' Their assaults demonstrate not only a disarming commercial energy, reinforced by an unequalled art of persuasion, they also allow a glimpse, behind the children's smiles and pleas, of *real* competition.

What do you do? Get angry? Push them aside? It is easy to say. From a

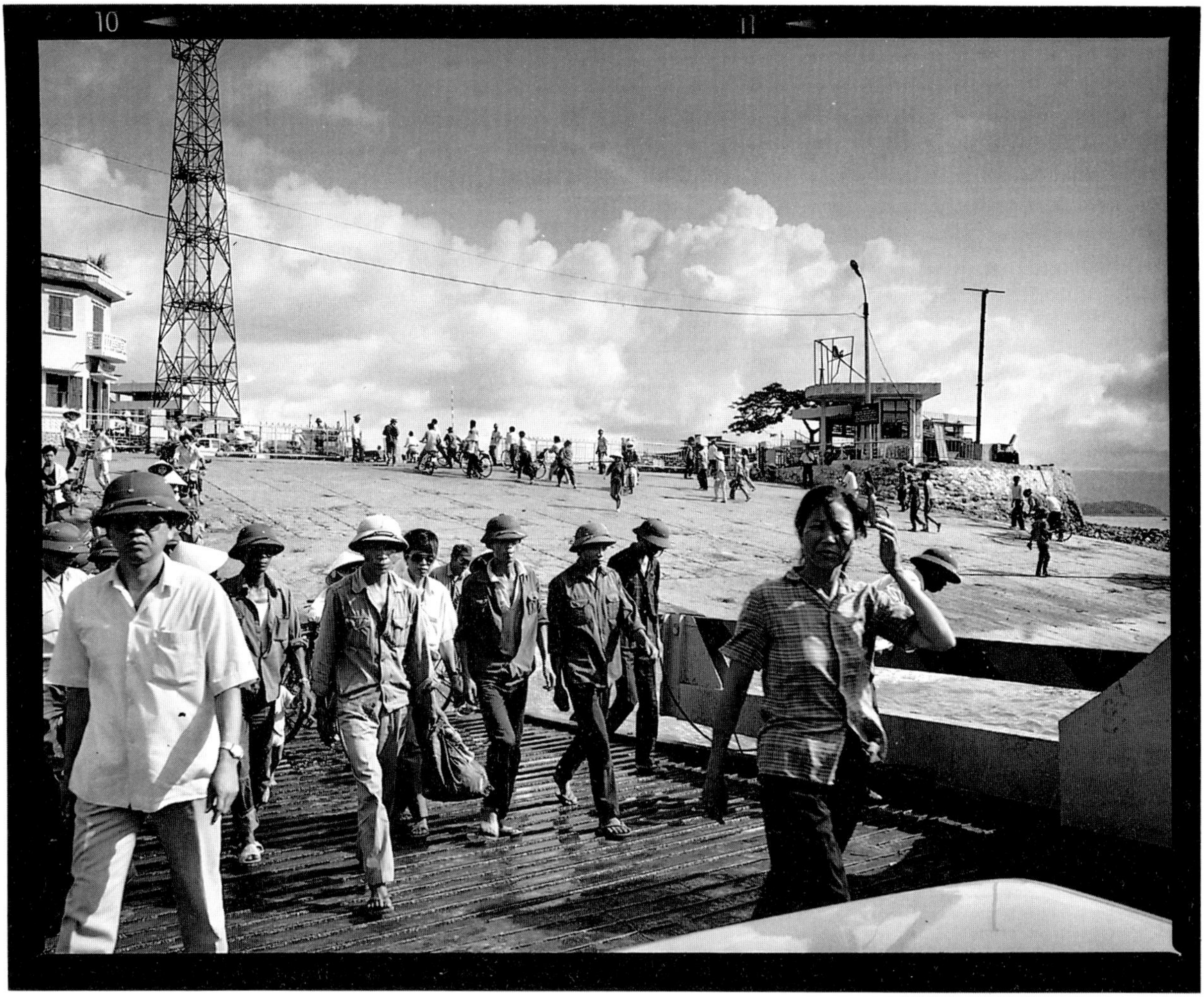

Haiphong . . . the port.

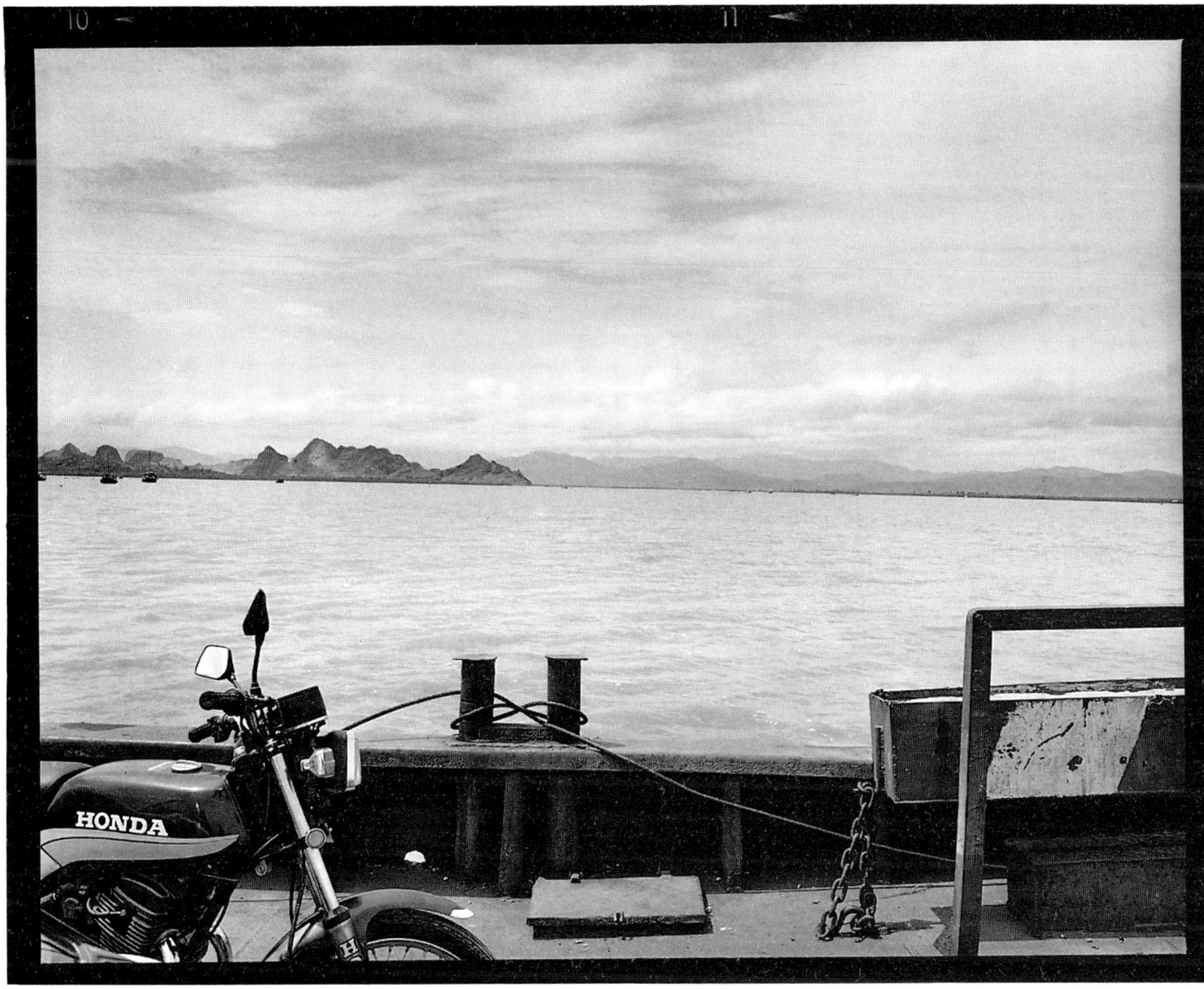

On the ferry.

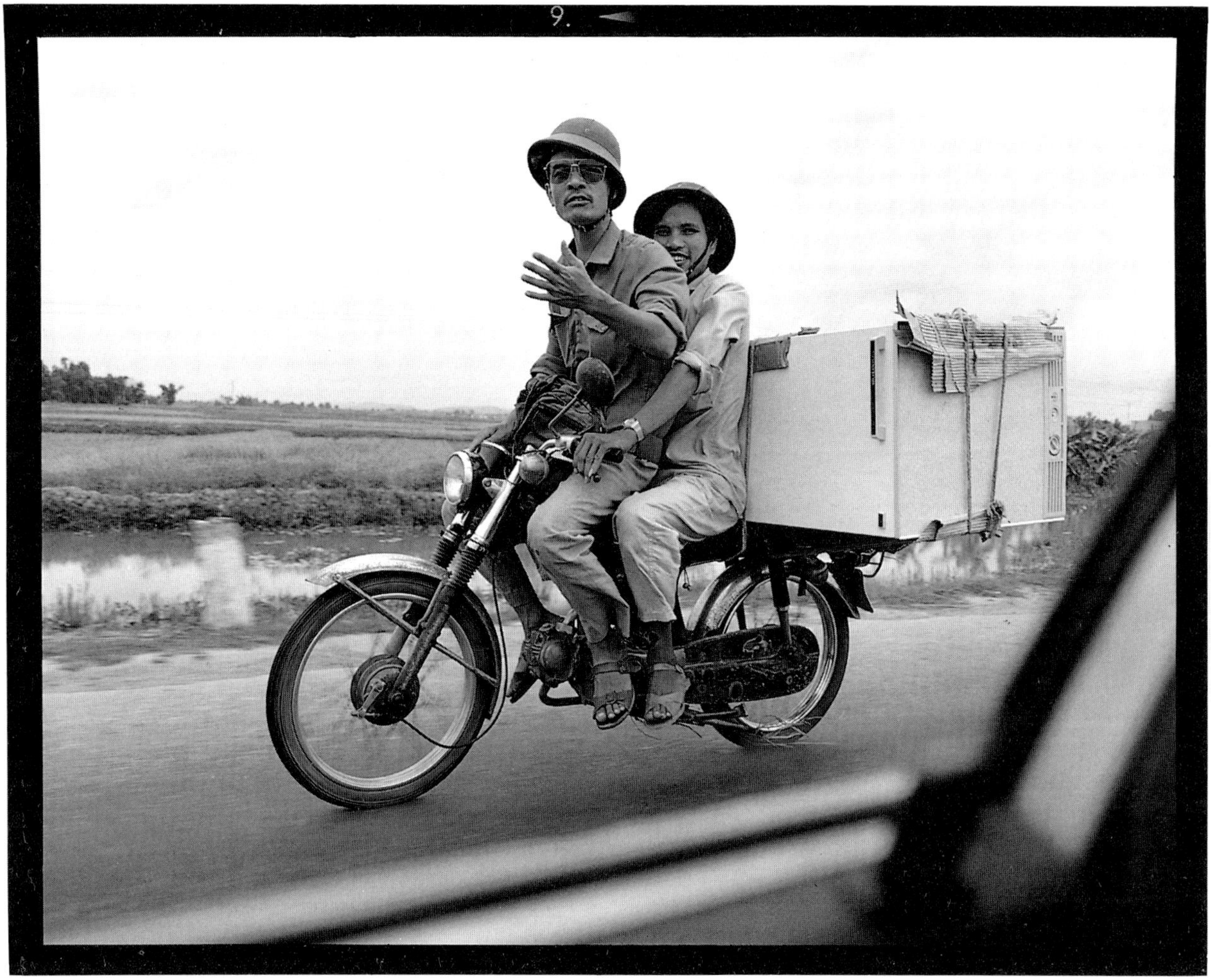

This is the North, with its own charms and its improvised solutions.

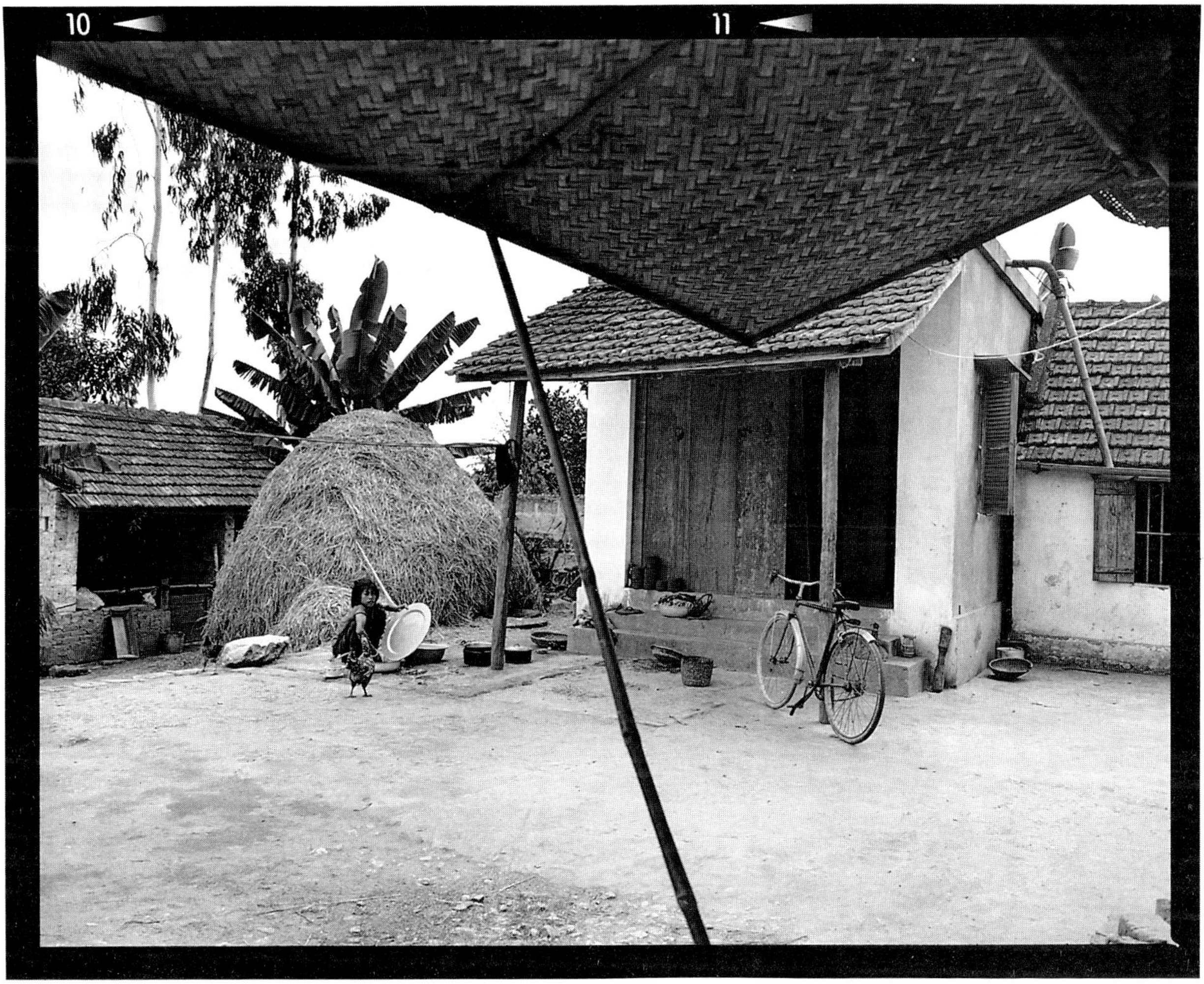

... a small farm and a little girl ...

distance, Raymond observes my embarrassment in the middle of this squealing little pack. He senses me giving in. One of them is selling cigarettes, another brandishes a Coca-Cola, still another – barely six years old – is waving packs of chewing gum. But the Coca-Cola is lukewarm, the cigarettes are made of light tobacco, and I don't like chewing gum. Joyous, vociferous insistence surrounds me, as in a game where everyone senses an approaching dénouement. Besides, the ferry is arriving at the opposite bank.

All in all, the cigarettes will not be entirely useless. I resolutely take a pack from the one selling them while declining, with a slightly annoyed gesture, the other propositions.

That is when the tears start. Real, serious tears, like a sense of hopelessness which suddenly can neither hide itself any longer nor call upon irony. The youngest girl, the one offering chewing gum, has just broken out in sobs. Loudly. Interminably. She hiccups, runs every which way among the passengers as they are getting off. Her lips are trembling, she rubs her eyes and smudges her face with black soot.

The other kids have taken off. I am left faced with this near-baby whose breathing is broken by the violence of her sobs. I hastily offer to buy all her chewing gum. And indeed more, if I must. It is too late. She no longer seems interested. I insist, but in vain. The little girl hides behind her hands, her tears redoubling. This time there is no longer just another little girl taking a chance playing buy-and-sell with a Western traveller. There is only the inconsolable despair of a poor child, an *immensely* unhappy child.

I buy everything she has, forcing her to accept, and stroke her hair.

Pathetic.

WHISPERS AND CONJECTURES

As in the past, of course, we also meet diplomats and colleagues, eminent advisers and politicians. In Hanoi we dash off to check the dispatches at the AFP headquarters, have lunch at the embassy, are told in detail what is suitable to know – or to suspect – about Vietnamese political affairs. It is a respectable ritual, a moment with which I have become familiar. Over twenty years I devoted the necessary time to these diplomatic conjectures, these meetings 'at a higher level', these detailed examinations of present and future. Naturally. There is always a moment during the trip when you have to evaluate the respective chances of 'liberals' and 'hardliners', to weigh the reality behind a diplomatic 'opening', to examine border 'tensions', calculate the economy's disarray, listen to the opposing sides in the back room of a café, wonder about the intentions – and the ways and means – of French diplomacy. And all the rest.

We can't avoid it.

I hear sombre prognostications in Hanoi about the determination of old guard communists to remain in power. I note what it is useful to know about the distancing of the 'Pro-Chinese'. I listen to more circumspect talk about the risks, always present, of a skid toward renewed civil war between North and South. ('A lot of resentment has built up. And, the regime is no longer in full control of the situation.') Others assure me, to the contrary, that the principal concern of Vietnam – that of returning to the Asiatic fold after being drawn into the Cambodian quagmire – is a guarantee of caution and flexibility. Still others insist on the 'decisive' step which would be represented by the official lifting of the American embargo, and the subsequent arrival of some of the bigger investors. Some Vietnamese interlocutors implore me not to hide the stupidity of the

Stalinist leaders of such a pathetic mess – leaders covered with the blood of cleansings, liquidations and successive eliminations, clinging today to power which no longer warrants any real confidence. ('Your love of Vietnam must not blind you to these things!')

But why on earth would I say nothing about that? Why wouldn't I write about what is – the foolishness and corruption, the betrayal of heroes and forgetting of sacrifices, the stubbornness and obstinacy of those bankrupt old men who only count the days and gain a little time before being swept aside by a flood of young people with a different perspective. Why would I be indulgent? I have no accounts to settle with today's Vietnam. (Who still does, anyhow?) I have nobody to punish or to spare. Vietnam has entered into the history of the Far East which is no longer our own. If we are still blind about Vietnam, it no longer has anything to do with a war of ideologies. It is simply a matter of indifference.

So I listen to these theses and antitheses, these analyses and 'excuses' with a freedom, a distanced coolness which used to be unimaginable. I object sometimes, courteously, and am responded to in the same tone. As if Vietnam had attained the status of a simply neutral object, interesting and hypothetical.

But what is it, this time, which blunts my curiosity?

A desire within makes me want to cut short each of these conversations. At Agence France Presse I quickly put down the batch of 'interior' dispatches with confessed weariness. The inexhaustible erudition of 'well-informed observers' no longer really interests me. I give up noting the countless ideological nuances, the presumed dosages of Politburo and Central Committee, where the conventional competition between hard- and soft-liners is played out.

Why?

In the end, I know very well.

Politics is not, or is no longer, the essential aspect in a Vietnam which has been seized by a great ferment and transformed, beneath the veneer of words and the dross of circumstance. For some time now, politics has had little purchase on anything but the short term and the superficial. As if from the depths a confused wave has emerged which has reduced the vaguely byzantine hypotheses of Marxology to empty rhetoric. Here in Hanoi I recall certain evenings in 1989, spent in Prague, Budapest or even Tirana. I listened to scholarly debates on the 'tendencies' and the 'currents' while, outside, the crowds swelled. Crowds which, rather than arbitrate between the players, soon changed the game entirely.

Certainly, no crowd stirs now in the cities of Vietnam. But in the streets, inside families, within minds – is not the game in the process of changing? Has it not already changed?

I have still other hypotheses. Such as: I can no longer think without anger of Vietnam twenty years ago and the use to which it was put. A use which sometimes entailed more polemical fever than solicitude, more cannibalistic haste than real curiosity, more voluntary myopia than real scrutiny. The rush to judge, to choose a posture, to define a 'line'! Ah, the narcissistic pleasure of bias and commitment! The 'sympathy' so abstract that it turned away again from its object when there were no longer any matters of 'dispute'. Were these politics anything other than a paradoxical alibi for a lack of interest, the cover-up for a simple dialogue with oneself? The real Vietnam was less important, in the end, than the cause in which, thanks to it, one cloaked oneself. To know and describe then counted hardly for anything. To judge was the principal urgency.

Pardon me: twenty years later, everything inclines me to prefer the opposite. Let's return to the streets.

THE GUNNER OF THE BAY OF ALONG

Every journey comes to an end. We end this one on the Bay of Along at the Hôtel de la Plage – a group of bungalows dating from the French colonial period, with a panoramic dining room, a veranda opening onto the sea, wicker chairs and carved wooden balconies. The antique buildings smell of sawdust and hot tea; they are surrounded by simpler structures, inexpensive Moscow-style hotels built toward the end of the 1970s. At a stone's throw from the Chinese border, Along remains the fashionable beach of North Vietnam. General Giap owns a villa which can be seen, flanked by a heliport, at the top of a hill. At the weekend buses bring veterans' associations and former prisoners of war. They mix in with the very 'nomenklaturist' crowd which invades the beach till nightfall.

Just yesterday 'Soviet comrades' were numerous on the Bay of Along. This is attested to by signs in Cyrillic, which no one dreams of removing. With somewhat harsh 'production-committee' elegance, the beach also evokes a time nearly past.

We are happy and idle. A little exhausted, perhaps. Every morning, Raymond counts his remaining rolls of film and tries to work out how to apportion his meagre stock. In the evening we walk beneath the filaos, the silver eucalyptus, the coconut palms and pines where cicadas are buzzing. On the sea mineral barges pass by, pulled toward the port of Hong Gaï by little tugboats; in the evening lobstermen cast off their boats toward the maze of three thousand islets to which the French once gave names: Revolver, Queen, Banana, Cythera, Hazelnut, Punchinello.

I don't know how Mr Huang B. suddenly appeared among us. Wearing a crooner's moustache and cotton pants, he is interested first of all, as a

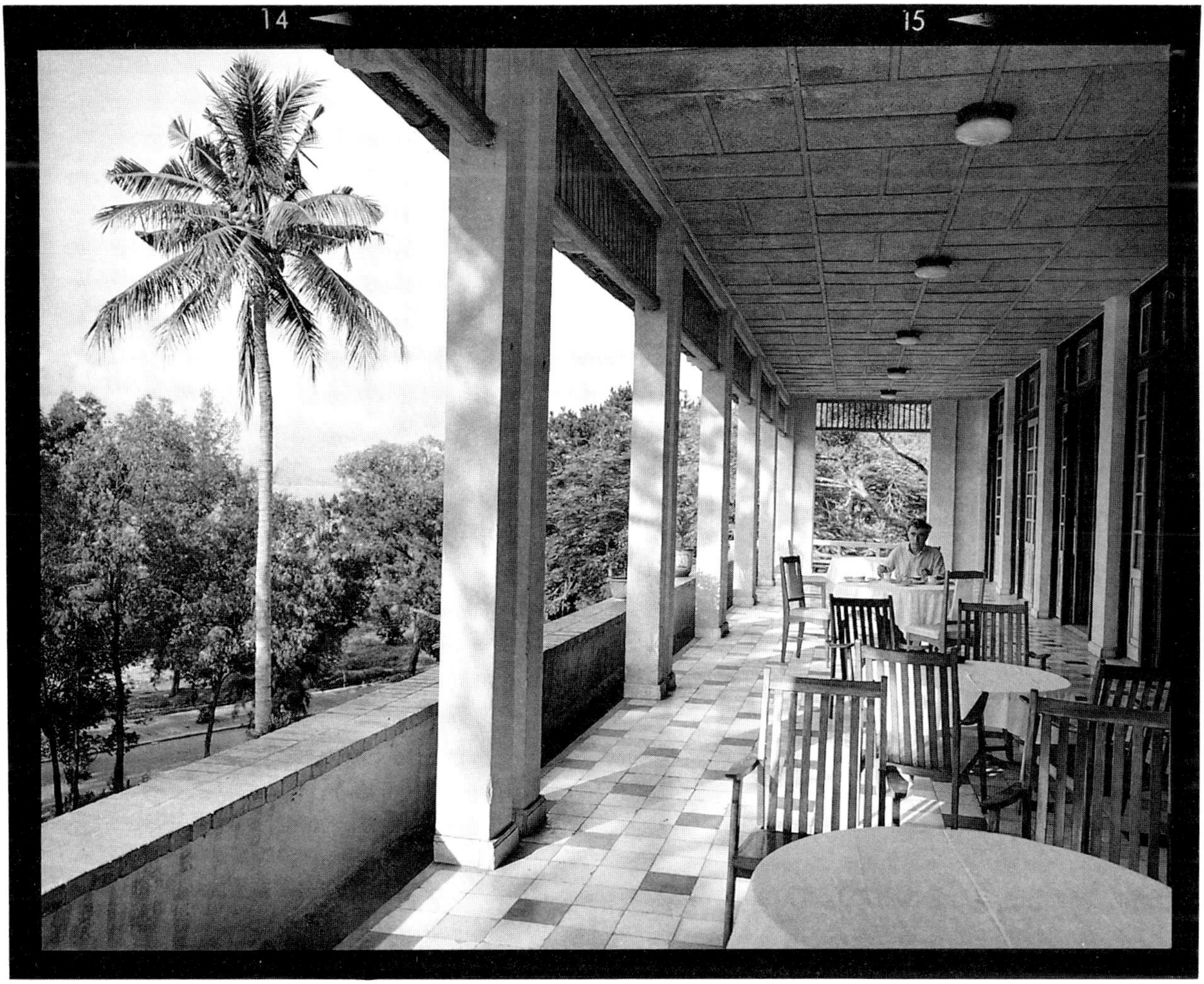

Hôtel de la Plage on the Bay of Along ...

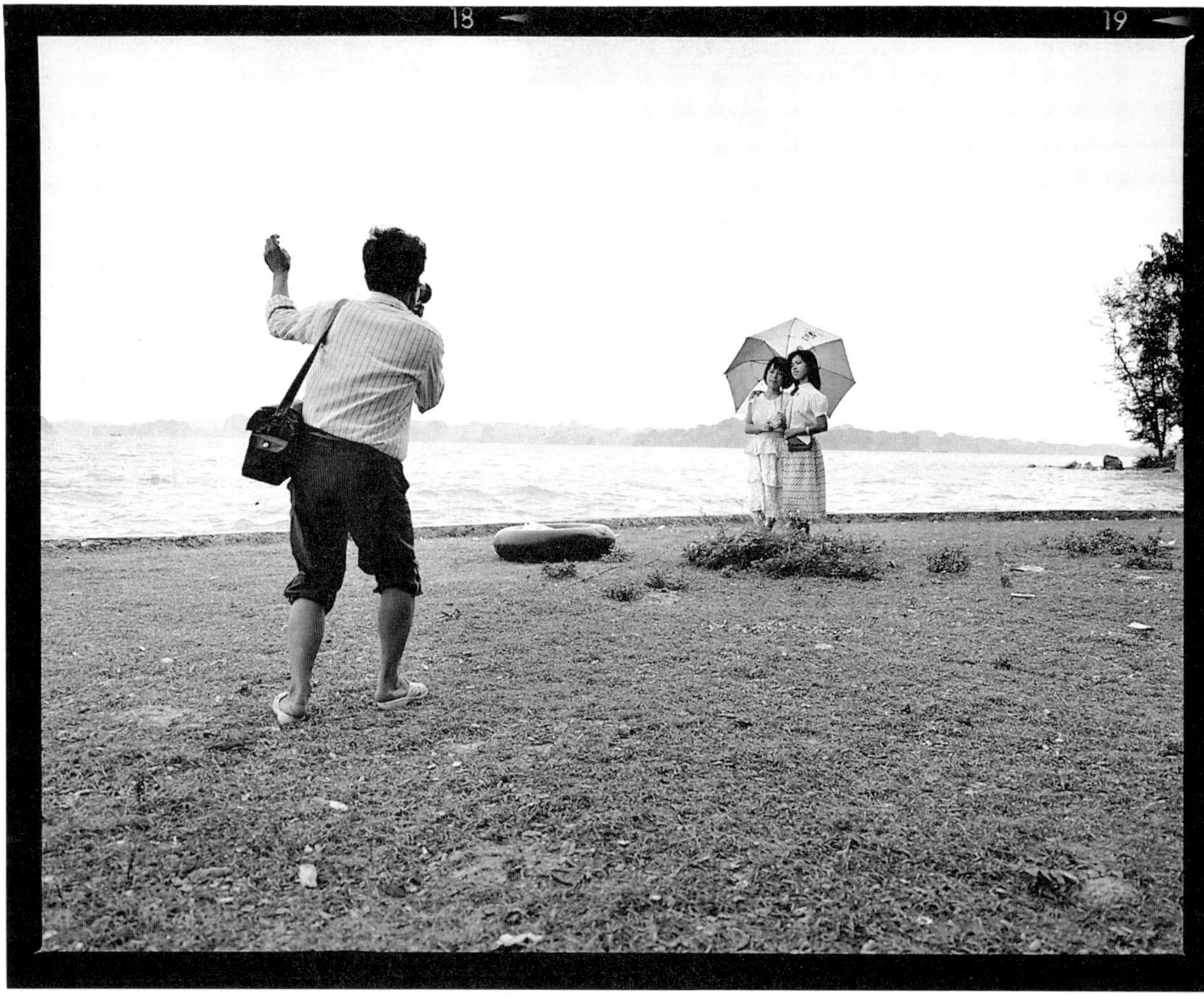

... so many photographers! ...

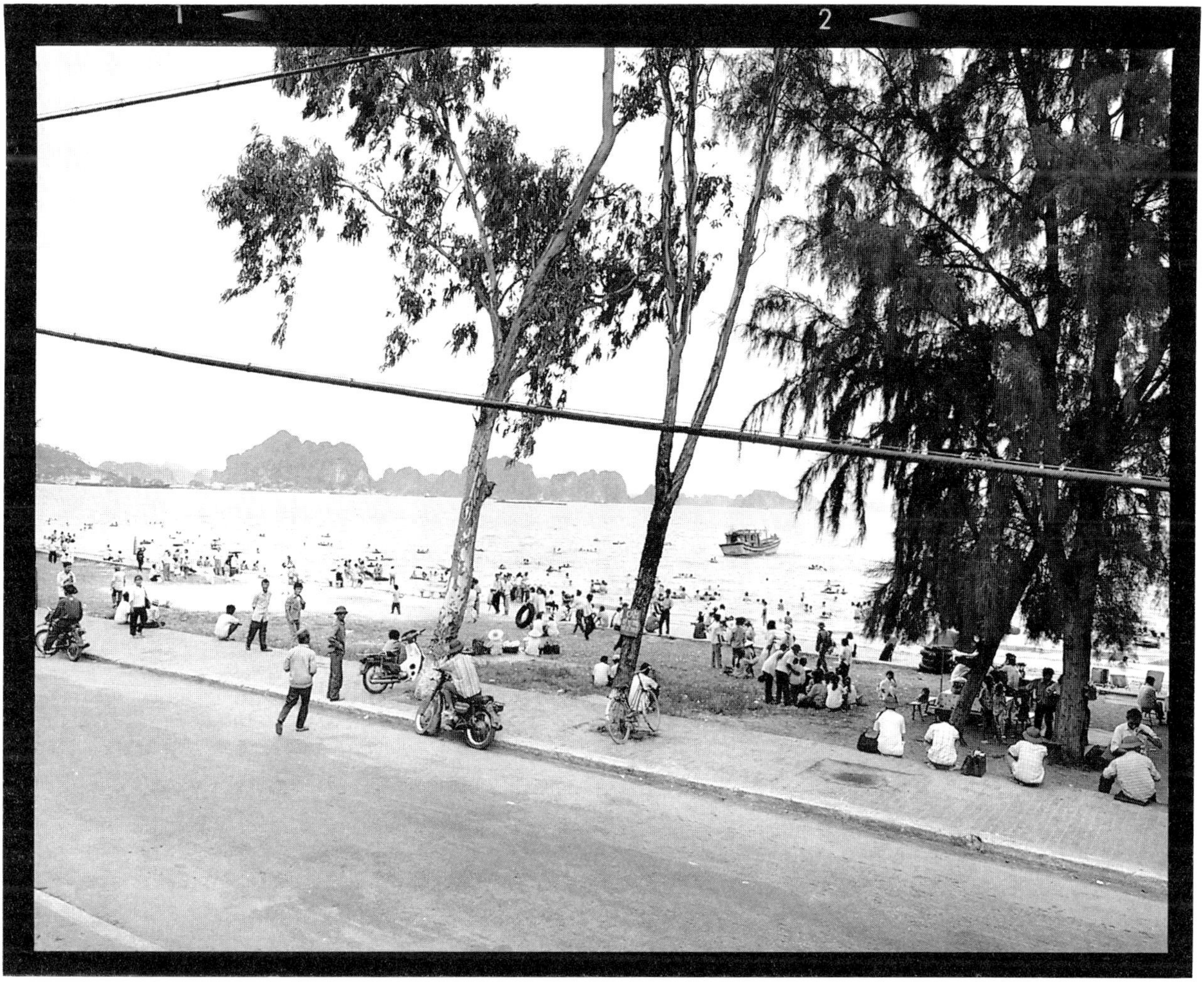

... and young people, on this beach ...

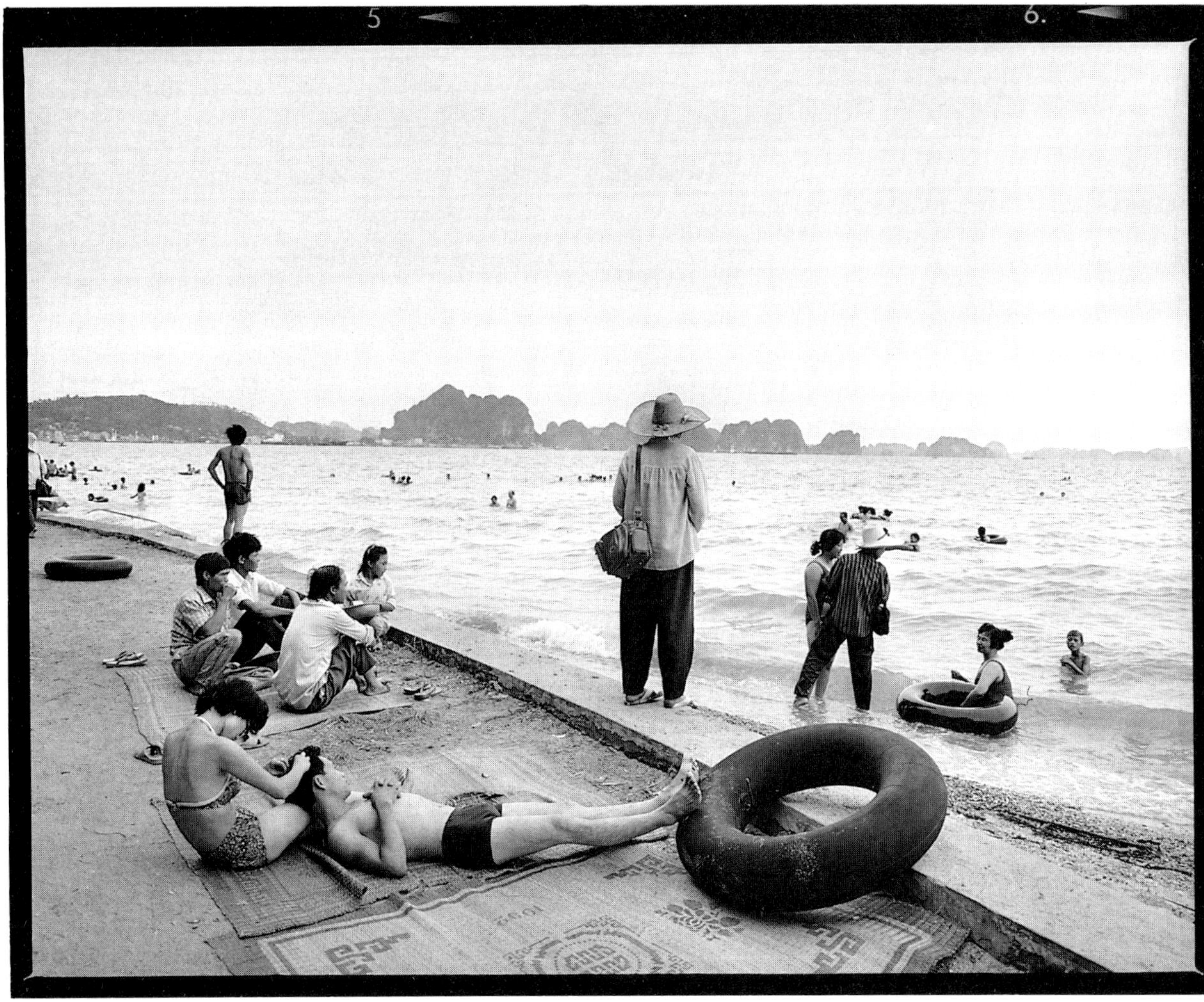

... here as well, it's summer and the holidays ...

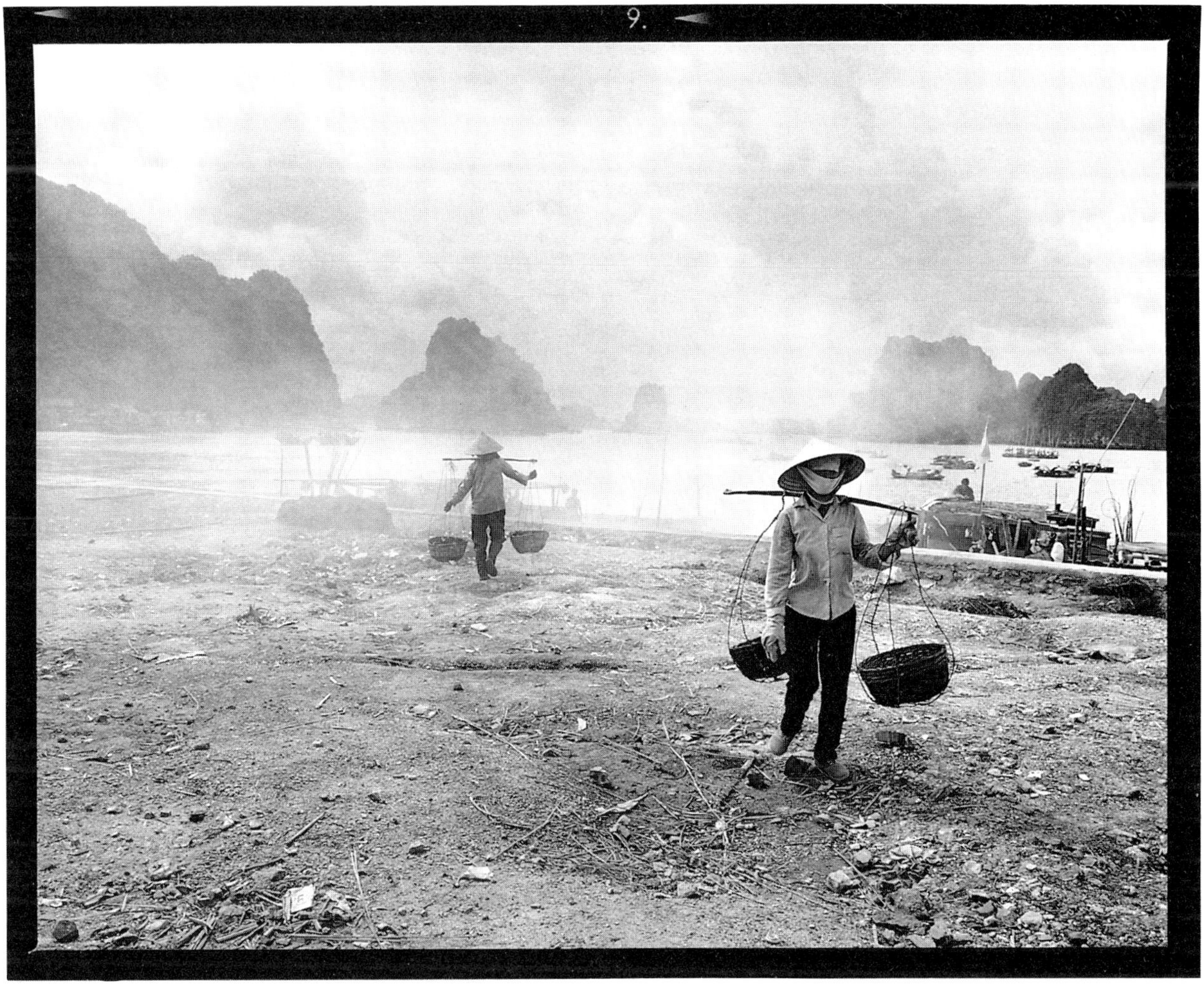

… but in the nearby town, work continues.

professional, in Raymond's camera. But we don't stop there. Mr Huang B. lacks neither political audacity nor news, nor the 'distance' which guarantees good information. A beach photographer with whom we become friends, Mr Huang B. was formerly an artilleryman at Haiphong, a communist cadre, a party hero and an immigrant worker in Poland – and then, in 1972, an appalled spectator of the American bombing of Quang Ninh Province. Today he is back from all that. In the most political sense of the term.

Is there an angel of providence for travellers? I don't know. The sudden advent of Mr Huang B. is a terribly theatrical stroke. At just the right moment he appears before us as if to recapitulate the journey and extract its lesson – even in spite of himself. We often see Mr Huang B. on the Beach of Along. We sit on a bench and he talks – a good deal, probably more than he ever has in his life.

In 1965–66 Mr Huang B., a young communist *bo doi* working in the navy yards, became an artillery officer in a suburb of the Port of Haiphong. He commanded an anti-aircraft battery when Lyndon Johnson launched the first bombing raids – Operation Rolling Thunder – on North Vietnam. He recalls neighbourhoods on fire in Haiphong, he still hears the sound of sirens and the indefinable whisper of bombs falling from high-altitude B-52s. At that height, the noise of the plane's eight jet engines doesn't reach the ground. Only the gentle hiss of air of the string of bombs dropping from the sky is audible. 'Murmuring death', the North Vietnamese used to say. In 1966, Lady Luck smiles on Mr Huang B: his anti-aircraft guns bring down an American Phantom fighter. Promoted to hero of the people's army, he is decorated.

The following year, as compensation for his feat of arms, he is sent for training to the Szczecin naval shipyards, in Gomulka's communist Poland. He recounts, in great detail, the incredible railway journey which took him from Hanoi to Warsaw, crossing Manchuria, Siberia, and the Ukraine – eleven days and nights for the young Vietnamese hero who had never left Quang Ninh Province. Huang B. thus found himself in Poland when the strikes erupted in December 1970 in the Gdansk and Gdynia shipyards, and then the workers' insurrection which chased Gomulka from power and forshadowed, ten years before it actually happened, the birth of Solidarity.

Consigned to his workers' hostel, like all the immigrant Vietnamese, Huang

B. nonetheless began to have his first doubts about the dictatorship of the proletariat and Marxism-Lenism. He learned Polish and, at the same time, how to make certain arrangements with dogma.

Returning to Vietnam in 1970, he took up his work again at the navy shipyards of Quang Ninh, equipped and aided by Poland. He was still there in April 1972, when the American bombing started up again, in response to Vô Nguyên Giap's offensive on the 17th parallel. The bombing lasted twelve days and nights, ravaging Quang Ninh Province and destroying the Port of Hong Gaï, on the Bay of Along. Recalling this time, Huang B. insists on showing us the former Japanese-Vietnamese Cultural Centre, running alongside the wharves, where hundreds of civilians were buried beneath the rubble. 'It took several weeks to extract the bodies,' he says.

He waves toward the horizon, to indicate the hotels and fishing villages. 'Everything was destroyed here. When they were coming back from Hanoi, the B-52s emptied their bomb bays here. We were living in underground passages.'

A long time ago. Twenty years.

Today, Mr Huang B. has quit the Party, he no longer believes in communism, or in revolution. Quang Ninh's naval shipyards are nearly bankrupt. Those workers who have not been laid off work only six months a year. The Port of Hong Gaï, the Japanese-Vietnamese Cultural Centre, and the hotels on the Bay of Along have been rebuilt. Mr Huang B. has turned himself into a professional beach photographer and works with a 24 × 36 reflex camera manufactured in East Germany.

He speaks softly, without anger, his illusions gone.

'Now, all the party cadres are corrupt. I preferred, myself, to become an ordinary citizen again. But I am worried for my children. It used to be that a person could find work and put his children in the university. Now that takes money. To enrol my daughter at the university, I would have to pay $150. I don't have it.

'Today, you see, everybody is fascinated by America. Even Russia, which is the source of communism. You would think that Vietnam will always be the slave of a great power. The day before it was China, yesterday Russia, tomorrow America. But what can I do? I am just a grain of sand on the Bay of Along.'

It seemed to me that Mr Huang B. was smiling as he said those last words. But I'm not sure.